Pacifists, Patriots and the Vote

Also by Jo Vellacott:

FROM LIBERAL TO LABOUR WITH WOMEN'S SUFFRAGE: THE STORY OF CATHERINE MARSHALL

BERTRAND RUSSELL AND THE PACIFISTS IN THE FIRST WORLD WAR

Pacifists, Patriots and the Vote

The Erosion of Democratic Suffragism in Britain during the First World War

Jo Vellacott

palgrave
macmillan

First published 2007 by
PALGRAVE MACMILLAN
Houndmills, Basingstoke, Hampshire RG21 6XS and
175 Fifth Avenue, New York, N.Y. 10010
Companies and representatives throughout the world

PALGRAVE MACMILLAN is the global academic imprint of the Palgrave
Macmillan division of St. Martin's Press, LLC and of Palgrave Macmillan Ltd.
Macmillan® is a registered trademark in the United States, United Kingdom
and other countries. Palgrave is a registered trademark in the European
Union and other countries.

ISBN 13: 978–0–230–01335–3   hardback
ISBN 10: 0–230–01335–X   hardback

This book is printed on paper suitable for recycling and made from fully
managed and sustained forest sources. Logging, pulping and manufacturing
processes are expected to conform to the environmental regulations of the
country of origin.

A catalogue record for this book is available from the British Library.

Library of Congress Cataloging-in-Publication Data

Vellacott, Jo.
    Pacificists, patriots, and the vote : the erosion of democratic
suffragism in Britain during the First World War / Jo Vellacott.
        p. cm.
    Includes bibliographical references and index.
    ISBN 0–230–01335–X (alk. paper)
    1. Women–Suffrage–Great Britain–History–20th Century.
2. Feminism–Great Britain–History–20th century. 3. Suffragists–
Great Britain–History. I. Title.

JN979.V45 2007
324.6'23094109041–dc22   2007018310

10   9   8   7   6   5   4   3   2   1
16   15 14 13 12 11 10 09 08 07

Transferred to Digital Printing 2008

*'When we use the word "patriotism" do we mean –
our country is in the right,
our country must get some advantage out of the war?
Or do we care, first and foremost, that our country should play
a worthy part, worthy of the best ideals we have for her?'*

Catherine Marshall, November 1914

Contents

Preface

The process of writing history from original documents is both fascinating and frustrating. Unless you are fortunate enough to have a complete microfilm, or the documents are available electronically, you study for long hours in collections here and there and hope to bring away with you all that will prove to be important – a pile of paper or computer notes and photocopies. What you find in collection B is sure to make you realize that you missed stuff in collection A that you now know you need.

When you finally sit down to write, you find yourself putting together a singularly interesting jigsaw puzzle – but always, always, a puzzle with some pieces missing, since you have gathered them from many different boxes rather than finding them stored neatly together in a single box closed with sticky tape. Even in the final stages of writing this book, putting the pieces together has shown me in some places more than I expected, and in some other places has made it evident that there are still missing pieces to be sought.

One of the last collections that I revisited provided me with hard evidence to confirm what I had thought might be the case – that support for peace work of one kind or another was greater in the National Union of Women's Suffrage Societies (NUWSS) than has previously been recognized. On another issue, what I found when I put the pieces together overthrew rather than confirming my former thinking. I had accepted the popular wisdom that the suffragists really had no option but to accept the limited franchise for women that was held out to them in 1917. Now I make a case that they could indeed have done better with a bit more courage and political will on the part of the leadership; this is not exactly 'hard' evidence, since you can never prove what would have been the consequences of actions that did not take place. But the evidence is very suggestive. Another surprise to me at the end was the self-damaging indifference of the Labour Party to the claim of women for a wider, less classist franchise; the party simply was absent from the positions and places where I expected to find it. The work of other historians suggests some general reasons that may have contributed to this; but there is clearly room for more detailed research here.

I have found it a fascinating experience and a privilege to try, if not to walk in the shoes of an earlier generation, at least to get a little closer to the reality of their lives. In those lives there is much that may resonate for us. On the micro scale, many of us work on committees of organizations identified by long acronyms, organizations which we hope are going to be able to effect change for the better; and we sometimes bog down in imperfect or abused process. On the macro scale, we are once more working against a background of war, less intimate and close for most of us than the war of 1914 to 1918 was for my protagonists, but potentially even more devastating in its consequences; like them, we look for ways to turn things around.

Because I hope to build some small bridges between different disciplines and to make this important story available to an even wider readership, I have been at some pains to give enough explanatory background to facilitate understanding. What theory there is – and indeed I hope there is some – emerges from the material, and is my own. I hope that telling the tale as I found it will enable scholars and general readers to bring to it understanding enriched by their own special knowledge and experience.

Acknowledgements

Because my life has been full of all manner of things – good, bad and indifferent – and because I am at best a slow writer, the work from which this book has emerged has been spread over many years. Throughout those years I have had invaluable help from many people, and I welcome the opportunity to express my appreciation.

Once more, primary help, exceptional skills, and comradeship in the research came from my colleague, Margaret Kamester, whose friendship has added a special dimension. I want also to pay particular tribute to the late Susan Shea, whose intelligence, good humour and patience made her a first-class research assistant, and who lived and died with courage. The skilled help and warm encouragement provided by Ruth Pincoe have been a special joy.

Douglas Newberry has given me invaluable support technologically, materially and with his unswerving respect for my work and love towards myself; Irene England has been his generous partner in all this. Mary Newberry and Gus Sinclair have fed my body with good food, my mind with conversation, and my soul with love, laughter and companionship. Among others who helped at an early stage with my research were John Isaac and Soo Newberry, and more recently (a particular joy) my grand daughter, Siara Isaac. Others who helped in different ways, from supportive friendship to technological rescue, have been Jean Dean, Phillida Hargreaves, Arpi Hamalian, Bert and Lyn Horwood, Charles and Daphne Maurer, Evelyn Reid, the late Eleanor Segel, and Mair Verthuy.

Conversation with the following in person, by telephone and by email spread out over a number of years has been of great help in broadening and clarifying my thinking and in some instances in saving me from error: Jo Alberti, Naomi Black, Ken Blackwell, Blanche Wiesen Cook, Sheila Fletcher, Brian Harrison, Sandra Holton, Tom Kennedy, Jill Liddington, Sybil Oldfield, Richard Rempel, and David Rubinstein. Special thanks go to Hal Smith, who has greatly and generously helped me with his knowledge of the subject, to David Doughan whose unrivalled knowledge of the women's suffrage collections now in the Women's Library has been so freely put at the service of more then one generation of scholars, and to Ursula Franklin with whom it has been my great privilege to exchange ideas on many subjects. They are not of course responsible for any errors.

I shall not repeat here the names of all the others who have contributed as research assistants both to this book and to my earlier work; they are mentioned in the acknowledgements to *From Liberal to Labour*, and my appreciation continues for their contribution and that of others who have had to be omitted from the list.

This work could not have been done without access to the Fawcett collection now at the Women's Library and to the Catherine Marshall papers in Cumbria Record Office. For information on the Women's International League for Peace and Freedom and its British branch I have made use of collections at the University of Colorado in Boulder, in the Swarthmore College Peace Collection, and at the British Library of Political and Economic Science, where the E.D. Morel papers also shed light on the early days of the Union for Democratic Control. Other rich sources have been the Labour Party archives, the suffrage papers at Manchester Public Library, and the International Archive for the Women's Movement in Amsterdam; in addition I have drawn on the Bertrand Russell Archives at McMaster University, the Fonds Duchêne, Bibliothèque de documentation internationale contemporaine (Nanterre), and the Clifford Allen papers at the University of South Carolina. Two of the collections were available to me only by correspondence at the time I used them and I appreciate the service I received in the use of the Lloyd George papers (then at the House of Lords) and of the Schwimmer-Lloyd Collection at the New York Public Library, from which Edith Wynner sent me selected documents.

I am grateful for the opportunities to use these remarkable facilities, and warmly appreciate the assistance offered by their staff. Particular mention must be made of the generosity of Frank, George and Eve Marshall in encouraging full use of the papers of Catherine Marshall, in sharing their memories, and in allowing me access to a smaller collection of papers kept by the family; and also of Barbara Strachey Halpern who allowed me to use her extensive collection while it was still in her house in Oxford.

I greatly appreciate the funding and/or facilities provided at various times by the following: the Canada Council; the Canadian Social Sciences and Humanities Research Council; the (now, alas, defunct) Canadian Institute for International Peace and Security (Barton Fellowship); Institute for Advanced Study in the Humanities, Edinburgh University; Lucy Cavendish College, Cambridge (Calouste Gulbenkian

Fellowship); Simone de Beauvoir Institute, Concordia University, Montreal; Queen's University, Kingston, Ontario; Woodbrooke Friends' Study Centre, Birmingham.

I appreciate the help I have received from Ruth Ireland and Michael Strang at Palgrave Macmillan, and of Shirley Tan.

Jo Vellacott
Kingston, Ontario: 2007

Abbreviations

The following abbreviations are used in notes and text. See also the abbreviations for collections in the bibliography.

AR	Annual Report
BCIWC	British Committee of the International Women's Congress (later WIL, qv)
CC	*Common Cause*
CCCWSS	Consultative Committee of Constitutional Women's Suffrage Societies
CCEW	Central Committee for the Employment of Women
EFF	Election Fighting Fund for Women's Suffrage
ELFS	East London Federation of Suffragettes (later WSF, q.v.)
FWW	Federation of Women Workers
IAS	Inter-Allied Suffragists
ICWPP	International Conference of Women for Permanent Peace
ILP	Independent Labour Party
IWSA	International Women's Suffrage Alliance
LL	*Labour Leader*
LSWS	London Society for Women's Suffrage
MG	*Manchester Guardian*
MWIC	Manchester Women's Interests Committee
NCAS	National Council for Adult Suffrage
NCF	No-Conscription Fellowship
NU, NUWSS	National Union of Women's Suffrage Societies
NU exec.	NU executive committee minutes
p/	postmarked (used for undated or partially dated letters, where they are accompanied by an envelope which can be assumed to be the original)
PLP	Parliamentary Labour Party
PSF	People's Suffrage Federation
TUC	Trade Union Congress
UDC	Union for Democratic Control
VFA	Votes For All
WCG	Women's Cooperative Guild
WFL	Women's Freedom League

WIC	Women's Interests Committee [and see MWIC]
WIL	Women's International League
WILPF	Women's International League for Peace and Freedom
WLL	Women's Labour League
WNC	War Emergency Workers National Committee
WSF	Workers' Suffrage Federation
WSPU	Women's Social and Political Union
WSS	Women's Suffrage Society
WTUL	Women's Trade Union League

1
Introduction: The National Union of Women's Suffrage Societies before the First World War

By the time the First World War broke out, the eventual winning of the vote for women within a few years had become inevitable, although those who wanted this to be so knew they had to keep up the struggle, and those who hoped otherwise still thought they might stave it off. In any event, the impact of the war altered the trajectory of the women's suffrage movement in ways that profoundly affected the outcome, and the nature of the feminism that prevailed. In the immediate pre-war years, new young leadership within the National Union of Women's Suffrage Societies (NUWSS, NU), the major non-militant women's suffrage organization, was embracing a fresh vision of democratic polity, going beyond middle-class women's drive to obtain the vote for themselves. The theme of this book will be the way in which the potential for realization of this vision would be a casualty of the war. This introduction will briefly review significant factors and events in the pre-war history of the NUWSS.[1]

Early years: 1897–1910

The NUWSS had been formed in 1897, as the result of the coming together of two London-based groups, and the formation of a federation of local societies across the country. During its first ten years, the growth of the movement took place mainly at the periphery; in the North of England in particular there was a substantial working-class constituency. Outreach was to men as well as to women, on the logic that the support of those who had the vote was needed, and that common cause could be made with those who did not, who included many working men. The women's campaign had contributed to the awakening of the consciousness of voteless men.

The executive committee, in London, was loosely formed of members from the constituent societies across the country; the active core group was made up mainly of London members, who also facilitated liaison with the pro-suffrage group in Parliament. But despite impressive delegations and petitions from northern textile and pottery women workers, parliamentarians spared little attention for the women's cause. However, the involvement of working women, propaganda amongst men, and the tradition of direct dialogue with Members of Parliament were all features on which the NUWSS would build.

From 1903, when the NU convened a National Convention in Defence of the Civic Rights of Women, the organization took a more active role in the parliamentary constituencies, with local committees pressing parliamentary candidates to pledge their support if elected. By 1907, the need for a stronger and more centralized organization was apparent, and a new and carefully democratic constitution was approved, under which executive committee members were elected for a one-year term by the annual council, and the executive was made responsible to quarterly councils of representatives from the affiliated societies. From this time, too, the NU had its own office and a paid staff.[2] The new constitution was an important advance, enabling the executive to act more effectively, but in some ways it further distanced the constituent societies from the day to day running of the NU, which continued until 1910 to be dominated mainly by London suffragists, members of the London Society for Women's Suffrage (LSWS).

The 1907 constitution provided the remedy for its own shortcomings, since actual policy-making rested in the hands of the elected quarterly councils, which increasingly became a forum for open discussion. By 1909, discontent with the concentration of influence in London was finding expression. Not only was a need felt for more direct and efficient regional administration of such matters as the travel and booking of speakers, but political and philosophical differences were just below the surface.

The NU's formation in 1897 had been strictly on a non-party basis, refusing affiliation to women's auxiliaries of political parties. While the commitment to political neutrality kept party bias from showing openly in the executive (and hence from appearing in the minutes), it did not prevent party loyalties from playing a part in decision-making and the formation of policy. Harold Smith has drawn attention to the significance of conservative influence within the LSWS, and hence on the NUWSS.[3] At the same time, the Liberal Party appeared to many suffragists, many of them long-standing Liberal supporters, to offer the best hope of success, and they were encouraged by the Liberal parliamentary victory in 1906. In the country at large, Liberal membership in the NU was certainly substantial.

Some suffragists, especially in the north, were moving towards a broader vision. The limited objective, to achieve the vote 'on the same terms as is or may be held by men', alienated some who felt that the NU executive was looking to obtain the vote only for women of property, and some supporters moved over to work for adult suffrage, in particular through the new People's Suffrage Federation (PSF), formed in 1909. Significantly, the new northern leadership now increasingly active in the NU stayed with the organization, but took a different route towards what Margaret Llewelyn Davies of the PSF (followed by Sandra Stanley Holton in her important book) named 'democratic suffragism', by moving NU outreach beyond the drawing room to the village hall, the minehead and the factory gate, widening both their audience and their membership to working men and women, and connecting in some areas with a long tradition of suffrage agitation. Between 1906 and 1910, with the pressure and opportunities provided by the important elections of the pre-war decade, and the spur of the attention-getting militancy of the Women's Social and Political Union (WSPU), NUWSS activity developed with extraordinary speed.

The control exercised at the centre by the small and large 'c' conservatives of the LSWS became increasingly irritating to some suffragists at the periphery, and by 1909, the Birmingham and Keswick societies in particular were advocating major change.

Constitutional reform: 1910

Among those most interested in seeing some regionalization of the NU were Emily Gardner of the Birmingham and Midlands Women's Suffrage Society, and Catherine Marshall, of the Keswick Women's Suffrage Association (KWSA). Despite the importance of Gardner's contribution at this early stage, she – probably from choice – did not continue with a nationally visible role, while Catherine Marshall became prominent. Marshall was from a comfortably off Liberal background, and had had an excellent liberal education at home and at St. Leonard's School in St. Andrews, with periods of travel, particularly in Germany; unlike many of the new leaders, she did not go to university. Her father was a housemaster at Harrow School, her mother (Caroline Marshall) and she were active in the Women's Liberal Association in Harrow, and after the family moved to Keswick in 1904, when Catherine was 24, she campaigned for suffrage and the Liberal Party in the 1906 general election. Even at this time, she was no drawing-room suffragist, but reached out in her campaigning to women and men of all occupations and economic levels. By 1908 it was clear that the Liberal government, under Asquith's leadership, was in no hurry to enfranchise women, and the Marshalls focussed increasingly on advocacy for suffrage, rather than support for the foot-dragging Liberal Party, forming the KWSA as a branch of the NU. After taking part in a major suffrage procession and demonstration in London in July 1908, Catherine Marshall's energy and most of her time were dedicated to campaigning widely for the cause in the Lake District, countering anti-suffragists, and promoting support in Liberal clubs and the Women's Liberal Association when opportunity arose.

Marshall's concern for some measure of regional organization had initially come mainly from a felt need to improve efficiency and cooperation with other societies, while Gardner's plan was more far-reaching. Both reform schemes had been mooted in 1909, and a specially appointed committee – on which both Gardner and Marshall served – brought a new and complicated proposal for constitutional revision to the NU Council in 1910.

Initially, the plan brought forward by the Gardner committee nearly bogged down in the difficulty some had in understanding its implications, as well as the hostility of a few who perhaps understood them only too well. Opposition came from several members of the national executive and from the LSWS.[4] Under the constitution which finally emerged, the general council, consisting of delegates from every society in the NU, would meet twice a year (instead of quarterly), and would elect the executive and officers at its February meeting. The local societies were to join together in regional federations, each with a committee made up of a representative from each of its constituent societies, together with a non-voting member of the national executive. These committees were charged with promoting the growth of new societies, improving the organizational framework, making arrangements for joint meetings and coordinating the use of travelling speakers, and conducting election work, if they so wished, in accordance with NU policy. A new provincial council was established to meet twice a year, and to consist of the national executive, together with two elected representatives and one officer from each federation. Although the provincial council could not make policy, which remained in the hands of the general council, it could take any action consistent with approved policy.[5]

The reformers – the increasingly visible democratic suffragists – helped to make sure that the new scheme went into effect: Marshall promulgated an explanatory leaflet, Helena Swanwick gave space for helpful articles in the *Common Cause*, of which she was editor. For most regions the advantages of the new constitution clearly outweighed the drawbacks, and federations were formed rapidly and enthusiastically.[6]

The results of the 1910 constitutional revision were quite dramatic, and probably went beyond the expectations of those who had framed the scheme. Federation had been seen as freeing regional groups to develop strategies suitable to their needs, and as enabling coordination of regional administrative needs. More important in the long run was its effect in making the up and coming provincial leaders known to their own constituents and much more visible nationally; the provincial councils provided them with a forum where they were both seen and heard, becoming better acquainted with each other and with the members. The result was the election of a significant number of new women to the national executive, where they quickly made their mark. The provincial councils also provided a forum for exploring common experience and developing initiatives which could then be brought to the general council. Less visible, but significant, was the change in the composition of grassroots support behind executive members. While the executive remained mainly middle class, they were no longer mostly elected from branches consisting solely of their like, but instead came from broader local and regional constituencies where working women had been a respected part of the suffrage movement for some time.

During the next two years the democratic suffragists took over leading roles in the NU executive, and there was significant change too in the makeup of those working at headquarters, among both honorary officers and paid staff. The relationship of the LSWS to the NU office underwent something of a role reversal: no longer was the NU national office dominated by traditional LSWS members; rather, the LSWS was significantly infiltrated by members of the now more radical NU staff, officers and executive, some of them born and bred Londoners, others immigrants from different parts of the country, and particularly from the north, resident in London only because of the demands of their suffrage work. Although the new members did not generally compete for office within the LSWS, leaving that control with the long-time members, there was a new tension at times between the NU officers, staff and executive, and the leading members of the LSWS.

Resisting reform: The London Society for Women's Suffrage

The LSWS had disliked and feared the 1910 constitutional changes from the start, had not shown sufficient interest even to send delegates to the first Provincial Council (held in Keswick in October 1910), and made no move to form its own federation until 1913, when a modified scheme for London was introduced by Ray Strachey at the LSWS annual meeting in November.

Ray Strachey, born Costelloe (in 1887), was raised in the main by her devoted grandmother, Hannah Whitall Smith, an American Quaker but far from any kind of orthodoxy in her views. Ray had a good formal education at Kensington High School and at Newnham, Cambridge, enhanced and sometimes interrupted by a remarkable variety of experience and of travel between her mother's residence in Italy and the home of her grandmother in London, with visits to relatives in the United States. As a student, she took part in a NU suffrage caravan tour in 1908, in the course of which she enjoyed the hospitality of the Marshalls in Keswick, and she had also joined the Reverend Anna Shaw in a suffrage tour in the US. In 1911, she married Oliver Strachey. Oliver's sister, Philippa (Pippa), had long been active in the LSWS, and when Ray renewed her interest in suffrage, Oliver too became active.[7]

The shape that would be taken by the LSWS federation involved important issues.[8] The class makeup of societies might differ sharply according to geographical location, and one of the ways in which the federal scheme contributed to democratization of the NU was in the value and voice it gave to each individual society, mandating that each local society was affiliated directly to the NU, and each federation committee was composed of representatives from every member society in its area. The model prescribed in the 1910 constitution would have made the LSWS more truly democratic by building in provision for an equal voice and equal control over funding to be given to the suffragists from the East End and from South London, rather than continuing the hegemony of the members from the city's West End and northern suburbs.

Ray Strachey's plan did not go nearly as far as the regular federation model, but most incoming and outgoing LSWS executive members liked it, including initially at least some of those associated with the democratic suffragists, notably Maude Royden. Helena Swanwick, however, more radical in outlook and well able to perceive the ramifications of a constitutional document, moved an amendment which would have initiated a London federation in complete conformity to the NU's normal rules of federation. A stormy and confused discussion ensued, with proposals and counter-proposals from every quarter. The Stracheys were in no doubt that the London Society was 'fighting for its life'.[9] The financial arrangements were the focus of the dispute. A clause in Strachey's plan by which branches would receive from the federation executive 'an annual income proportionate to their annual subscriptions' Strachey euphemistically described as 'financial independence' (a phrase which Marshall marked with an exclamation mark in the margin of her copy of the proposal). Although this was an improvement on the previous arrangement, under which all subscriptions were absorbed by the LSWS headquarters, it still left the poorer areas heavily disadvantaged and the LSWS executive in control.

Equally significant was the structure for the appointment of the executive. Since the LSWS had always operated as a single unit, despite the existence of branches, its twenty-member executive had no built-in representation of the various London regions, with their different class populations, and this was to be maintained. In Strachey's words, this arrangement ensured that it was 'possible to choose the most competent people, no matter where they live';[10] in practice it meant that the executive could continue to be drawn predominantly if not exclusively from middle- and upper-class west, central and north London.[11]

So serious were the disagreements that no resolution was reached at the November meeting of the LSWS, and an adjourned meeting was called for the following month. Although the NU as such carefully took no position on the matter, the perception inevitably was of the NU headquarters pitted against the LSWS executive, but by the time the adjourned meeting took place, tempers had cooled and a compromise was reached. Strachey's scheme was adopted in the main, and Swanwick withdrew her total opposition, resting content to introduce amendments to the financial arrangements, and to insist on the use of the term 'federation'. Liberty was given to branch societies in the London region to affiliate directly to the NU if they preferred; a number would soon take advantage of this, causing considerable consternation in the LSWS executive. The revised constitution was approved at the February 1914 council of the NU, granting the LSWS 'the status of a Federation, with all its rights and responsibilities, though, owing to the special character of its work and organisation, the Society does not adopt the ordinary federation rules.'[12]

The London Society had successfully resisted the more democratic features of the federation scheme, and the same group of people remained in control. Its continuing narrow outreach lends credence to the persistent view of the LSWS and of the NU when under its domination as something of a social club for the well-off. Although the dominant London members were right that London had particular problems and might not fit the regular model, their motivation may have derived as much from inherent classism as from strategic considerations.

Some tensions continued between the LSWS and the NU headquarters, but on the whole the two cooperated with wary mutual respect until the war. What is significant, however, is that the modified federation structure of the LSWS gave those who held influence there some coherence, security from radical infiltration, and protection from having to answer to a large and unpredictable constituency from across London. Although they still had good representation on the NU executive, they had lost their dominance there after the 1910 reforms, but the same leaders – in particular the Strachey family – retained it in the LSWS. At the side of the stage now, they would be available to step on to centre stage again when the unforeseen events of 1914–15 took place.

Democratic suffragism takes hold: 1912–14

Developments between 1912 and 1914 may be summarized quite briefly. Successively, hope in a private member's bill, in a bill uniting some members of all parties (the Conciliation Bills), and in the good intentions of the Liberal Party was lost. After the débacle of 1912, when the Speaker ruled that the Liberal government's Reform bill could not be amended as promised to include women's suffrage, the NU focussed its attention on by-elections and the next general election, due in early 1915. Trust in the power, if not the good faith, of the many individual MPs of all parties who had declared themselves committed suffragists had been shown to be misplaced. The objective now was to ensure that whatever party came to power in the general election had a firm commitment, as a party, to a measure which would extend the franchise to at least some women. To this end the NU courted the Labour Party, coaxed the Conservative Unionists, and threatened the Liberals.

The Labour Party was wooed in several different ways. A huge grassroots campaign worked with those already active for women's suffrage; much was done to raise the consciousness of the many men still excluded from the franchise; strong connections were made with working women's organizations; the Trade Union Congress (TUC), a numerically very significant part of the Labour Party, was infiltrated and converted, largely by the brilliant work of Margaret Robertson, the NU's leading paid organizer, and herself a Labour sympathizer; individual Labour leaders were targeted; the Independent Labour Party (ILP) was kept on its toes. Despite its name, the left-wing ILP was an integral part of the Labour Party, with representation on the National Executive, and was always the section of the party most supportive to women's suffrage. By stages, the Labour Party affirmed its support for women's suffrage, and by January 1912 became the only party pledged to reject any franchise reform that did not include women. The NU decided on a radical new policy, developing the Election Fighting Fund (EFF), through which it was able to offer Labour candidates substantial financial help and probably even more valuable organizational skills and resources in selected constituencies where there would be a three-cornered contest. The training and employment of a number of working-class women as election organizers built further bridges of respect and common interest. At the same time a scheme called the Friends of Women Suffrage increased outreach to working women by enrolling and keeping in touch with declared sympathizers who were unable to afford the expense of time or money involved in full NU membership.

The development of the EFF policy was unpopular in some NU societies, including the LSWS, and with some individuals,[13] especially in those constituencies where Liberalism was strong within the NU branch, and where suffragists felt they had a strong supporter in their local Liberal MP. But it was upheld by a strong majority in the executive, and found support in most parts of the country. The EFF raised substantial funds and took an active role from 1912 on, pursuing its negotiations with the national ILP and Labour Party meanwhile. The final key agreement – affirming commitment on both sides – was made at a meeting of NU and EFF representatives with the National Administrative Council (NAC) of the ILP at Glasgow in January 1914, and confirmed comfortably at the Labour Party annual conference and by the NU Council, although not without a certain degree of obfuscation. Interpretation of this 'Glasgow agreement' would be highly controversial in the changed circumstances of 1915.[14]

Work developed as a series of particular understandings in the constituencies selected for EFF work. Selection was by NU criteria, focussing for instance on seats held by anti-suffrage Liberal ministers or on seats of particularly pro-active Labour suffrage members, and was made cooperatively with the local Labour Party and the local WSS – which might have its own EFF committee. In some constituencies, no Labour candidate would have stood had it not been for the promise of EFF support. The nature of the support might be of several kinds; EFF organizers trained and paid by the EFF worked on voter registration ahead of the expected general election or a by-election, and on setting up constituency offices, public meetings, canvassing, press work, mailings and so on during an election.

Most visible was work in a number of by-elections, in most of which the EFF contributed significantly to an increase in the Labour vote, although no seats were won.[15] Less visible, but potentially of greater importance, was help in preparation for the expected general election, where an approved Labour candidate in a targeted constituency might be given support far beyond what the party could have furnished, with a full-time organizer, trained and paid by the EFF, providing on-the-spot expertise and working in effect as a Labour Party staff person. Voter registration, in particular, played an essential role under the cumbrous regulations of the time, particularly among the working class; the Labour Party, for lack of staff, often lagged behind. Especially in targeted constituencies, the local WSS also often provided substantial volunteer help. Work had begun in twenty-two constituencies, of which seventeen had already named candidates by mid-1914.[16]

Although there was no likelihood that Labour would come to power in the expected general election, the EFF policy was the cornerstone of the NU's political pressure campaign through 1913 and 1914, and not just for its direct effect on that party. The NU had cultivated friends and suffrage sympathizers in every party, and set to work through them to reach the party policy-makers. The Liberals were invited to dread three-cornered contests which would deprive them of their majority in some constituencies, and to fear the possibility of a stronger Parliamentary Labour Party to which they might have to make policy concessions in the House of Commons; the alternative was to root out the leading anti-suffragists from their number (and especially from the Cabinet) and make an open commitment to franchise reform that would include women. The Unionists were asked to confront the likelihood of the introduction of a wide franchise by conceding the need to enfranchise women, and committing themselves to enacting at least a narrower measure more to their liking, should they win the election.

In his biography of Millicent Fawcett, David Rubinstein shows her to have been, at least by 1912, substantially free of party interest.[17] The cause was all-important to her, and it was her outspoken and uncompromising devotion to it – together with the respect that she always commanded from friend and foe alike – that made her for many years a great leader for the NU. Not a great strategist herself, she relied on a relatively small group of women around her to set the agenda and carry things forward. From 1910 to 1915, this group was comprised of the leading democratic suffragists.

Fawcett, now already in her mid-sixties, enjoyed the comparative youth and vitality brought by Kathleen Courtney and Catherine Marshall, the two with whom she worked on almost a daily basis. Marshall had demonstrated her administrative abilities and political skills, and after substantially increasing the visibility of the NU while she served as press secretary, she was temporarily appointed Honorary Parliamentary Secretary on the resignation of Edith Palliser in 1912, and was elected to the position in 1913, defeating Chrystal MacMillan, herself another forward-looking influence in the NU who had been a member of the executive for several years. MacMillan already had played a dramatic role in suffrage history, having pleaded the final unsuccessful appeal of Scottish graduate women on their claim to the vote before the bar of the House of Lords in 1908. Kathleen Courtney, meanwhile, had been elected honorary secretary of the NU in 1911, replacing Edith Dimock. Courtney had grown up in London, taken her degree at Oxford, had worked at the Daisy Club (a girls' club in Lambeth, London) and for several years in a paid position as secretary to the North of England Society for Women's Suffrage, in which Margaret Ashton was another influential democratic suffragist. Although Fawcett was never demonstrative, a great deal of warm affection undoubtedly grew between her and the two new officers, Marshall and Courtney.[18] Emily Leaf, who took over from Marshall as press secretary in April 1911, was another of the younger ones, an eager disciple of Marshall's in the art of getting good media coverage locally and nationally. Ida O'Malley, a young Oxford history graduate, became honorary secretary to the literature committee. Helena Swanwick, somewhat older and always more astringent, brought great ability and uncompromising honesty to the editorship of the *Common Cause*. Maude Royden, later to be a well known preacher, was young, enthusiastic, and a good speaker and writer; she took over editing the *Common Cause* when Swanwick resigned. Isabella Ford, a Quaker and trade unionist from Leeds, was one of the older NU stalwarts and one of the very few democratic suffragists whose friendship with Fawcett both pre-dated the campaigns of 1912–1914 and survived the divisions of 1915.[19] All of these served on the executive, which met monthly; most were from outside London, although some were living there to facilitate their suffrage work. O'Malley and

Royden, however, had been active in the LSWS for some time. All, except O'Malley, were personally moving left politically, or were already there. But the nominally unchanged non-party principle and the demonstrably effective strategic rationale for the arrangement with the Labour Party shielded these women from open discussion of their party sympathies on any but the suffrage issue.

The new leaders covered a wide range of age and personality, but they also had a great deal in common. All of those named above were from middle to upper middle class families; most were enabled to do their suffrage work because they either had their own independent means or had the political and financial support of their families. Most of the active younger women had benefited from the great advances made in the education of privileged women, and in particular from exposure to remarkable teachers at certain enlightened institutions where freedom of serious discussion was encouraged. Correspondence between Courtney and Royden (cited in Fletcher's biography of the latter) during and after their time together at Lady Margaret Hall, Oxford University, often brightened by a sense of fun, nevertheless brings vividly to life their sense of mission, of important work to be done. Class privilege for them was seen as entailing responsibility; and several went further, making a serious effort, without condescension, to understand the lives of the less fortunate by working in settlements, or (in Ford's case) with women trade unionists.[20] A frequently discussed but now mercifully obsolete ethical dilemma which forms part of the background to the availability of such unpaid talent to the suffrage movement was the issue of whether it was morally justifiable for young women whose fathers could support them to compete for paid work with those who really needed it.[21]

A second long-affirmed principle, along with the non-party stance, was that the NU was working for suffrage for women on the same terms 'as is or may be' given to men. Not incidentally these were both principles dearly held by Millicent Fawcett, although not with complete consistency: the failed Conciliation Bills of 1910 and 1911 had been cautiously supported by the NU, although they offered a franchise even narrower than 'as is'. A good many suffragists, including Fawcett, held that any opportunity should be taken to break the gender barrier, however narrow the breach. The new leaders trod carefully around Fawcett's sensibilities. The EFF policy was constructed and named as a strategic arrangement with the Labour Party, rather than as an alliance, and therefore as no departure from the non-party principle. And in rousing the dormant demand for enfranchisement among the many men who did not have the vote, what the democratic suffragists were doing in effect was to shift the emphasis from work for the vote 'as is held by men' to 'as may be held by men', and, they hoped, making sure that the voteless men made common cause with the voteless women. Adult suffrage would become a compelling drive without having to be so named.

For a number of the most active of the NU's new leaders, moving into the new relationship with the Labour Party had been an education. Closer acquaintance with articulate women trade union leaders and men and women of the ILP had provided them with a better theoretical understanding of democratic socialist ideals, which for some resonated with what they had formerly believed to be the direction towards social justice promised by liberalism. Perhaps even more important were the grassroots personal connections being cultivated. It was nothing new for women's suffrage speakers to draw their examples of women's need for the vote from the sufferings of working women, but Catherine Marshall's speeches, for example, took on a new conviction and a fresh basis in reality after she came to know more and more working women who knew they wanted the vote, knew why they needed it, and had been working for years to make the trade unions and the Labour Party understand their position.

The new NU leaders, especially those from the north, counted as colleagues women of all backgrounds. The LSWS, meanwhile, valued the working-class connection in rather a different way, mainly for the spice that these working women added to suffrage occasions. For example, in October 1911, when a group of women pit-brow workers were in London protesting a threat to their work, Pippa Strachey asked Fawcett for 'the loan of two or three of the pit-brow girls' for an At Home; and in January 1913, Pippa wrote to Susan Lawrence asking if she could provide a party of charwomen for an Albert Hall meeting, saying 'I am a great enthusiast for charwomen whom I consider the salt of the earth.'[22]

The position of the suffrage issue at the outbreak of war was summed up in November 1914 by Marshall, NU Parliamentary Secretary, in her report to the Council. Although no women's suffrage bill had come before the House of Commons in the last session, Marshall pointed to several occasions on which the cause had been aired in Parliament. Admitting that the Irish question had dominated the 1914 parliamentary session, Marshall claimed 'there had been every indication that when that was settled Women's Suffrage would loom large ... and be a prominent issue at the General Election'. This she attributed to the pledge of the Labour Party, to growing interest within the Conservative Party, with a move towards the adoption of a definite policy, and to increasing uneasiness among Liberals, in reaction to Conservative interest in the question and even more in response to the pressure resulting from the NU's Election Fighting Fund policy. 'All parties', she said, 'realised that the Women's claim was becoming yearly more difficult to refuse or evade.' She mentioned other bills affecting women, and spoke of progress made both in South Africa and in New Zealand, where the suffrage victory of 1893 might soon be followed by eligibility to sit in Parliament; she also spoke of the visit to London in June of the international board of the International Women's Suffrage Association (IWSA), commenting that those spokesmen from all parties who had welcomed them had 'expressed their opinion that the next Government, whatever party was in power, would be obliged to deal with the question of Woman Suffrage.'[23]

Marshall's review consciously brought together all the most hopeful signs. But it did not depart from the truth. To focus too narrowly on this or that delaying factor in British politics is to ignore a wider trend which indicated that by 1914, in the western (and commonwealth) world a measure of women's suffrage was an idea whose time had come. But by the time the review was presented, the country had been at war for three months, and suffrage hopes and fears were on hold, though never far from feminist consciousness.

2
Response to War: August to October 1914 ·

Feminist response to crisis

The British people became aware of their country's impending declaration of war only at the final moment, the last two or three days of July, in part because of the difficulty the Cabinet had had in agreeing to go to war. During the August bank holiday weekend (31 July to 3 August) a belated but substantial campaign was mounted, protesting and calling for British neutrality by petitions, letters, meetings and in a wide range of the press; only the conservative press, which had long wanted a showdown with Germany, showed some satisfaction. But by that time, the decision had been made, and because the declaration of war was indeed made by a Liberal government, the Liberal press almost instantly fell into line and expressed support. The voice of those still protesting was muted, only able to find an outlet in, for instance, the *Labour Leader*, the weekly paper of the Independent Labour Party.[1]

For good reasons, many anticipated that the war would bring economic ruin, and the first few weeks seemed to promise that the gloomiest predictions would be fulfilled. In the event, experience varied sharply according to economic status. Many of the least well off lost their jobs or the family breadwinner almost instantly, and suddenly faced a critical present and an uncertain future. Prices rose enough to be catastrophic for those who were already marginal, or who were among the many who altogether lost their source of income. A vast number of people lived almost literally from hand to mouth, with nothing left over from the week's pay packet by the time the next week ended. Only the flimsiest social safety net was provided – and that for relatively few – by the recently enacted Health and Unemployment Insurance Acts. Auerbach described the crisis as she saw it:

The magnitude of the financial disaster in which this country is involved is not easily grasped – It is almost impossible for any commercial firm to tell whether they will be solvent or not when normal business is resumed and perhaps you can imagine what effect that is going to have on the trade of the country. I am haunted day and night with the thought of the unemployment and distress that I see coming and that we shall be helpless to alleviate except to an infinitely small extent. I believe our Societies will rally with fervour in support of any scheme that we can frame for work.[2]

Within London the worst effects were naturally in the poorer East End, and here the fullest feminist firsthand account of wartime experience comes from Sylvia Pankhurst, who was known to and trusted by many of the poorest women.[3] She described how reservists and volunteers, often the main family breadwinners, left almost at once for unknown military destinations, leaving their families uncertain what measure or source of support would be available to them. In some cases either the serviceman or his closest relatives, or both, were unable to read and write, with the result that, at best, no news was sent or received for a considerable time, and at worst, no allowance came through. Government provision for the payment of allowances to the dependants of soldiers was inadequate, inefficiently administered, and erratically paid. Even the men who had flooded to volunteer were incompletely provided for, and were expected to find money for necessary clothing, bedding and so on, while appeals were made to the public to send shirts, socks, cardigans, wool helmets and even handkerchiefs for the soldiers – although by the end of the month the embarrassed War Office was denying the need.[4]

If the condition of the soldiers' families was bad, that of some others was as desperate. Numerous factories and large and small businesses closed, temporarily or permanently. Many of the well-to-do carried out their personal economies, which they saw as patriotic, in ways that added to unemployment – for instance, by dismissing some of their domestic staff, at that time a very large and particularly vulnerable group. There were countless reasons for being thrown out of work; for example, many jobs involving horses were lost instantly as the army commandeered the animals, although in some cases the men working with them were offered the choice, on short notice, of enlisting with the commandeered animals, as were the drivers of requisitioned motor vehicles.

Despite the extent and suddenness of the crisis, the NUWSS responded promptly and effectively, and with a strong sense of its own identity. The activities of the NU at the beginning of the war provide striking evidence of the centrality of the role that the non-militant women's suffrage societies played in the lives of their members by this time, and of the extent and efficiency of its network. There has not been sufficient recognition of the role of the non-militant women's suffrage movement in educating a large body of women throughout the country in self-confidence and in an understanding of women's history, position, needs and potential contribution that went far beyond the demand for the vote.

Already, on 3 August, the day before Britain declared war, the executive had sent out a letter to all the constituent societies, asking for their views on what should be the action of the NU. Meanwhile, a number of women's organizations had asked them to coordinate an opportunity for the voice of women to be added to that of the many groups trying to delay British involvement in the war; working with several IWSA members who were in London they organized a mass women's meeting at the Kingsway Hall on the evening of 4 August.[5] On 5 August, with war now a fact of life, the women – staff and leaders – turned their attention to the best way to meet immediate needs.

By the time the executive met on 6 August, more than two hundred replies to the letter of 3 August had been received, and Courtney reported that all except two 'had been in favour of the Union using its organisation at this time for the help of sufferers from the industrial and economic dislocation caused by the war.' With this kind of mandate, she had felt free to go ahead, especially as people were flocking to the office spontaneously to offer help 'in a variety of capacities' and in such numbers that she had already set up a card-index system (the latest in technology)[6] to keep track of the information. Courtney also 'stated that she and Miss Marshall had taken the responsibility of offering the services of the Office to the Local Government Board for its work of dealing with offers of help, but had not yet received a definite reply.' The committee unanimously endorsed these actions, which had been mirrored all over the country by societies offering help to the local authorities, and members pooled what information was available on the combined plans being made by the 'Lord Mayors, Mayors, and Chairmen of the local Councils' to raise and administer a Central Fund (known as the Prince of Wales' Fund) to alleviate distress, discussing where they could best fit in and have an effect.

The NU office collated a long list of suggestions from societies and individuals on ways in which the Union could best use its resources. They cover a range of objectives from relieving distress to giving direct help to the government in its prosecution of the war. One or two jar unpleasantly in the twenty-first century: in particular a scheme 'for boarding-out children under five years old in the houses of the well-to-do', seen as a useful service to be performed by, amongst others, 'rich people living in the country who cannot do much to help in other ways.' An even more chilling variation of this plan, evidently from another source, proposed that 'Babies under a certain age belonging to parents with less than a certain income be taken charge of by an organisation who would make themselves responsible for them either opening nurseries on a large scale or getting private persons to undertake the care of them. If possible, send them to the country.' Such suggestions reflect grossly classist attitudes in some branches; however, they were atypical and were quietly dropped at headquarters. The majority of the suggestions were closer to the line already being taken, and make it clear that suffragists were aware of the strength of their administrative network and its potential for coordinating work and maintaining a strong feminist presence throughout the country.[7]

The executive recognized that the war was forcing it into a major departure from usual practice in making policy decisions on behalf of the whole Union – in particular the decision to use the organization for purposes beyond the one of suffrage – which would ordinarily have had to be made by a properly called national Council. They accepted the burden of decision consciously and after serious discussion, feeling that the emergency was too extreme to do otherwise, and that it would be irresponsible to try to call people together at such a time of disruption, but reassured by the generally supportive response already received. They agreed, apparently with little discussion, that 'ordinary political work will have to be suspended during the war,' and did not attempt to define exactly what this meant. Indeed, by 28 August, the *Common Cause* was at pains to explain that the NU was not abandoning all political work.[8] The habit of thinking politically underlay most NU action, and the considered response to the crisis was far from the 'unreflective, almost knee-jerk reaction to war, [turning] to work that emphasized gender divisions' ascribed to the NU by Susan Kingsley Kent.[9]

Already, at this early stage, the executive was able to spell out certain important principles which must inform the contribution of the NU. All were agreed that they must act quickly, both because of the urgent need and also because 'it was essential to the interests of the N.U. that the members should be kept together in their various societies. It was essential to organise as a Union and thus keep together. It would be an irreparable misfortune if members were drafted off to other associations.'[10]

The committee rejected the idea of the NU starting a project of its own, but was clearly conscious of the value of suffragists having a high profile in the crisis. The importance of gaining representation on the Citizens' Committees being formed all over the country for relief work was spelled out, and NU societies were urged to put forward the names of women, whether NU members or not, who were particularly fitted for this service. Little mention was made of anything in the way of more direct support of the military effort, except that Chrystal Macmillan proposed 'that the Union should equip and staff a hospital.' The idea was rejected; Auerbach thought that hospitals should be 'part of the national scheme.' Later, however, the Scottish Federation, of which Macmillan was a member, successfully initiated the Scottish Women's Hospitals.[11] The NU also decided, before the end of August, to play no role in recruiting for military service, although their help had been invited. A leader in the *Common Cause* said roundly that women could take the place of men who enlisted, and that the NU would try to ensure a decent wage for them, but since women were sick of being told what to do, they were not about to start telling men what they should do; according to Fawcett, 'it was not [the NU's] function to lecture men on their duty but to encourage women to do theirs'.[12]

By the end of their first wartime meeting on 6 August the executive had a detailed set of proposals to send out to all constituent societies.[13] Significantly, all the action was under the rubric of 'the relief of distress caused by the economic and industrial dislocation', but all favoured provision of work, not of handouts. The NU executive specifically decided against fund-raising for the Prince of Wales' Fund (the major central relief fund which had sprung into existence). In rejecting this role they were refusing both to accept the stereotypical middle-class feminine activity of fund-raising, and to become mere auxiliaries to an organization they did not control. Instead they rejoiced in the realization that Auerbach's farsighted management of the NU's funds, and her insistence on 'keeping a reserve in case of emergency', now 'enabled the Union to keep its organisation together.' Not only was the staff at headquarters maintained and kept busy with work related to the crisis, but by the end of August the decision was made that none of the trained professional political organizers throughout the country – about fourteen in number – were to be dismissed. They would be employed on war-related work where possible, and held on a retainer where no immediate work was seen for them. Although new appointments which were to have taken effect in the autumn were cancelled, even these women were not to be left high and dry; where there was seen to be any financial hardship, they would be employed for a month, giving them time to look for other work.[14]

This kind of security was no small thing. The NU entered the war equipped with a democratic structure by means of which decisions could be made by the organization as a whole, with financial security sufficient to maintain its office and field staff, with confidence in its own administrative expertise, and with the freedom to choose in which direction to offer its services. The case of the militant Women's Social and Political Union (WSPU) was far different. Emmeline Pankhurst was later to claim that 'at the outbreak of the war' she had 'set a whole organization to work'.[15] But in fact the deliberate rejection by Emmeline and Christabel Pankhurst of a democratic constitution makes it as hard to see just what actions were taken by WSPU branches throughout the country on the outbreak of war as it had made it to see anything before the war but the smoke of the arson campaign; recent research has shown great variations of emphasis from branch to branch and significant dissatisfaction among its membership.

The WSPU's initial reaction to the war was similar to that of the constitutional suffragists; all feminists inclined to see the disaster as the inevitable and logical outcome of male dominance in politics. But beyond that, responses differed. For the WSPU, as reflected in the very visible action of its London leadership (primarily Emmeline and Christabel Pankhurst), the outbreak of war led to the cessation of the arson campaign, the release of all the suffragette prisoners, the suspension of publication of the *Suffragette*, dismissal of WSPU organizers with a week's notice, the transformation of Christabel and Emmeline from outlaws into government-sponsored military recruiters, the final rejection (as lacking in patriotism) of Sylvia Pankhurst by her mother and sister. There was a great deal of controversy and divergent activity among the organization's members across the country, who scarcely knew what use was now being made of the London offices, or what had become of their funds, and who had no opportunity to influence statements emanating from their society. Dissent expressed by WSPU members regarding aspects of the Pankhursts' wartime policies and the control of funds exercised by Emmeline and Christabel suggests that when the unity around suffrage and the personal loyalty engendered by the harsh imprisonments, particularly of Emmeline, were dissolved, WSPU members became more conscious of the lack of democracy in their own organization.[16] There were also significant variations within other national suffrage bodies, including the NU, but the democratic constitution of the latter set limits to the variations.

The *Suffragette*, renamed *Britannia*, resumed publication in April 1915, promulgating the anti-German views of Emmeline and Christabel Pankhurst. Jacqueline de Vries has analysed the patriotism of the WSPU leaders, emphasizing their gendered interpretation of the war, by which all that was 'good' (Britain and her allies) was seen as feminine, and all that was 'bad' (Germany) as masculine.[17] Although this can be stretched into lending a feminist theoretical flavour to the WSPU's attitude, the representation of Germany as the male bully and Belgium as the assaulted maiden was also much used by both government and press for pro-war propaganda.

Throughout August, knowledge of distress and of national and personal need flowed into the NU office in a confused and seemingly endless stream. Several specific areas of concern were seen by government, public opinion, and even the women of the NU as suitable for the ministrations of women: for instance, the supply and conservation of food at a domestic level; care of the wounded and of children; social order (in particular, questions of alcohol consumption and of prostitution).

From the start, certain characteristics emerge in the NU's response to the confusion of the early weeks of the war. Remarkable care was shown by the executive to evaluate issues in feminist terms, and to refuse to jump into any activity just because others thought they should, because it was what was expected of women, or because their help was solicited in new and complimentary terms. Tensions as to the nature of true feminist patriotism would surface later, and were in fact present from the beginning, but, especially during those few weeks when the prevailing view was that the war would be over quickly, the NU executive made many decisions with conviction and feminist wisdom. They chose where to put their energies, and they laid down their own conditions. The direction taken by the LSWS differed in some significant ways from that laid out by the national executive; we shall return later to look at this.

A syllabus drawn up by the NU in August and revised in September gave guidelines (and suggested speakers) for lectures which local branches were urged to offer on 'Women's Work in Time of War'; the syllabus goes far beyond the earlier mere listing of suggestions.[18] Individually, many members of the NU must have wanted to rush off to volunteer in any capacity that would enable them to feel they were being of service. But here we find very different advice, and a real attempt to channel all this enthusiasm in a feminist direction, with sensitivity to the needs of working women. The first heading is 'Unemployment', and members are cautioned against adding to distress by 'doing any voluntary work, which would oust paid labour' and specifically, for example, against 'Doing voluntary secretarial work on Local Distress Committees under the L[ocal] G[overnment] B[oard]', since 'There are hundreds of efficient clerks and secretaries out of work'.[19] Rather than making articles 'which would be bought through the ordinary channels and paid for by Government', readers are urged 'to support with gifts of money and material the emergency workrooms which have been opened by the N.U. and other organizations, for out-of-work seamstresses.'

Under 'Schemes for Stimulating Employment' suggestions are made which members can urge on the government and local authorities, but it is noted that 'government plans for stimulating employment benefit women only indirectly or slightly', and concrete schemes are outlined to help women: the 'opening of Workrooms in which clothing may be made for future distribution'; helping women to move to places where work is available; training women for 'trades in which there is always a shortage of labour'; setting up laundry service for the needs of newly enlisted soldiers in camps and for military hospitals.

These suggestions addressed the critical distress by looking to provide work which used the existing skills of the women hardest hit by the war. Even so, the list of occupations in which women could replace the men who went to the Front included – especially in the later draft - many that were outside the traditional expectations of women at that time, such as gardeners, farmers, chefs, tram and bus conductors, cart and van drivers, special constables, clerks, commercial travellers, chefs, waiters, shop assistants and shop walkers, and civil servants.

The first of the NU workshops, set up in Whitehall near the NU head office, immediately proved useful. By 18 August work had been found for almost all those (presumably seamstresses) who had applied at that time. In the same spirit the NU sought a constructive solution to the disastrous situation threatening the harvest, opening an office to coordinate offers of help with the harvest; their aim was to ensure that the shortage of workers was supplied, but supplied from the large pool of unemployed rather than by volunteer labour. Every effort was made to encourage conservation of foodstuffs by disseminating information on bottling and preservation.[20]

The NU had positive suggestions for volunteers (who would be mainly from the middle class), focussing on needs that would not otherwise be met, and work that would not cut into jobs available to those needing paid work; suggestions range from 'social work' at baby clinics and maternity centres to service as interpreters for refugees and wounded foreign soldiers. The NU characteristically went at its decision to press for full representation of women on Government Relief Committees from both ends, urging women in the branches to seek this locally, and at the same time making sure that the President of the Local Government Board went on record as wishing 'that women should be adequately represented on these Committees'.[21]

The first months of the war saw heavy casualties on both sides and brought disillusionment to any who had thought that the Allies would walk over the German armies and be home in time for Christmas. Heavy fighting at Mons, around Ypres, and on the Marne in August and September failed to check the German advance, which finally ground to a standstill just short of Paris in November 1914, by which time both sides had already suffered enormous losses; casualty lists – published daily – soared. Very rapidly, the war affected every aspect of life.

Many issues exercised the NU executive and officers. They struggled with tension between the wish to prevent young women from being drawn into prostitution and the need to monitor government infringement of the human rights of suspected prostitutes; they experienced increasing concern over maternity and child care in time of war, over the need to train midwives and nurses, over the loss of jobs by professional women, over the establishment of homes for convalescents and for children, over the treatment of the wives and families of soldiers and sailors, over poor working conditions for women moving into new areas of employment, and over the spread of atrocity stories and the effect this had on inflaming the population to commit acts of violence against citizens of German ancestry or with German names.[22] In addition to finding work for the unemployed, the NU monitored the behaviour of any employers thought to be exploiting women workers, following up, for instance on 'repeated rumours that the *Times* is working its clerks overtime and at reduced pay during the current crisis', and keeping in touch with government and labour bodies over such cases.[23]

The work of the NU did not pass unnoticed, and as labour organizations as well as government strove to put some kind of order into the mass of initiatives which had arisen haphazardly to deal with the distress caused by the war, an attempt was made to enlist their competence and good sense in a more formal setting. Mary Macarthur, a noted women's trade union leader and pre-war adult suffragist, had been appointed as honorary secretary to the Central Committee for the Employment of Women (CCEW), an official body under the Local Government Board and closely connected with the Queen's Work for Women Fund.[24] Macarthur's appointment to the CCEW – and the help that she called on – was part of a bridge between this official body and the War Emergency Workers' National Committee (WNC), on which she represented the Women's Trade Union League (WTUL).

The origin of the WNC is of interest. Ironically, Arthur Henderson had convened a meeting of the National Executive Committee (NEC) of the Labour Party on the eve of war, hoping to form a broad National Peace Emergency Committee which would 'supply a united proletarian response to the threat of war' and urge 'the strictest neutrality possible in the present crisis'.[25] Among the fifteen organizations which were to have been invited to join the major official Labour Party and trade union bodies in this organization was the NUWSS, a significant indication of the standing it had achieved in the regard of some of the Labour leadership by 1914, though it is highly unlikely that the NU would have felt free to join.[26] By the time the NEC met, Britain had declared war; by a majority the NEC gave its *post facto* support to entry into the war, although committing the leadership to work towards obtaining peace as soon as possible. The WNC was transformed at birth into a broad coalition of labour groups and organizations dedicated to relieving distress and preventing the exploitation of workers, and had value in its ability to speak for a wide constituency.

As one of its earliest successes, the WNC negotiated the setting-up of the CCEW by the government, in response to its strong protest against the 'appeals ... being made for women to work for nothing, while hundreds of thousands of working women were out of employment', an issue on which, as we have seen, the NU executive had been equally sensitive from the outset. The WNC was responsible for the appointment of five representatives of working women among the total of fourteen CCEW members.[27]

In the CCEW, Macarthur called on those whose work she already knew – in particular some strong women with labour experience or connections. She asked the NU to loan the service of either Courtney or Marshall to serve on a subcommittee, whose function would be 'to provide schemes for the production of useful articles to be distributed to persons who have no purchasing power, and also schemes to employ workers in various ways. The proposed members ... are Lady Myddleton, Lady Askwith, Miss Susan Lawrence ... and Miss Bondfield.' This was a distinguished group (and not because of the titled names) clearly designed for serious work, so the request was not to be taken lightly, and Marshall agreed to serve for a limited time to get it up and running, realizing that the work she had already been doing in 'collecting ... information as to avenues of employment for the people who apply at our shop in Whitehall' would be relevant, and that 'its activities would to some extent take the place of what I am doing at present.'[28]

Marshall described the CCEW to her mother as 'the very valuable Committee which has emerged from the Queen's Needlework Guild, whose original proposals were so pernicious'; at the outset, the Queen herself had urged unoccupied well-to-do women to set up amateur sewing circles to make some of the garments needed by the army and navy, and had been forced by public pressure to retract the suggestion.[29] What little material survives suggests that the trade union and feminist women handled the relation between 'The Queen's Fund' (QF) and the CCEW with admirable skill. Well-meaning wealthy women had their use as donors and fund-raisers: spending principles could better be set by women with more knowledge of conditions and an understanding of feminist issues. Flyers headed 'Queen's "Work for Women" Fund' describe in fact the work of the CCEW, and are clearly designed for use in fund-raising, keeping the QF organizers and their contributors well-informed of the good use to which their money was being put, highlighting a few cases of particular hardship which had been relieved, and indicating where there was a current need for donations of cash or material.[30]

There is a striking closeness between the terms of reference for the CCEW workshops and the model already set up by the NU in Whitehall, which Marshall had been running throughout most of August. Even the rate of pay was to be exactly the same. Marshall may well have already taken advice in setting the NU rate from another pre-war political contact, James Middleton, assistant secretary to the Labour Party, who was now also serving as secretary of the WNC. Although the amount, ten shillings a week, was then and has since been criticized as low, the original government proposal for family relief from the Prince of Wales Fund had been only six shillings per week for one adult, rising to fourteen shillings and sixpence for a family of four; negotiation by the WNC had resulted in a somewhat better rate, although short of what the WNC itself recommended.[31]

The principles set out by the CCEW were quite strictly circumscribed. In particular, help was to be given to women who had lost their own livelihood directly because of the war, and not to women who were in straitened circumstances because the male breadwinner had enlisted; again the CCEW was in line with WNC policy in insisting that soldiers' dependants were the responsibility of the War Office. And although the term 'relief' was often applied to the opportunity offered by the CCEW, there were no handouts; what was provided was a chance to work, or in some instances to train or retrain for semi-skilled or skilled work. Workrooms were only to be set up where it could be shown that there was 'abnormal need'; and any set up under the CCEW were non-profit, often operating in space provided free and making use of donations of money and materials collected by the Queen's Fund. Care was taken to ensure that they did not compete with any commercial enterprise, especially the hard-hit cheap clothing trade, so they generally produced clothing to be distributed to the very poor, and in particular made baby clothes (out of donated material and used clothing) and cradles (out of banana crates) to go to distressed areas.

Further support was given to commercial workshops by helping them obtain replacement workers and contracts for products for which there was a new wartime demand – for example, the army was calling for vast numbers of men's shirts. In London, many if not the majority of the women thrown out of work were dressmakers and seamstresses, some of whom had worked for companies, some of whom had worked privately for individuals or families. Many well-to-do families, in addition to discharging domestic workers, economized by doing without new dress clothes for the women, a saving made easier by the cessation or changed nature of many social occasions; in addition, distress further affected the sale of cheaper clothes, and export markets were lost. Conversion from ladies' dressmaking to the mass production of men's shirts was not necessarily as easy as it sounds, so the CCEW set up a training course in its workshop in Park Lane specifically to help 'Distressed Dressmakers become Shirt Makers'. Some seamstresses who had done only stitching were trained in the skill of cutting out, by more all-round dressmakers who had also lost their jobs. Contracts facilitated by the CCEW had to contain a 'fair wages clause', and the employed women were to be covered under the National Health Insurance Act.

The work of the CCEW was not confined to London. The closing of many cotton and woollen mills made the situation even more desperate in some parts of the north; many coastal and fishing towns saw a sudden and almost total disruption of customary occupations. The CCEW strove to address problems wherever there was dislocation causing loss of work in a variety of trades and jobs, notably among women clerks.[32] Every effort was made to ensure that work provided under the CCEW itself was temporary, and a large part of the committee's work was directed to finding new permanent employment for the women in need. Marshall continued the research she had already begun into where women workers could be used; for example, she wrote to different parts of the country to find out what part women customarily played in harvesting potatoes, whether this role might be expanded, and whether the need for workers was well supplied locally. Training in a variety of domestic skills might also be provided, some directly related to jobs for which there might be a demand, and some to improve the students' own homemaking skills, for example by knowledge of simple home cooking, or of how to 'make over' secondhand garments, or of more efficient home laundry, or of child care. Although the London workrooms seem to have been the first to get going, help was offered wherever there was need, care being taken to ensure that the CCEW retained control, with the Queen's Fund relegated to the fund-raising role.[33]

Unquestionably the heavy emphasis in most such relief work fell within the traditional sphere of women's occupations. Some elements, too, may suggest to us a taint of middle-class paternalism, but the strong trade union component in the Central Committee must have been satisfied; these were women who knew women workers. Whenever possible, the NU and the CCEW pressed for women to be trained to take the place of men who had joined up, and to be given fair wages in jobs that they might fill in this way.

The idea of turning the war deliberately into an opportunity to free women for employment in occupations previously regarded as male preserves was not the dominant motive, although there was always an undercurrent of anxiety on this score from the men leaving for the front. On the contrary, feminists were motivated by an urgent desire to see the lives of women not made worse by the crisis – and they felt understandable satisfaction when the ability of women to undertake jobs previously reserved for men had to be acknowledged. Some found it less than flattering that such a fuss should be made when it proved to be possible for a woman to accomplish such an undemanding task as that of a tram conductor. In more substantive areas, they took the opportunity to further the feminist cause. For instance, we find the NU urging – as feminists already had unsuccessfully before the war – that women be considered for the civil service; a proposal was prepared, including even a list of suitable names (and diplomatically stressing it as a way to release men for the war), to bring to David Lloyd George, the Chancellor of the Exchequer and an old political sparring partner of Marshall's.[34] The NU also had considerable correspondence on the subject of midwives; the shortage of doctors offered hope for improved conditions of training and work long seen as desirable by many women.[35]

The work of the NU and the CCEW in the first weeks was a direct and well thought out response to the crisis into which the war plunged many women's lives, in an age when many lived so close to the poverty line that a week without work meant quite simply a week without food for themselves and their families. Working with what skills the women had and what jobs were available, they were able to save many from acute distress. By using donations to set up workshops, rather than for direct handouts, they preserved the dignity of the recipients and bought time for them to be trained in new skills and to find employment, again with the aid of the NU or the CCEW, in any area of work where a demand existed; whether it had previously been seen as men's or women's work was not the issue, though employers sometimes needed more persuasion for the former.

In a Fabian tract published on 1 September 1914 Sidney Webb had urged that local relief committees include working people, not just 'prominent citizens' (always of the male sex), friends of the Mayor or Chairman, and professional philanthropists', and specifically described as 'a fatal mistake' the ignoring in many areas of 'the local organizations of working women such as the Women's Trade Unions, the Women's Co-operative Guild, the Women's Labor [sic] League, etc.'[36] Although it took a few weeks to come, the appointment of such women as Mary Macarthur, Margaret Bondfield, and Susan Lawrence to the Central Committee was savoured by many as a triumph for feminism as well as for Labour, and their insistence on Marshall's appointment, brief only at her own wish (and the insistence of her parents),[37] was an affirmation of the NU's pre-war growth in vision, developed as the NU worked alongside Labour for the extension of the suffrage.

Wherever the NU worked to relieve distress, they injected their own feminist yeast into the mix. Several particular examples illustrate the extent to which the NU, in the early days of the war, retained its feminist consciousness, and set its organization and its reputation to the service of feminist causes.

The NU had some serious complaints about the rights of soldiers' and sailors' dependants: payment of allowances was slow, often irregular, and at times attended with a condescending attitude suggesting welfare to the improvident poor, rather than an earned right. The Soldiers and Sailors Families Association, to which the War Office delegated the administration of dependants' allowances, was a charitable organization, and at first treated the legitimate claims of the soldiers' relatives at best as if they were charity cases.[38] But military chauvinism went further, paying little attention to women except in their more or less regrettable relation to men. A wife might lose her allowance if her husband was discharged as unfit, or if he was placed under arrest; at one time, no separation allowance was to be paid if the marriage had taken place after 4 August 1914, or after enlistment; it was a struggle to get any allowance for a child of a common-law marriage, or adequate support for a serving man's mother with whom he had lived and whom he had helped support until he had enlisted.

Home Office and War Office circulars authorized the police to monitor the behaviour of soldiers' wives, and in particular their sobriety, to make sure that none of those receiving money (in lieu though it was of their husbands' pre-war earnings, and as part of their pay) were undeserving of this beneficence, and this Marshall took up with indignation, marking the most offensive passages in a copy of the orders, arranging to meet with the Home Secretary Reginald McKenna, raising the issue in her talks with other political leaders, and later, when revisions made to the War Office circular were found to be still unsatisfactory, drafting a detailed condemnation of the provisions in a letter to the *Manchester Guardian*.[39] Maude Royden, meanwhile, suggested that it might be appropriate to subject all recipients of government pay – and specifically Cabinet Ministers and ambassadors – to the same kind of supervision, and asked 'Who knows whether their private conduct would commend itself as "worthy" to the police?'[40] This was perhaps a more pointed question than she intended, since she may or may not have known – to give two of many possible examples – that Asquith was a heavy drinker and Lloyd George had a mistress.

As casualty lists lengthened, questions around pensions became more pressing. The NU's creative stance is well illustrated by the plan presented to the government Select Committee which (put briefly) suggests that instead of a small lifelong pension, a young childless widow should be given the opportunity to get a thorough training for some work 'of real value', receiving the full cost of living and tuition while training, instead of being 'pensioned off as if her work in the world was of no account because she had no husband'. In listing the jobs for which the widows might be qualified, the NU put in a plug for 'a new Public Health Service'. NU representatives also met with Lloyd George and Andrew Bonar Law, and Marshall enlisted the support of James Middleton.[41]

Another significant issue addressed by the NU was protection of the civil rights of suspected prostitutes. Nineteenth-century feminists, led by Josephine Butler, had won a legendary victory in their campaign for the repeal of the notorious Contagious Diseases Acts, under which women could be picked up and examined or forcibly confined on suspicion of prostitution: the Acts had been suspended in 1883 and abolished in 1886. With the coming of the war, women were again threatened with the same provisions, instituted at first by local regulations introduced in areas where troops were stationed, notably in Cardiff and in Plymouth, and later reinforced by provisions of the Defence of the Realm Act (DORA). Feminists were quick to draw attention to what was happening; Marshall and others raised it with pre-war contacts, and made it clear that the provisions of the Contagious Diseases Act would not be allowed to slip back in unnoticed.[42]

Marshall also brought to the politicians' attention, as indicative of the general suspicion of women common to many of those in authority, the new provisions adopted by publicans' organizations in some regions, on the advice of the police, to forbid women entrance to public houses before 11:30 am. The NU hoped to see some general restrictions placed on hours – as was soon to happen – but resisted what they saw as a tendency to put the blame for increased drinking entirely on women, and to discriminate against them.

The International Women's Relief Committee (IWRC), operating from the overcrowded office of the IWSA, worked with registration and hospitality for Belgian refugees, and occasionally called on the NU's political know-how to help out. For example, in mid-November Marshall had a letter from Ellen Walshe at the IWRC, begging to be put in touch with any MP 'of a waspish turn of mind' who would pressure the government daily to take action on the Belgian refugees. Walshe had visited refugees living in appalling conditions in camps in Holland, as had Mary Sheepshanks and Chrystal Macmillan, and had ample offers of hospitality in Britain, but, she said, the government would not bring them over, nor allow anyone else to do so. Walshe wrote confidently, 'You know all about how to work things in parliament.'[43]

Marshall sent her a long list of MPs of all parties worth approaching, with suggestions on the best way to do this, and herself wrote to Lord Hugh Cecil and some others. Within a few days, the government agreed to bring over another two thousand refugees weekly, for which Marshall rightly took some share of the credit.[44]

The many political and press contacts developed before the war came in useful, and were sought on behalf of a variety of causes. Much of the day-by-day work of advocacy for women's rights in wartime was undertaken on an *ad hoc* basis by whoever would pick it up – mainly Marshall, Kathleen Courtney, and Chrystal Macmillan (whose legal knowledge was invaluable) – but the importance and extent of work under this rubric, and the continuing need, became so clear to the executive that a special committee was formed. The 'Personal Liberties Committee', which was soon changed to the gender-specific but otherwise wider 'Women's Interests Committee' (WIC) held its first meeting on 1 January 1915. The manuscript minute book is only extant for the period from the committee's inception to mid-April 1915; together with scattered papers and records from later, it constitutes a strongly feminist record. Not surprisingly, the most active continued to be Marshall and her cohort; Rackham also attended at the outset and Fawcett regularly brought her keen interest in women's rights. Non-traditional employment, particularly farm work in the early months and later industrial production, especially of munitions, was another major and increasingly important focus of the committee.[45]

To see the concern for women's well-being underlying the work of the NU and the CCEW as anti-feminist, simply because it did not give priority to enabling women to take on previously 'masculine' roles, is to step away from a lived reality and to impose an ahistorical theoretical analysis that makes no sense in the context of the time. My analysis differs markedly from that of Susan Kingsley Kent,[46] who argues that the NU abandoned feminism at the outbreak of war, and jumped back into what she sees as anti-feminist 'motherhood' roles. True, as Kent points out, a writer in the *Common Cause* rejoiced in the news of Sylvia Pankhurst's toymaking workshops set up in the distressed East End, and saw toymaking as appropriate women's work; but the main issue here was that toys had previously been almost exclusively imported from Germany, and that the demand had not altogether dried up, so here was a product which could be sold. Use was indeed made by feminists then (but also before the war) of the rhetoric of motherhood, but action tells us at least as much as rhetoric. Most feminists of that time believed (a belief I share) that true feminism can and should be able to accept motherhood unapologetically as one of women's roles, while rejecting any attempt to make it the only or defining role. Helping women, whether mothers or not, to retain their independence and their ability to support themselves and their families was not only compassionate, but was also a statement of solidarity.

I argue that, at this early stage of the war, the NU showed more feminist independence in choosing its causes than did those suffragists who hastened to do whatever the government asked of them, falling, as ever, into the expected support role. There is a fundamental difference between rushing to enter a man's world on his terms and wanting to enter it on terms which would enable women to bring a new perspective. It was of course not by definition anti-feminist to support the war effort, nor illegitimate to see the opening of opportunity in non-traditional jobs to women as, at the very least, proving a point many feminists had long seen as obvious. What emerged was that suffragism, not inappropriately, contained within it several different feminisms. When the war, and not the vote, took pride of place in suffragists' lives, differences surfaced, and the unity imposed by the single cause threatened to dissolve.

Variation in response: The LSWS

The break in unity was occurring within the NU as well as between the response of different wings of the suffrage movement. A distinct difference of emphasis emerged between the actions of the LSWS and those of the national executive during these first few weeks of the war.

LSWS leaders had also worked throughout the August Bank holiday weekend that saw the war begin,[47] but not apparently in close conjunction with the NU leaders, although there was some overlap of membership between the two executive committees, and many individual connections of friendship and past suffrage labours together. Fawcett had served on the LSWS executive until the end of 1912, and had been instrumental in keeping it within the constitutional fold during a threatened militant takeover in 1908–09, although her involvement had lessened after she became president of the NU in 1907.[48] The LSWS had long been well served by Philippa (Pippa) Strachey, its long-time secretary and a most effective manager and organizer; according to some accounts, Ray Costelloe married into the Strachey family in order to enhance her opportunities to work alongside Pippa. Now remembered particularly as the historian of the NUWSS and biographer of Millicent Fawcett, Ray Strachey was still a young woman, twenty-seven years old in 1914, and married since 1911 to Oliver Strachey, thirteen years her senior. During the years 1913–1915, one or other or sometimes both Oliver and Ray would serve on the executives of the LSWS and of the NU. The Strachey presence on the LSWS executive also included Mrs Elinor Rendel, older sister to Oliver and Pippa;[49] less vocal than Ray and Pippa, she was of like mind with them on most matters.

Not constrained by any felt need to consult with the London branches, by the end of the weekend the London executive had come up with their own plans to address the crisis. Although different shades of opinion were represented, the prevailing tone was strongly in favour of support for the war effort, and their plan emerged under the general rubric of a scheme for women's service.[50] As Holton says, the LSWS 'provides perhaps the most extreme example [in the NU] of undisguised involvement in the war effort itself. Their Women's Service Bureau was established specifically to release men needed at the front by providing women workers to replace them. Organisers were withdrawn from relief work for this purpose.'[51]

Over the next days and weeks Bureaus for Voluntary Workers were set up by the LSWS to place volunteers with other organizations and with municipalities, to work on the supply of needed goods and of information, to help raise money for the Queen's Fund, and to operate clubs for soldiers. The brief report contained in the LSWS Annual Report makes no mention of care being taken to avoid volunteering for work which could be done by a woman thrown out of work by the war, a caveat stressed by the NU executive.

As the need for immediate relief diminished, the work of the Women's Service Bureau became increasingly relevant to the perceived demands of the time. The LSWS, and in particular Ray Strachey, showed foresight in anticipating the areas of work that might open up to women, and the skills that would help them move into these areas. Quite early in the war, they began to provide instruction for girls in such military adjunct activities as signalling, and would soon move into training for the soaring production of munitions, even setting up an Acetylene Welding School.[52] Strachey would demonstrate a brilliant capacity for supplying women to serve the munitions trade, but would only occasionally pay more than lip service to their need for fair wages, and would show no skill – nor inclination – towards conciliating the trade unions who might have supported the women's position.

Mary Berenson wrote later that Fawcett and Ray Strachey had seen the future benefit to women in doing war work, and also felt it important not to undercut men and 'lead to bitter sex antagonism, the very thing we want to travel away from'. From the outset of the war Strachey saw her role and that of the suffragists to be in 'placing women in various "war works" and trying to see that they are used in such a way that they don't ruin the whole labour market by taking low wages',[53] a worthy enough goal perhaps, but not consciously feminist in its wording, since the emphasis is on support for the war rather than on the needs and rights of the women.

The tenor of the LSWS response, while not unfeminist – indeed, its provisions for moving women into previously male occupations will be seen by some as more feminist than retraining dressmakers to make shirts – had as its primary goal service to the war machine, and unlike the early plans of the NU executive, did not put first the needs of the distressed women, nor pay much attention to making sure that the terms of employment did not discriminate against them.

Like the NU, the LSWS made efforts to place needy women in work, setting up a useful Employment Exchange. They took the same position as the wider NU on a number of the political feminist issues, for example condemning the police surveillance of soldiers' wives. Minor bickering took place between the LSWS and the NU over meetings held and workshops set up within the London area; this was nothing new, but the differences of focus and of philosophy evident in the approach to war work were striking.

As we have seen, when war came the NU executive built on its pre-war labour connections, working cooperatively with trade union and labour initiatives with mutual respect, and particularly closely with some of the rising women trade union leaders. Women such as Marshall, Courtney, and Margaret Robertson Hills had worked hard before the war to overcome the hostility towards feminism among some trade unionists, and while their influence prevailed in the NU, the NU would continue to do what it could to integrate women into both trade unions and new jobs, trying to ensure them adequate training and good wages, which in turn, it was hoped, would help lessen the fear of dilution of the work force by large numbers of non-unionized unskilled women willing to work for low wages.

During those first few months, the NU leadership had worked with confidence, choosing its causes, and at the same time operating from within the pre-war network of which it had become part, where the women's suffrage goal had widened towards a truly democratic suffragism, expanding to become a vision of equality across both gender and class lines. The different direction taken by the LSWS was an irritant to some – indeed, a mutual irritant – but in the early days of the war, the depth of the chasm was not yet apparent, and the freedom of the London society to follow its own course could hardly have been challenged even had the will to do so existed. Response to the war varied considerably between local societies, although the initial strength of the desire to have some direction come from the national executive has been shown above.

Towards the end of 1914, the worst of the unemployment crisis was over, especially for men, but much was still to be done for women, including those who were threatened with new or old forms of exploitation or discrimination. Nevertheless, the demand for workers soon exceeded the supply, and the NU had different challenges to meet, challenges which would drive the wedge much deeper between the differing feminisms of the pre-war NU leaders and of the leaders of the LSWS.

3
Division Threatens

Cultural conditioning: Marshalls and Stracheys

Before the war, the NU executive had kept its essential unity intact, though not without a struggle. Now that work directly for the vote was in abeyance, unity crumbled. The tragedy was that the external circumstance of the war set the scene for a disintegration which would naturally have occurred in part, and possibly with little ill-feeling, when the cause was won. After all, the purpose of the whole campaign was to gain for women the right to vote, as men did, for whatever was their choice among existing political parties, and no one knew better than the members of the executive that they would not all find themselves in the same political camp when they could go to the polls.

The differences of approach of the NU and the LSWS to relief of distress and to war work were important and suggestive. While there was still hope that the war would be short, an increase of the long-present tension could be tolerated. However, the different ways of handling the immediate crisis were clearly indicative of more serious disagreement regarding response to the war itself, and as it gradually became clear that the war was going to go on for many months, it became impossible to hide the width of the divide.

Divisions within the NU had deep philosophical and cultural roots, at least as reflected and acted out by some of the leaders on either side of the divide. Nearly all came from the middle or upper middle class and were well educated and comfortably off, so it was not class that divided them: but differing attitude to class was a real factor. Differences of party affiliation also divided the factions, but untidily and not along a straight line.

A look at the Marshall family, from which Catherine came, and the Strachey family of which Pippa was an offshoot and on to which Ray Costelloe had grafted herself by her marriage to Oliver, provides some illuminating background. Of course, neither family was all of one shade in its beliefs, nor were those beliefs static; but the contours of Catherine's feminism and the dissimilar shape of Ray's can be seen to have sprung from roots underlying their respective families, and to have been fertilized by different nutrients. Although neither side of the divide can be fully represented by one or two individuals, a look at the familial climate of these two may be suggestive.

Barbara Caine titled her fascinating study of the Strachey family *From Bombay to Bloomsbury*, neatly summing up its most pervasive characteristics. Those members of the family with whom we are most closely concerned – Pippa, her brother Oliver and his wife Ray – seldom spoke of empire at the time of our interest, and were not central in the Bloomsbury group, but both their gifts and their limitations were redolent of these influences. Pippa, Oliver, and the better-known Lytton were three of eight children of Sir Richard Strachey and Lady Jane, formerly Jane Grant, a member of another influential Anglo-Indian family.[1]

The Stracheys had worked their way into the upper middle class in the course of the nineteenth century through public works and administration in India, the Marshalls through success in the flax spinning industry in Leeds.[2] By the end of the century the Marshalls were gentry holding several pieces of land in the Lake District, and more than an arm's length from their industrial origins, while the Stracheys in the early twentieth century were gradually withdrawing from their Indian involvement and, according to Caine, suffering some discomfort from having to accept a less affluent and exalted position in British society. In common with all families of means at that time, both families employed servants, but both Stracheys (once away from India) and Marshalls had a lifestyle that was comfortable rather than lavish.

Both families invested substantially in the education of the younger members, and provided opportunity for the development of their considerable gifts. Lytton Strachey's literary brilliance stands out, but other Stracheys were visible as literati of the Bloomsbury world. The Marshalls' bent was more towards careers in education; Catherine's cousin Tom would later become a Cambridge professor, her father, Frank, was a house master at Harrow, close friends included distinguished academics, and even after they moved to the Lake District, she had many opportunities for discourse with intellectuals, particularly in economics and politics. Her early reading included J.S. Mill's classical Liberal texts. And always, ideas were not set out as dogma, but were up for discussion.

Both families, interestingly, had an inherent (though not of course universal) strain of organizing ability, manifesting itself markedly in Catherine and Pippa, and also apparent in Ray. Both families were well in advance of their time in supporting the feminist claim to equality; there were strong women in both families, and there were also supportive males. Caine shows this for the Stracheys, and as early as 1873 Henry Marshall had chaired a suffrage meeting in Keswick; the following year Frank Marshall and C.E. Colbeck, another Harrow house master and brother of Caroline, who was soon to marry Frank, were among those named as supporting the suffrage campaign at a meeting in Harrow.[3]

The differences between the two families are more subtle than the similarities, but more important.

Although the long years in India were undoubtedly undertaken, particularly by the earlier generations, with a sense of service, Caine shows the Stracheys from the start as seeing themselves as dedicated rulers, 'bringing civilization and good government to the benighted natives', and brings out clearly the lack of interest shown by the Stracheys, including and perhaps especially Pippa during her time in India, in the conditions of Indian women or the Indian poor, even during a time of famine. The one exception was the unfortunate Margaret, the ill-chosen wife of Ralph Strachey, who much preferred his sister Pippa (wanting even to take her along on their honeymoon). During her time in India in 1908, Margaret, though unsure of herself over this as over everything else, met socially with some Bengali women, something never done by the other Stracheys; her comments on what she had learned of 'the hatred of the native ... for the white races' which she saw as encouraged by 'our government and its mistakes' left her scared but unheard, serving to show again how poorly she fitted into the family pattern.[4] What Lady Jane Strachey and her daughter Pippa brought to the suffrage campaign from their Indian experience was a sense of personal empowerment, a sense that they, of all women, knew how to govern. Ironically, their insistence that there was no parallel between the right of British women to emancipation and the struggles of colonial peoples was used as an additional argument to counter the fears of some that female enfranchisement would seriously weaken the British Empire.[5]

The Stracheys brought a sense of entitlement and superiority from their imperial background and personal privilege. Aspects of Catherine Marshall's early experience could have imbued her with the same sense of superiority and entitlement. In Harrow, she grew up among some of the most privileged British youth (but excluded by gender from their activities); in the Lake District, she wrote a short story about the delight of a young local girl entering domestic service; she was exposed to and identified with the constant difficulties of her mother in obtaining servants; she tried to teach clean living to groups of local boys and girls; she improved her knowledge of dairying and even of the art of ironing, perhaps in order to be better able to instruct the lower class in how to do these things well.[6] But there was always a counter-balance; the Marshalls saw their privilege as carrying obligations; notably, for example, Frank Marshall, in his retirement, worked to extend secondary education and delight in music to those less privileged, and the singing lessons Catherine gave locally were a part of this.

Catherine never learnt to treat those less well-off than herself as inferior, quaint, or threatening. She did not see the suffrage movement as simply a campaign to extend a male privilege to women of her own class. Once involved in suffrage, she quickly became familiar with the needs and difficulties of women – factory workers, miners' wives – and of the men themselves, many of whom also did not yet have the vote.

Party leanings were often known but seldom referred to in the NU before the war, but they also underlay attitudes to the extension of the democratic principle. The climate of the early twentieth century was more open to hope than has been possible at any time since 1914. As feminists, the suffragist Stracheys had to believe in change and progress, but for them, change should be slow and conservative in its nature; there was no need to look beyond the desired outcome of gaining the vote for propertied women. Catherine Marshall and her parents had been deeply rooted in the Liberal party and in liberal idealism. Finding themselves betrayed (as they saw it) by a party that first failed to move on women's enfranchisement, and then took the country into the war, they were ripe to move towards the idealistic socialism of the ILP.

Catherine Marshall, much more of a political theorist than the Stracheys (although unfortunately a less prolific writer than Ray), came to see the common factors behind different forms of oppression. By 1913 she was inveighing against 'the old enemy which has always barred the way to progress – the spirit of monopoly and privilege, the opposition of those who possess power to those who demand liberty, the reluctance of those who have to share with those who have not.'

Class-barriers and sex-barriers, she claimed, were 'in reality part of the same fence.'[7] Soon this concept came into even sharper focus for her, and gained a third dimension very probably after reading an important article by Beatrice Webb. In an interview with Sir Edward Grey in December 1913 Marshall spoke of the close relations developing between suffragists and the labour movement, and linked the coming struggle between capitalism and labour to a sense of kinship with the 'struggles of [the] subject races'. It was her hope that a right outcome to the women's franchise issue could play a positive role in the other two areas of controversy.[8]

I am far from laying out a great theory that explains all in terms of extended family background. After all, many do not follow the same course as the families from which they come. The Strachey family was indeed divided over the war: while Pippa, Ray and Oliver were enthusiastic supporters, Ray's sister, Karin, together with her husband Adrian Stephen, and Oliver's brother, Lytton, were notorious for taking the side of the conscientious objectors. And Ray Strachey was raised by a Quaker grandmother, although I could explain this away by a disquisition on the idiosyncrasies of this particular doting grandmother. But Caine's work on the Stracheys opens the door to my less extensive overview of the Marshall family: at the very least, the comparison may be suggestive. Carried into the suffrage movement, the 'Strachey attitude', following through on the Anglo-Indian belief in the mission to govern, led to a resistance to democracy within the LSWS, a sense that the leaders knew how best to run the society, and that the rank and file were there to be called on when numerical support was needed or when (as in the case of the pit-brow workers) some exotic colour was wanted. The 'Marshall attitude', on the other hand, encouraged and promoted democracy in the NU, and was shown in respectful outreach to working women and men, a seeking to come to know them, hear their views, bring them in, and work alongside them to serve the needs of all. The differences that can be illustrated in these two families were surely replicated to a greater or lesser extent throughout the suffrage movement.

Controversy

On 31 July 1914 an 'International Manifesto of Women' had been circulated to embassies and the Foreign Office in London by the International Women's Suffrage Alliance (IWSA). Drawn up presumably by the members of the IWSA executive who were just concluding a meeting in London, and signed by Millicent Fawcett, the manifesto spoke of the horrors of war and called on governments to 'leave untried no method of conciliation or arbitration for arranging international differences which may help us to avert deluging half the civilised world in blood'.[9] Because press and public in Britain had been kept so much in the dark while the cabinet moved towards involvement in the war, the IWSA, with representatives present from several countries in Europe, where war had already broken out, may have been at the forefront of awareness. Following the manifesto and in line with its direction, on the very eve of war Fawcett had chaired the large gathering of women at the Kingsway Hall in London on 4 August, called to protest against Britain's involvement (and had had her wrist smartly slapped by a Unionist suffragist politician for doing so).[10]

Almost without exception, the new leaders, those who had done most to put the NU in the centre of political action during the last two years, were deeply in sympathy with the IWSA's public declaration, and held back from overt support of the war effort, relieving distress and meanwhile seeking a way in which they could contribute to enduring peace. Catherine Marshall, Kathleen Courtney, Isabella Ford, Maude Royden, and Helena Swanwick, among others, were committed to finding some way to channel women's energies towards work for lasting peace, and understandably must have felt that in this they were in line with the stated position of the international suffrage movement.

But Fawcett was at heart a traditional patriot and once Britain was in, she, like many others, could not bear to be seen as being other than wholeheartedly behind the nation in the crisis. Tension in the NU executive was not only between those in sympathy with the LSWS's focus on war work and those favouring the avoidance of direct war support, but also increasingly between the NU president and those who had been her most active supporters before the war.

One of the first challenging policy decisions arose around Rosika Schwimmer, a noted Hungarian feminist who was in England at the outbreak of war. She gave up the paid position she had held in the IWSA and began to focus all her attention on plans to enlist the help of neutral countries, and in particular the United States, to bring the war to an end as soon as possible through an active mediation scheme which could be brokered by the neutral nations. Before leaving for the U.S. at the end of August, Schwimmer talked her plans over with Marshall, who was able to provide introductions to a few potentially influential contacts there.[11]

In the United States Schwimmer stayed with Carrie Chapman Catt, president both of the National American Woman Suffrage Alliance and of the IWSA. Remarkably enough, Schwimmer quite soon succeeded in meeting with President Woodrow Wilson. On 21 September she cabled Isabella Ford, reporting that she had been given a long audience on 18 September, and that the President had 'accepted suggestions of manifesto as valuable help assured petition will carry great weight in his further considerations'.[12]

Meanwhile Schwimmer's request for support came before the NU at the executive meeting of 27 August. Nothing of the discussion – which may well have been uncomfortable – was minuted, only that 'The Committee did not feel able to offer the support of the Union in the present circumstances or without summoning a Council meeting.'[13] The decision was probably the only one that could have been made at that time, much as many members of the executive may have wanted to pursue the plan.

In the nation at large, and in the suffrage movement, the first three months of the war saw some definition of attitudes, and a clarification of who stood where. Although in the opening weeks the case for Britain's entry into the war, put by the ruling Liberals, had made a convincing showing in the press – since the major papers had all fallen in line behind the Liberal Party as soon as war was declared – some people, however reluctantly, were unable to take the question as settled. While the Labour Party had decided to support the government in its decision to go to war, the small Independent Labour Party (ILP) had remained critical, in and out of Parliament, publishing on 11 August a manifesto indicting the secret diplomacy of the pre-war years, condemning the alliance with Czarist Russia, and speaking of socialist solidarity with the workers of all nations.[14] Prominent members of the ILP were those who had worked most closely with the NU on behalf of suffrage. A small group of renegade Liberals had also been opposed to Britain's entry into the war and now helped to lend credibility and visibility to the efforts of the ILP. The *Labour Leader* became one of the few outlets still available to critics of the war, and was soon being avidly read by those who became increasingly uneasy with Britain's role – and that of the Foreign Secretary, Sir Edward Grey – as more detail of the events immediately preceding the war came to light.[15] Dissidents began, too, to examine international relations with a view to establishing means to prevent the recurrence of war.

Among suffragists, the WSPU leadership (Emmeline and Christabel Pankhurst) was gaining favour with the government and some of the public for its vociferous support of the war effort, while Sylvia Pankhurst's East London Federation of Suffragettes (ELFS) had come out in criticism of the war. Opinion in the Women's Freedom League (WFL, the home of Emmeline and Frederick Pethick Lawrence) was divided on the issue, but the WFL kept its focus on suffrage and feminism, and was vocal on all questions of women's rights. The WFL worked on the same issues also taken up by the NU, from the alleviation of distress to the protection of women from regulations similar to the Contagious Diseases Act; but where the NU tried to work with the government where this seemed in women's best interests, the WFL's criticism was open and often confrontational.[16]

Meanwhile prominent leaders in the NU saw their organization, the largest suffrage body in the country, as paralysed on the central question of the time, despite the wish of most of the executive to take a stand. Unminuted discussions did go on in an attempt to deal in some way with the difficulty caused by the rift between the uncompromising support for the war shown by Mrs Fawcett and some others, among them a number of prominent LSWS leaders, and the increasingly questioning attitude of most of the other leaders; a temporary solution, unsatisfactory to all, was a half hearted and ill-kept commitment on the part of both sides to stay away in public from the issues of war and peace.

Feminists who were clear in their need to work for peace reluctantly explored other outlets for their energies. The first and for some months the most significant organization arising as a forum for critical examination of the war and Britain's entry into it was the Union for Democratic Control (UDC), which attracted a considerable number of those who had expected Britain to maintain neutrality, who had remained unsatisfied by the arguments which the government had given (*post facto*) to justify involvement, and who were frustrated by the lack of public or even parliamentary influence on decisions of war and peace: a number of NU supporters were drawn to it.[17]

Factions harden: October to November 1914

The executive minutes for August and September shed little direct light on divisions within the NU. It was not the regular practice (although there had been exceptions) to record how the voting went, and for this period the minutes do not even indicate whether there was a vote; only the action or the decision not to act is noted, often with a brief note of the rationale behind the direction chosen. In part, despite tensions, the initial public display of agreement surely reflects a wish to maintain the visibility and enhance the good name of the organization while serving the needs of women in distress. Had the war been short, the NU might have come through unscathed.

By mid-October the division of opinion could no longer be kept off the executive agenda. Not only the London-based executive members and those working at headquarters were concerned about the NU's silence, or about what seems to have been the understood policy enjoining leading members throughout the organization to refrain from taking a public stand. On 6 October Dr Ethel Williams, a leader in the Newcastle-on-Tyne women's suffrage society, wrote to Marshall, marking her letter 'Private and confidential', and asking quite bluntly, 'We are exceedingly anxious to know what lines, if any, the NU is going to take on the question of peace.' A branch of the UDC was about to be formed in Newcastle. Although Williams approved of its work, she had some doubts about the way the UDC was constituted and, for instance, would need assurance that men and women members would be treated as equals. But those showing an interest had included a number of prominent local NU members, and felt their first commitment to be to the NU, where they did not want to cause dissension. Williams's question was, 'If the N.U. is not of one mind in the matter or sufficiently of one mind to avoid schism, would it not be best to leave us free, at least for the present?'[18] But many hoped that their own organization, the NU, would give leadership.

The NU's public attitude to the war clearly could not be a matter for simple majority decision. Not only were strong convictions held on either side, but strong emotions towards the organization itself, and towards fellow members, made it a heartbreaking issue. And in particular, there was Millicent Fawcett. Brian Harrison describes 'Fawcett's feminist leadership [as] anything but charismatic', but admits that 'Her followers grew to love her.'[19] Perhaps she had never worked so closely with her disciples, or been as much loved by them, as she did and was in the immediate pre-war years, when the women of the newly radicalized NU executive had in fact been as much teachers as pupils, propelling her gently, with her eyes open, along the path they were determined to travel. Now Fawcett could no longer lead in the direction they wanted to go, would no longer either follow or keep silent, and manifestly could not be stepped around.

Two letters written by Isabella Ford in October 1914, one to Fawcett ('Dearest Millie') and one to Marshall, well illustrate the agonizing dilemma of the time. Ford – Quaker, socialist, trade unionist, suffragist –

was of Fawcett's own generation and had long been a personal friend as well as an admirer of her leadership. Fawcett told Ford of her anxiety about an upcoming public meeting to be held by the NU, at which both would speak. The theme would be 'Women's Work in Wartime', a topic which it had become apparent could mean very different things to different people. Ford's response was a passionate avowal of her respect and love for Fawcett and her wish to do and say nothing to hurt her or cause dissension. She urged Fawcett to air her opinions on German guilt freely, and promised that she would not 'look tiresome' or even 'feel hostile'. But she had to conclude her letter by making it plain that, however much she herself might 'hate Prussianism', she did not think 'that war ever destroyed war – and real salvation can only come to people and nations from within', and she admitted that there might come a time when she felt she 'must take some other line than what you approve'. Ford's letter to Marshall, written later, after the public meeting, is more outspoken. Of the difficulties in the NU, she wrote, 'of course, as you know well Mrs Fawcett is our stumbling block. She is not so bad quite, as I expected – for she [was] most unspeakable during the Boer war – till she went to the Camps.'[20]

The minutes of the NU executive meeting of 15 October 1914 contain the first minuted discussion of differences over the European war, stemming from a resolution introduced by Helena Swanwick, the intent of which was to summon a General Council in November 'to consider whether any policy should be adopted with regard to the European War, and ... the political situation which may arise on any proposal for terms of peace'.

In her introductory remarks, Swanwick focussed on the need to clarify what liberty of action was to be allowed to the members, officials and component societies of the NU on the subject of the war. Should the officials remain neutral? or should they be allowed to act as individuals 'without involving the National Union'? or should the NU 'take some broad line carrying out in detail the Resolution passed at the Kingsway Hall Meeting on the eve of the War'?

The ensuing discussion was ostensibly confined to the issue of whether a Special Council should be called to meet before Christmas, but inevitably focussed at least as much on the question of whether the NU should, as Margaret Ashton (of Manchester) urged, 'speak as a body on the question of peace and War', and on the more significant and divisive subtext, just barely below the surface, of what should the NU position be? Among the officers and the most active executive members, it was well known already where their colleagues stood.

Those who favoured holding a Council were, in the main, those who had increasingly been chafing at being confined to relief work, and included a few who were associated with the UDC. Those who opposed holding a Council were, with a few exceptions, those who believed the Union should not declare a position, and who not only favoured support of the war effort, but were in some cases already engaged in it. While this may suggest that Fawcett, the outspoken leader of this faction, and her followers, may have been afraid that they could not carry a Council with them, they may also have been motivated by fear of division, and by the thought that even to discuss the question was unpatriotic. At the same time, this group spoke strongly in favour of freedom for the individual to express opinions.

There are signs that Millicent Fawcett was in pain at this executive meeting. Strong as was her emotional support of the war effort and her sense that 'it was not desirable to hamper the Government in their conduct of the greatest crisis in history', her recorded remarks suggest that she was bitterly unhappy at the impending loss of closeness with the women who had been most active in the immediate pre-war campaign. Ruthlessness, an indifference to personal relations with all but a very few of her colleagues, sometimes characterized Fawcett's behaviour,[21] and would soon reassert itself to an egregious degree on this question of feminist response to the war. But on this occasion she seems to have been begging for understanding from those who opposed her point of view, and even appears a shade ambivalent about the ground on which she stood; it was, after all, not long since she had appended her signature to a plea for a peaceful solution to the crisis. She hedged her strongest statements. While reiterating that a German victory 'would be a great blow to the women's movement and to all representative institutions', she admitted that 'she was not prepared to dispute the fact that the proposals outlined by the Union for Democratic Control would be what the National Union as a whole would desire should Great Britain be successful in the War'. Although she opposed calling a special General Council, and advocated leaving 'Members of the Executive ... free to express their views as individuals on the European War', she concluded by reaffirming the view 'that if women had had a voice in the Councils of all the nations concerned they might have prevented the War. War was a gigantic crime, only to be stopped by awakening to its horrors the classes most affected by it'.

The Special Council was voted down: Swanwick and her friends had lost the first round. Worse, as they had feared and predicted, the situation remained without clarity. Although it was spelled out that

freedom to express views on the war as individuals entailed an obligation to make it plain on every occasion that the views expressed were
only personal and not those of the NU, Millicent Fawcett, the most
visible of them all, would continue to fail to make the distinction.
Meanwhile, 'Attitude of the National Union to the War', and 'The
meaning of the Physical Force argument' were accepted among several
topics suggested for discussion at the upcoming Provincial Council
(not empowered to make new policy). At the same executive meeting,
Maude Royden, as editor of the *Common Cause*, received approval to
run a series of articles discussing the causes of war, 'without the
National Union being involved in any of the opinions which might be
expressed'.

Those who wanted the NU to take a position saw the issue of peace
and war as integral to the women's suffrage question. At the executive
meeting Helena Swanwick stated bluntly and undiplomatically, in
response to Fawcett's claim that the NU could have an opinion only on
suffrage, 'that the question of peace and war, involving as it did the
question of the relations of reason and physical force, was at the basis
of the whole Franchise movement and that therefore, to follow the
line proposed by Mrs Fawcett [that is, to refuse the attempt to speak
with one voice] would be to put the question of Women's Suffrage
second'.

If the 'peace' faction deplored Fawcett's inability to control her
public tongue, the 'patriotic' faction had some reason to resent
Swanwick's open avowal of her views outside as well as within the
executive, especially when she reiterated them in the October 1 issue of
Jus Suffragii, the organ of the IWSA.

Once it had been established that the November Provincial Council
would openly air the issue of attitude to the war, NU leaders were free
to let their personal views be known. Speakers were in great demand at
NU branches, where members wanted to know more about the role the
national office of the NU was playing in the changed lives of women,
and many branches were equally exercised about future directions. At
the beginning of November, Marshall spoke to the Cambridge WSS on
behalf of the NU, and in conclusion on her own behalf as well. No one
could give a better informed account than she of what had been done
to relieve distress and protect women's rights, and she reported fully
on these. But now she felt compelled to build into her talk her
thoughts on what seemed to her 'to be the most important duty of all
which falls on women in such a time as this – I mean the duty of
working to secure a satisfactory issue of the war. ... Women have been

busy binding up the wounds which men are busy inflicting on each other. ... But ... I believe it is our duty not only to try to remedy the evils when they have been committed but to look ahead and take our share in trying to prevent their recurrence.' It was essential, she said, to foster a real spirit of conciliation – lasting peace could only be built on good feeling and trust between nations.

Marshall gave the reasons why she thought that women had special responsibility for setting the climate. As 'the mother-sex', women's function should be 'to give reality to that vision of the brotherhood of all humanity which has been preached ... through all the ages'. As 'the sex which does not fight' women should be better able to avoid war fever, and had time 'now, whilst the war is going on, to be thinking constructively about the future foundations of peace'. And surely women of the women's movement should not delay having an opinion on 'the most vital problem that can confront any country' until they could vote. Further, war was a setback to all the reforms for which they had been working. Marshall also stressed the 'common ground of friendship and co-operation with the women in other lands' developed by the international women's movement, asking if it could not be used to further the cause of peace, and to prevent the sorrow and desolation experienced in 'the homes of the world'. Making a point seldom mentioned, she urged her listeners to think not only of the suffering of 'our soldiers and sailors, but ... also ... of the suffering we send them forth to inflict – not from choice of theirs but because we have found no better way. ... Let us do our part, that their sacrifice may not be in vain.'[22]

Such arguments have been read as redolent of maternalism and of essentialism, but the view bears a second look; we need to distinguish between vocabulary and action, and to situate the discourse in the context of the time. The most ardent anti-feminist would not deny that women's approved sphere enlarged in wartime, without changing her essential support role, which she was temporarily licensed to fulfil in the wider public field outside the home. When the leading anti-suffragist Mrs Humphry Ward campaigned among workers for more and greater effort in support of war production, and went to the Front line to encourage the troops, she – like Emmeline and Christabel Pankhurst – was conforming to the role expected of women in wartime, and urging others to do the same. On the other hand, the women who were standing out for the right to be heard on questions of war and peace were radically rejecting their assigned role as docile supporters of men's wars.[23] Proud as the suffragists had reason to be of their contribution to relieving distress, Marshall for one felt strongly that to 'succumb to [the] temptation to do what wins us universal approval' would be mere 'moral flabbiness'. She recognized bitterly that suffrage was 'never so popular as since we ceased to mention it', and that praise of their work often came with the insulting tag: '*Now* you are doing something useful'. For her, there was indeed 'a connection between suff[rage] and relief work: [and] equally a connection between suff[rage] and work for peace'.[24]

Provincial Council at Wallasey: November 1914

Within the executive, preparation for the NU Provincial Council at Wallasey (12–13 November 1914) was fraught with tension. The selection and exact wording of the resolutions for discussion was an excruciatingly difficult and delicate task. Even a proposal from several sources that the suffrage issue again be urged on the government – because events since war began had demonstrated both women's need for the protection of the vote and their worthiness of full citizenship – had to be worked and reworked; it was hard to word it in a way that was convincing without any show of bias towards fervent patriotism on the one hand or over-emphasis on women's potential as peacemakers on the other.[25]

Yet more difficult was the task of setting out the issues directly concerning the NU's attitude to the war. A rather generally worded resolution drafted by Mrs Fawcett led to discussion that was unsatisfactory where it was not acrimonious, with Swanwick challenging Fawcett's categorization of 'the British Empire [as] fighting the battle of representative government and progressive democracy all over the world', by a pointed reference to Britain's war alliance with the extremely illiberal Czarist Russian state. The resolution was eventually put on the Council agenda, with the offending passage removed; in its final form it applauded the response of the constituent women's suffrage societies to the war emergency, and urged 'the societies and members ... to continue ... all efforts which have for their object the sustaining of the vital strength of the nation', a wording that blurred any distinction of principle between relief work and direct war work.

Much of the discussion at the executive turned on procedure, but dissension surfaced between those who clearly feared any public discussion of controversial issues and those who saw that it could not be forever avoided; particular heat was generated as soon as the question of a possible NU role in education for peace was raised. Lady Frances

Balfour,[26] at one end of the spectrum, asked 'what statecraft would think of a body sitting in the middle of a war and affirming its belief in arbitration and conciliation as opposed to war?'. Swanwick, at the other end, was determined to get a clear decision on whether how peace should be made could now be openly discussed by NU members. Millicent Fawcett, despite her bias towards support of the government at this time, seems to have striven to keep a balance between the two opposing views.[27]

When the Council convened at Wallasey, Fawcett's resolution, ambivalent but inoffensive, was easily approved. Then followed discussion on 'Attitude of the N.U. in relation to the War: Meaning of the Physical Force Argument'. For Swanwick, rejection of the 'Physical Force argument of the anti-Suffragists' was central both in the suffrage campaign and in determining the attitude the NU should take to war. If it were accepted that 'Women can't fight, therefore they can't vote', and that 'the constitution of the State will be stable only if Government remains in the hands of those who can enforce it', women never would achieve the vote. Swanwick urged the Council to face up to the implications: the suffrage issue could not be separated from the physical force issue, 'for war was the supreme assertion of the Physical force argument, and Votes for Women was the supreme negation of it.'

The attempt to keep the argument to principle broke down as soon as the discussion was opened to participants; Fawcett led off with a virulent attack on German philosophy, policies, and practices, which was not only irrelevant but beyond ordinarily insensitive in view of Swanwick's partly German parentage and Bavarian birth.[28] Little in the way of cogent argument followed on either side, though the report suggests that, while some feared a line of thinking and action that might alienate them from their compatriots, others showed some genuine interest in understanding what could be done, in practical terms, while the war was still on. Maude Royden strongly supported Swanwick's position, and perhaps with more practicality, emphasizing the immense educational resource that lay in the NU and the responsibility that laid upon them.

The internationalists genuinely believed that an Allied victory gave the best hope for a good peace, but no matter how often they repeated this, they were constantly accused of taking Germany's side. Wrapping up at the end of the discussion, Swanwick commented rather bitterly on the way she had been represented as defending Germany, and more clearly made her point, saying that 'she believed public opinion on right lines could be made and the N.U. ought to help to make it.' 'They could help,' she said, 'by making Mr Asquith or Mr Churchill or any other Minister feel when he talked in a civilised way about the settlement after the war that at least the suffragist women would back him, because they believed in the guidance of reason instead of war and in the domination of physical by moral force.'

Swanwick's final remark led directly towards the resolution (forwarded from the executive) that Marshall was to move after the lunch break, which called upon the Provincial Council to support a recent statement made by the Prime Minister, Asquith, regarding the 'principles which should govern the settlement after the war', and to recommend that the General Council call upon 'Societies and members of the Union to work for the building up of public opinion on these lines.'

The so-called peace faction had been pleased by Asquith's speech in Dublin on 26 September, in which he had defined the end to be kept in mind during the war. A part of Asquith's speech had been reprinted in the agenda. He had spoken not only of the repudiation of militarism (often, at that time, a mere euphemism for the defeat of Germany) but of independent existence and free development for smaller nations, and most important of all, of 'the substitution for force ... of a real European partnership based on the recognition of equal right and established and enforced by a common will.' There was nothing disingenuous about the use of this speech in the resolution; encouragement of the better impulses of statesmen was what the idea of an education campaign was about. But there was a delightful irony in challenging the faction which saw itself as having a monopoly on patriotism to support – or to refuse to support – the nation's leader.

Two chief obstacles had to be overcome by those NU women who wanted to use their organization for the education of public opinion on issues of peace and war. The first was the question of the relevance to women's suffrage, which had been addressed at a theoretical level by Swanwick. The second was the uneasiness surrounding any talk of peace as possibly unpatriotic and, worse still, as unsupportive of the soldiers now fighting. The second was probably overwhelmingly the more important, because it carried immense and deeply personal emotional baggage; there were few NU members who did not have close relations at the Front, and too many were already bereaved. Mrs Fawcett herself had many young male relatives who had enlisted: who can wonder that she did not want to seem to separate herself in any way from their cause? By the end of the war no less than twenty-nine of her extended family had been killed.[29] Talk of peace could be felt as threatening, either because it was thought to weaken the war effort, or because even to suggest that there was a better way to order international relations might mean, unbearably, that the sacrifice made was futile.

In presenting the resolution to support Asquith's statement, Marshall did not discount emotions but tried to enlist them on the side of her argument; she presented the case for 'looking ahead to the time when the war was over' as the truest support for the soldiers. 'The present war is to be a war to end war, and our admiration, our gratitude, our loyalty to those now at the Front, ought to lead us to see to it that the sacrifices that they are making are not being made in vain.' She argued that success meant arriving at a settlement sufficiently conciliatory to last, and that the government would need the support of an educated public opinion to achieve this. Concluding, Marshall defined her idea of patriotism, asking 'when we use the word "patriotism" do we mean – Our country is in the right, our country must get some advantage out of the war? Or do we care, first and foremost, that our country should play a worthy part, worthy of the best ideals we have for her?'

Courtney, seconding the resolution, addressed the argument that the NU would be going outside its mandate if it became involved in discussion or an educational campaign on the nature of peace making. She argued that the NU had an obligation to help contribute to a well-informed public opinion, and pointed out that the NU had conducted education campaigns on other topics before, and could well conduct one now on 'the causes of war in general, the causes of this war in particular, what had been the basis of former peace treaties and why these peace treaties had not led to a permanent peace'.[30] She could relevantly have pointed to a good many of the wartime issues being addressed by the NU, which, though strongly feminist, were not strictly suffrage issues. Mrs Fawcett herself had never been inhibited about using the strength of the Union to support feminist causes in which she was interested, in particular the sexual exploitation of women and especially of young girls,[31] although there had also been times when a controversial issue had been sidestepped by ruling it peripheral to suffrage.[32]

The discussion that followed was confused, but does indicate that, although there were strong feelings among leading women on either side, there were still a great many women who were undecided. Eventually, after a number of amendments had been rejected, the resolution passed by 23 votes to 9. Another resolution saw Royden, as editor of the *Common Cause*, achieve an important point in getting approval for the paper to publish articles on the causes and prevention of war; the following months saw an impressive array of short articles by leading writers from outside the NU, as well as stimulating correspondence and leading articles from the membership.[33]

The Provincial Council had not been mandated to make decisions on how the NU should respond to the war, only to open the discussion more widely. What came out of it was an affirmation of feminist action to that date, anticipation of the annual General Council set for February, and a continuing anxiety about the NU's future felt by leading women on both sides of the debate.

Just before Wallasey, Millicent Fawcett had had a long letter from Helena Auerbach, one of her closest suffrage friends and long-time treasurer of the NU. Describing 'Miss Courtney, Miss Royden, Miss Marshall, Miss Ashton' as 'some of the dearest people in our Union', Auerbach expressed her indescribable 'feelings of exasperation' with what she clearly saw as their campaign to bring the NU into line with the views of the UDC, which, she believed, could only embroil the NU in disastrous controversy, however desirable a better informed public might be. Fawcett's brief reply, written just after the Council (and evidently enclosing some kind of report, if not the final one), is of great interest. Not only did she express satisfaction that her resolution had carried without opposition 'virtually pledg[ing] the NUWSS to use its utmost endeavours to support the country as long as the crisis caused by the war lasts', but she also confessed herself 'very much impressed by Catherine Marshall's speech [which] showed a real grasp of the essentials of the situation'.[34] The exchange suggests that, at this time, Fawcett, although wilfully blind to the ambiguity of her resolution, was still able to distinguish between a lack of patriotism and a desire that peace should be made, when the time should come, in a climate free from revenge. Among historians and biographers on both sides of the debate about the appropriate role for the NU, Fawcett has generally been represented as unremittingly opposed to any kind of peace work. Yet there is enough evidence here that, at least briefly, she could speak (and write privately to her friend) as if she was prepared to make some compromise, possibly for the unadmitted reason that Marshall and Courtney had been her closest associates for the past two years and she had come to rely on their judgement and political wisdom, and to take inspiration from their fresh approach.

Unfortunately, while Fawcett presented so rational a front to Auerbach, it may have been less visible to Marshall and her friends, discouraged and angered by her venomous response to Swanwick at the Provincial

Council and by her unpredictability. If Fawcett was indeed attempting to meet them halfway and to support the kind of programme of peace education they were advocating, she failed to make this clear. Yet Fawcett's approval of Marshall's speech was also a tribute to the moderate line which the latter was taking; she and Courtney were more careful than some of the other peace advocates, at this time, to focus narrowly on the climate in which the peace would be made, staying away from any particulars of what the peace should look like, or when it might come about, and clearly they were less confrontational in manner than Swanwick. Auerbach's accusation of 'strong leanings towards what the UDC calls its "policy"'[35] was not without foundation, especially in respect to Swanwick. But then again, neither the policy nor the methods of the UDC were ever radical enough to account rationally for the extreme anger and fear the organization met with among the public, or indeed among some of the NU executive.

Can a way forward be found?: November 1914 to February 1915

Many continued to hope that a middle way could be found on which the NU could move forward. Alice Clark thought that the Wallasey Council 'had been useful, that it had drawn people together instead of separating them'. Writing to Marshall, she reflected on 'the situation in the N.U.', seeing 'at one end Mrs Fawcett and doubtless many other people of less importance who are much more inclined to really militarist ideas than she is', and at the other Maude Royden, Helena Swanwick, and Isabella Ford who believed Britain could have kept out of the war 'and watched Germany beating France.' To Clark, 'from the point of view of practical politics and the prevention of war in the future these two extremes are equally dangerous.' Marshall and Courtney (and herself), she saw as being in the middle. She went on to express her hope 'that as both extremes are equally loyal to the N.U. it will be possible for the middle party who is bent only on the prevention of future wars to play off one extreme against the other and obtain a compromise which will be really of practical utility. It seemed to me,' she added, 'that you and Kathleen [Courtney] did this at the Prov. Council. I feel it will be worth Mrs Fawcett's rather unwilling acquiescence, the evident sacrifice which she felt she was making to preserve peace if it will induce the others to temper their ideals to practical aims.'[36]

For a short time Courtney shared Clark's optimism, and had 'great hopes of finding a 'modus vivendi' in the N.U.' She believed that

Fawcett was moving towards acceptance of some involvement in education for peace, and she reported that the latter had 'even drafted a resol[ution] for the Ann[ual] Meeting in order to make a departure from our objective constitutional'.[37]

Sandra Holton, in her more recent work, cites Clark's letter at length as evidence of serious disagreement within the peace camp, but I cannot agree with her analysis. Clark's letter was hopeful, not a forecast of doom; the distinctions she made were valid, but the lines between the three groups were far more blurred than Holton infers, and what differences there were between the 'peace' groups turned more on what role the NU could play than on what they should aim at. Swanwick, Royden, and Ford may well have held, as Clark said, 'that England could have kept out of this'. To support keeping out was a tenable position, although the pacifist hope would have been for Britain not to stand by uncaringly 'watch[ing] Germany beating France', but to use diplomacy and moral strength to help bring the war already being fought in Europe to an end. Clark nowhere says, as does Holton, that Swanwick, Ford and Royden 'wished to commit the NUWSS to an outright stop-the-war position like that of the UDC'. Clark's letter, in fact, does not mention the UDC.[38]

Significantly, Holton's critique also embodies a serious misdescription of the UDC. The UDC was not an 'anti-war organisation', especially during the early months of the war, and it was far from seeking 'the immediate cessation of hostilities and arbitration between the two sides'. Although the UDC was pilloried in some newspapers, notably including the WSPU's *Suffragette*, as a subversive pro-German organization, and its public meetings would become the target for physical attacks, it was in fact a very mild and initially almost timid body; some leading members were eager to have it understood that their concern was only with changes to be implemented after the war should be over, to make the administration of foreign affairs a more open process. The UDC's programme had nothing to say about how to end the present war, and stuck carefully to trying to devise means to prevent future wars. Indeed, the obsession of some UDC leaders with keeping a low profile was a source of frustration to some. Courtney wrote a lively letter to Marshall in October, describing a 'rather disappointing' meeting she had attended, at which Lowes Dickinson 'seemed almost the only person really in earnest', 'Mr [Arnold] Rowntree and Mr [Carl] Heath nearly came to blows in the interests of peace', 'some of the others were quite dears, but oh, so academic', and 'the wet blanket was heavily provided by W.H. Dickinson who is all for working in secret and getting *names* with which to dazzle an astonished public at the moment of making peace. He didn't seem to realize,' she added, 'that public opinion needs to be educated *now*.'[39]

Inevitably there were differences of emphasis among those advocating a role for the NU in peace education: Royden was a Christian pacifist; Swanwick was forming a firm idea of the political structures she saw as necessary components of a postwar settlement and saw support for these specifics as a desirable and probable outcome of making people better informed; Marshall, always interested in process, was concerned for the climate of peace-making, and believed open and honest discussion was essential; those most inclined to pacifism might have been well pleased had the NU been willing 'to lead an anti-war campaign', but were too realistic to expect this. I cannot agree with Rubinstein when he says that 'they were unable to act unitedly'.[40] Courtney, and indeed all of these women, desperately wanted to work towards helping the public gain some grasp of the international issues that would necessarily underlie the making of peace, and they believed that the suffragists might give leadership in resistance to the climate of hatred and the demonization of the enemy that would poison the climate for peacemaking after the war. They believed that the wide and deep NU network was an instrument to be used to these ends. Later, when this instrument was lost to them, they would take separate but overlapping paths within the peace movement.

Marshall had spoken privately at the Wallasey Council meeting with Eleanor Rathbone, and had evidently indicated that she 'and ... four others' (presumably Courtney, Royden, Swanwick and Ford) were actively considering resignation from the executive if their policy did not go through. Rathbone was 'aghast' at the thought, and felt such an exodus 'would mean ... the break up of the Union and also probably, the break up of Mrs Fawcett', and would 'give the Antis and the militants the satisfaction of seeing the N.U. split into two and finally crumble and disintegrate.' Rathbone wrote of the five as 'those of you on whom she has manifestly so leaned'.[41]

Despite this conversation, Marshall must have found some hope in the deliberations at Wallasey; she still hoped for a workable solution that would keep the NU together without paralysing it. At the end of the month she wrote to Fawcett from her home in Keswick, where she had gone after leaving her work with the CCEW. Like almost all of Marshall's correspondence with the NU (including that from before the war), the letter cannot be found in the NU collection, from which it may have been purged in the bitter aftermath of the wartime dispute;

fortunately she kept a copy of part of what she wrote. She began with an attempt to clarify the influence she thought women ought to have on 'the spirit in which [the war] is fought, and the temper in which the nation finds itself when the time for settlement comes'. In a striking passage, she wrote of the importance of keeping 'clearly in our minds the difference between the noble and the ignoble motives which drive men to war. ... Readiness to *give* one's life *is* a beautiful and noble thing ... but *enjoyment in taking life* (as shown, alas, in a good many letters in the press and private letters from men at the front) is an ugly and cruel and horrible thing.' In the margin of her copy, Marshall pencilled in a quotation from one such letter (presumably not in the original text sent to Fawcett), 'Best chance of big game shooting I am likely to get in my lifetime.' Women should not go along with the idea that such an attitude was 'manly and commendable – women who taught those same sons, when they were little boys, to be gentle and loving, and to reverence the teaching of Jesus Christ.' Marshall's terminology is of her time – although the Christian reference is rare for her – but what she is saying, in twenty-first century terms, is that women should not let themselves be seduced into accepting a brutal macho attitude as a praiseworthy norm for men.

Stressing again the need for suffrage propaganda to urge women 'to *think* and form an educated opinion', Marshall declared her hope that 'We can surely do this without advocating this or that conclusion'. More personally, she believed that Fawcett had 'in some ways misunderstood what it is that I, and those who feel as I do, want the N.U. to do ... and that the idea of what you *think* we want to do is causing you great worry and uneasiness.' She acknowledged that there was a real difference of opinion between two sections in the NU executive; 'one group cannot admit that even *this* war was wholly justified and inevitable, whilst the other cannot understand how there can possibly be any difference of opinion on what seems to them an obvious case of right and duty'. If the difference regarding events now past could only be recognized and barred from further discussion, Marshall believed 'that there is much ground for united action', adding 'the two groups must be careful to avoid accusing one another on the one hand of being "pro-German" and on the other of being "pro-War" – two equally wounding forms of misrepresentation.'

Urging that the NU must 'take *some* part in forming public opinion in this grave crisis', Marshall said that to attain this end she herself 'would refrain from doing a good many things which, as an individual, I should like to do, if only the Union will take some corporate action,' and concluded by stating plainly that 'If the Union cannot act, then I (and others, I believe) will feel bound to free ourselves to act with some other organization, even if that should necessitate leaving the N.U. for a time. This question is, for some of us, such an integral part of the whole question of women's political duties.'[42]

To see both Fawcett and Marshall expressing some willingness to meet each other halfway over the question of education increases the tragedy of the breach that was to come, centring now mainly on feminist international action.

4
Crucial Forum: The National Council, February 1915

International links debated: December 1914

During the run-up to the NU's Annual Council in February 1915, which would also involve the election of officers and executive, the divisions among the leaders hardened. To the issues of attitudes and actions relating to the war, on the domestic front, was added the complex question of the response of the international suffrage movement – should and could it make one? and if so, of what nature? Should the IWSA hold a congress? And if so, could discussion of the nature of peace form part of the agenda? These questions added measurably to the tension, including, very specifically, to Mrs Fawcett's personal anxiety and to the distrust of her felt by the peace faction.

Remarkably, international feminist communication, although rendered more difficult, had not been shut down by the outbreak of the war. The IWSA headquarters was in London, and the IWSA organ, *Jus Suffragii*, continued to be published with Mary Sheepshanks[1] doubling as Secretary to the organization and editor of the journal. Sheepshanks was a strong independent woman and a convinced pacifist internationalist. She was something of a loner and sometimes dour – perhaps as a reaction to having grown up as the eldest of the seventeen children (four of whom died in infancy) of a clergyman in a cramped and dingy household. She had however been able to go to Cambridge and was now one of relatively few among well educated prominent suffragists who had to earn their own living, which she did for long periods within feminist organizations; but the position of a paid employee was never quite on a par with that of voluntary officers.

Jus Suffragii was a genuinely international publication, open to contributions from any affiliates of the IWSA, and Sheepshanks saw to it that it continued that way during the war. Remarkably, articles continued to arrive, not only from Allied and neutral countries, but even from German sources, channelled through members in neutral nations. A great deal of the material reaching Sheepshank's desk inevitably came from women who were interested in what contribution the international sisterhood could make towards the cause of peace. She did her best to maintain a balance, and to give space to both sides of any question, although her own bias lay with the advocates of peace.[2]

Fawcett herself found *Jus Suffragii* a useful forum at times. Early in the war she aired her view that enfranchised women might have better managed the international situation: had they had the power of full citizenship, she wrote, 'it is impossible to doubt that [it] would have been used to ensure such a political reorganisation of Europe as would have rendered it certain that international disputes and grievances should be referred to law and reason, and not to the clumsy and blundering tribunal of brute force.'[3] It was perhaps a defensible view that once in, the war had to be fought; it was less rational to reiterate the claim, as Fawcett continued to do, that war was the product of male mismanagement, and that the preservation of peace in the future would be best assured by the full participation of women in the political process, and yet to stigmatize as tantamount to treason the actions and views of those who wanted to begin to lay the groundwork for that future.

As peace and patriotism increasingly came to be seen as opposite poles, Fawcett regarded what she saw as the pacifist tone of *Jus Suffragii* with increasing suspicion. Sheepshanks sometimes found Fawcett too close for comfort, in her role as first vice-president of the IWSA, and the only one on the spot.

The IWSA biennial conference was due in the spring of 1915 and was to have been held in Germany. As early as September 1914, the *Common Cause* and *Jus Suffragii* both carried correspondence debating the possibility and wisdom of holding some kind of international women's peace conference, and some suffragists had soon seen the idea of making use of the scheduled IWSA conference as a way to carry this forward although it clearly could not be hosted by any belligerent country. Suffragists and peace advocates from the neutral nations, free from any implication of disloyalty to their countries, took the lead in urging that the conference not only should go ahead, but should discuss the way to make a better peace. Some British suffragists had taken a great deal of interest in a Dutch group called the Anti Oorlog Raad (whose material Marshall hoped to send out to all the NU branches) and had also corresponded with the Women's Peace Party formed in the United States.[4]

As first vice-president of the IWSA, and geographically close to the headquarters in London, Millicent Fawcett was in correspondence with Carrie Chapman Catt (USA), president of the IWSA, and the question of whether to hold the 1915 conference quickly came to the fore. From the first, Fawcett was opposed to holding the conference, believing that 'feeling is running too high'. Others thought it 'rather a confession of failure not to make an attempt to hold the Congress even in the present circumstances.'[5]

The NU executive of 3 December 1914 had before it a letter from Aletta Jacobs, a leading Dutch suffragist, asking that the suggestion be discussed. A motion that the NU propose that the IWSA hold a 'business congress' was carried, with only Fawcett and Palliser recorded as dissenting.[6] The responsibility now lay with Fawcett to make an official report of the proposal to Catt, but no stretch of the imagination enables her letter to Catt to be seen as carrying out the decision of the executive. In effect she warned Catt that Chrystal Macmillan (on the NU executive and also an officer of the IWSA) was writing to all the IWSA officers urging them to support the calling of an international women's convention of which a major purpose would be 'to discuss the principles on which peace should be made and, if agreed, to act internationally'. She told Catt she was strongly opposed, averring as her main reason that '... it would hardly be possible to bring together women of the belligerent countries without violent bursts of anger and mutual recrimination. We should then run the risk of the scandal of a Peace Congress disturbed and perhaps broken up by violent quarrels and fierce denunciations.' This kind of thing, she wrote, was common at 'Socialist and other international meetings: but it is of less importance there: no one expects the general run of men to be anything but fighters. But a *Peace Congress of Women* dissolved by violent quarrels would be the laughing stock of the world.'[7] A cleaned-up (but still strongly-worded) version of her letter – omitting the references to socialists and to men – shortly appeared in the *Common Cause* and *Jus Suffragii*; here she claimed that the better way to defend the now 'feeble flame' of internationalism was by shielding it from the risk of 'outbursts of uncontrollable nationalism' which would be unavoidable at such a conference.[8]

Fawcett's attitude was crucial, and both personally and structurally beset with contradictions. She had had a deserved reputation as an imperialist all her life, and had been fiercely pro-British in the Boer

War. She had, indeed, proved capable of some criticism when she was sent to South Africa to report on conditions in the camps in which women and children had been placed to prevent them from providing support for the Boer commando units, but she had not been able to carry this to the extent of directly assigning any serious blame to her country or her country's soldiers. Her writings show her to have shared the underpinning of imperialist assumption which we have seen in the Stracheys.[9]

Structurally, the anomaly in Fawcett's position derived from her holding office as president of the NU, and also as an officer – first vice-president – of the IWSA. Her feeling against the proposed conference was so strong that she made up her mind from the very first that it was not an issue on which she could go along with a majority should her opinion not win the day; she told Catt that if the conference went ahead she would sooner resign her office in the IWSA than attend.

Preparing for the Council

The question of the possible international conference gave the debate focus and urgency beyond that which had arisen around the issue of education towards a better understanding of international relations. Ray Strachey, who never did anything by halves (an attractive quality in many circumstances) now entered with relish into what she saw as a campaign to defeat the 'pacifists'. She was pregnant at the end of 1914, and the much-wished for pregnancy was not going well (and later terminated in a miscarriage). Probably for this reason, Strachey did not herself stand for election to the NU executive in February 1915, but Oliver did, while she worked vigorously behind the scenes, having, as she told her mother 'great tactical and technical conversations about our suffrage crisis'.[10] For her, it seems never to have been a matter for searching for a forward direction that all could live with, but simply of which side would win.

Once the question of support for the war became front and centre in the struggle, Strachey's first move was not subtle. Early in January, Marshall and presumably all the other candidates for election received a list of five questions, with a covering letter from Strachey. They read, in full:

1 Do you consider that the National Union should advocate anything, however good in itself, if by so doing it might impair its influence in Parliament and the nation and so endanger the cause of Women's Suffrage for which alone it was created?

2 Do you consider that any propaganda undertaken by the National Union at variance with the present strong national feeling concerning the present war would so impair its influence?

3 Do you consider that it is possible to conduct any educational or other campaign concerning the general questions of war, peace, diplomacy, arbitration, or armaments at the present time without an application, implied or expressed, to the present situation?

4 Do you consider that if active propaganda is undesirable a declaration of the attitude of the National Union is nevertheless advisable?

5 If so, would you wish its attitude to be at one with the nation or otherwise?[11]

While a questionnaire was a legitimate way of testing the opinions of candidates, Marshall was surely justified in her comment that 'Your questions are as incapable of an answer by "plain yes or no" [as Strachey claimed] as the proverbial poser: "When did you stop beating your wife?"'. Interestingly, Ray seems to have sent her questionnaire out on her own behalf even though the LSWS executive had (despite its general support of Ray's position) declined to adopt them to be sent out officially, and had instead arranged for Ida O'Malley (who supported the focus on the war effort) and Helen Ward (who favoured peace education) to draw up a more balanced set of queries.[12]

Considering the rather jejune wording of Strachey's questions, it was perhaps generous of Marshall to spend time on them. Nevertheless, after the one acid comment, she settled down to 'try to give you the information you ask for as simply as I can.' But after a careful and serious answer to the first question, in which she admitted that there was a difference of opinion on this in the NU, and suggested that the will of the majority would be made clear at the Council, she became increasingly irritated, and was prompted to counter-questions. The last question provoked a final burst of impatience. Marshall declared that 'The only appropriate answer I can think of to this very enigmatical ... question is the answer of Tweedledum: "Nohow".' What, she asked, did Strachey mean by 'At one with the nation or otherwise?' Was the NU resolution supporting Asquith's principles (as articulated in his Dublin speech) 'otherwise'? If so, did Strachey consider that Asquith was not 'at one with the nation'?[13]

Strachey responded to some of Marshall's counter-questions with a startling directness: 'propaganda at variance with the present strong national feeling concerning the war' meant for her, '*any* propaganda that wasn't of the nature of a recruiting campaign'. And while Asquith was 'at one with the nation' in the principles articulated in his Dublin speech, he would cease to be so if he campaigned for those principles 'because his business now is to support the war, and ours to support him in doing so'. Marshall's refusal to answer with a simple yes or no did not prevent Strachey from reading what she wanted into her explanations; she rightly assumed that Marshall thought that for the NU to conduct an educational campaign on war and peace would not injure the suffrage cause; less accurately she assumed that Marshall thought it within the NU's mandate 'to conduct a campaign on questions *other than suffrage.*'[14]

Marshall was at pains, once more, to explain that for her questions of peace and war were intimately connected with suffrage through the suffering of women in war and more importantly through the belief that social relations should be based on the recognition of mutual rights and not on force. Here too was a chance to prove women's ability to think intelligently about 'the larger questions of politics'. It was rare for Marshall to display openly the degree of irritation that shows through her correspondence with Strachey over this 'examination paper'; her replies hardly conceal mounting frustration, probably because she felt that Strachey's mind was closed, and because she foresaw how much easier it might be for the Strachey faction to polarize the NU than to accept that patriotism might also comprise working towards a right ending of the war, or 'helping to prepare public opinion to make right use of victory when victory comes'.[15]

The National Council: February 1915

When 4 February 1915 – in Ray Strachey's words, 'the critical day we've been working and plotting for for weeks' – finally arrived, poor Ray was obliged to stay in bed to try to save the pregnancy, depending on Oliver for reports.[16] When the Annual Council meeting convened, tensions were running high. Matters peripheral – but not unconnected – to the main controversy were disposed of in the first two resolutions to be carried, which endorsed the decision to suspend 'ordinary political activities' and also 'the rules which restrict the work of the National Union to gaining the Parliamentary franchise for women', so as to allow the organization to be used for relief work and 'in such other manner as may be directed by the Council.' In order to protect the commitments made to the Labour party, Marshall then moved a resolution authorizing the NU to continue work at any by-election, along its approved policy lines and at the initiative of the executive; the resolution passed, though not without opposition.[17]

The first resolution relating to the attitude of the NU to the war proposed that no declaration of any kind should be made on the war or on the terms of peace, but first an amendment to take out the words 'the terms of peace' was carried and then the whole resolution was lost. A vaguely-worded (but 'patriotic') resolution from members of the LSWS proposing that the NU should identify itself with 'the cause of the nation as supported by the three Parliamentary parties' was also rejected, according to Marshall's notes, 'by a huge majority'.

Now the real test began, with a resolution, moved by Ashton and seconded by Ford, spelling out the link between the suffragists' denial of the physical force argument and their belief in arbitration between nations, and urging the government 'to do its utmost to ensure that in the future, International disputes shall be submitted to arbitration or conciliation before recourse is had to military force, and that the nations shall bind themselves to unite against any country which breaks the peace without observing these conditions.' An added paragraph called upon 'the organised women of the world to press the same policy on their respective Governments', and to work for the vote to put power behind the demand.[18] Despite efforts to have it weakened by amendment or better yet, rejected, the resolution was passed in the end by a 'large majority'.

A further resolution again affirmed the conviction that women's political participation at every level was 'of vital importance' in furthering international peace, and (not surprisingly) passed 'nem. con.' Another, moved by Royden and seconded by Marshall, called on 'the Societies and members of the Union to take every means open to them' to promote international understanding, and oppose any 'spirit of hatred and revenge'; the same resolution sent friendly greetings and sympathy in present suffering to 'the women of all nations who are striving for the uplifting of their sex', and expressed the hope that after the war united work on enfranchisement might be resumed. An attempt was made to lay the responsibility for the work for goodwill between nations on individual members, leaving out mention of the societies, but this was lost. But just over half of those present – including Mrs Fawcett – were sufficiently fearful of anything that smacked of criticism of the war effort to refuse to express an 'ardent hope that Peace may soon be attained', and had these words removed by amendment.

The peace faction must have been on the edge of their chairs by now. Nothing vital had been lost, but the potential strength of the opposition was apparent. Now came the attempt to build on Asquith's declaration – as near, perhaps, as the British government was ever to come to a statement of war aims – repudiating militarism, advocating protection of the rights of small nations, and favouring the substitution for force of 'a real International partnership, based on the recognition of equal right and established and enforced by a common will.' The resolution brought forward by the executive and proposed by Fawcett herself accepted these principles 'as a fundamental consideration which should govern the settlement after the war', and called upon the societies and members 'to work for the building up of public opinion on these lines'.

The Cambridge society had put forward an amendment to eviscerate the resolution by removing the last phrase. Marshall, sensing that 'on these lines' would be seen as too specific, made a last-minute attempt to replace the words with 'in support of these principles', but although she gave notice of a motion, she was not recognized by the Chair (Mrs Rackham) and 'never got the chance' to move the change. Instead, the last three speakers before the vote was taken, according to Marshall, were all supporters of the amendment, and 'directed their opposition against the advocacy of detailed terms of peace. Their attack was therefore beside the mark, directed against a proposal which no one had put forward.'[19] In any event, the amendment was carried; since no breakdown of the voting was given, an uncontestable majority must have been apparent.

Marshall would later describe the Council bitterly as having been willing to clap, but not to vote. And Dr Ethel Williams, one of the speakers in favour of the original resolution, was so angry that she moved the Previous Question to the resolution (moved, that is, that the whole resolution should be dismissed without further discussion); she was seconded, ironically, by a member of the Cambridge WSS, which had brought forward the amendment. The Previous Question was lost by a narrow margin, 250 to 266.

By this time the atmosphere was electric. Lady Frances Balfour, president of the LSWS, a member of the NU executive, and one of those most scornful towards what she saw as a lack of patriotism, moved an amendment to tie the achievement of 'the ideal of public right as the governing idea of international politics' to British victory, and included a clause recording the gratitude of the Council for the heroism of the soldiers, potentially making it impossibly invidious to vote against it. With presence of mind, Courtney separated the effect of victory from the heroism of the soldiers. The amendment was defeated, and Courtney's urgency resolution expressing 'undying admiration for the heroism of those who are now serving this country in the defence of the Empire' was passed unanimously.

Courtney, seconded by Maude Royden, now successfully moved a resolution recommending the organization of educational courses to encourage the study of the causes, consequences, and prevention of war, on the lines of previous educational campaigns undertaken by the NU.

Not surprisingly, members ended the day confused. What views could they express publicly? What must they avoid speaking against? Were there views which they were obliged to promote actively on behalf of the NU? Under the educational campaign, while members might speak in accordance with the views adopted by the NU, should speakers be brought in with a variety of views? The rulings would be the subject of continuing argument and revision over the next weeks.[20]

Mrs Fawcett's role during the actual Council sessions – although no report of speeches made is preserved – appears hard to fault, and her influence seems to have been exerted towards achieving a compromise that would avert the loss of leading members. But her circulated election address[21] had been strongly pro-war and imperialist, and if the pro-war faction had any remaining doubts as to whether her sympathies were wholeheartedly with them, they were dispelled in the evening, when a public meeting was held to make known the most important of the decisions taken at the Council. In the perception of the peace faction, Fawcett used the occasion to make just the kind of jingoistic speech which most upset and angered them, and which was indeed singularly inappropriate when her job was to report decisions which had on the whole favoured the move towards peace education. As reported in the *Manchester Guardian*, she mentioned support for the principles laid down by Asquith, but then included a long and scarcely relevant dissertation on the course of the war so far, emphasizing the heroism of the Allies. She averred that 'the first national duty was to get Germany out of Belgium and France', and worse still, went on to say 'Until that is done I believe it is akin to treason to talk of peace', although, in Rubinstein's apt words, she 'meaninglessly claim[ed] to speak for herself alone'. But Fawcett evidently continued to believe that she had given a fair account of what had occurred, stressing what had been carried and minimizing the importance of what had been lost.[22]

The Council made one other decision, significant in principle and as a measure of the membership's will at this time. The Manchester society brought a resolution to endorse the executive's decision to cast the NU's IWSA vote in favour of the holding of a congress, to be convened by the IWSA. Attempts by the LSWS to express regret rather than approval of the executive's action, or, failing that, to advocate holding the congress only after the war, were voted down and the resolution carried. This deepened the anomaly by which Fawcett's role as vice president of the IWSA, and her personal opinion, put her at odds with her obligation to vote according to the decision of her national organization. The procedure in the IWSA for making a decision between congresses was at best poorly defined. In fact, as Catt would explain in a letter which came to the NU March executive, the IWSA constitution gave the officers the power to settle all business between conventions, but she had thought the arrangement unfair since it deprived of a vote any auxiliary that did not happen to have an officer as a member. With an airy disregard of procedure (prescribed, if admittedly faulty) which is rather startling from one at the head of an organization so concerned with process, Catt had therefore 'always submitted the vote to officers and auxiliaries', leaving unresolved the question of what to do if the vote of an officer was contrary to the vote of her auxiliary. The present case, where Fawcett's view was contrary to that of the NU, was the only occasion when this had happened. Catt's report in March on the progress of voting so far would indicate a clear majority of officers opposed to holding the conference, and a shaky majority among auxiliaries of the same view, and she declared the proposal lost, though holding out encouragement to think in terms of a conference to be held immediately the war came to an end.[23]

The Council resolution supporting an international congress made no provision for what to do should the IWSA decline to call one. Not surprisingly, the doors were wide open to contradictory interpretations, with those who opposed the idea maintaining that the IWSA decision closed the case, and those who wanted to see an international women's gathering believing that the spirit of the resolution was in favour of meeting with or without official IWSA blessing.

Election of the NU Executive: February 1915

Historians have generally concluded that, while a majority at the February (Wallasey) Council was in sympathy with those who favoured work for understanding of peace, the minority was in fact much more representative of opinion in the NU throughout the country. This assumption shortchanges the NU's democratic process. Those at the

Council were, after all, delegates from the constituent societies, and the resolutions had gone out ahead of time; it would have been rare indeed for the delegates to be ignorant of opinion in their own societies, and on important issues it was the practice for their local societies to instruct them on how to vote, although they must have had discretion on the all-important amendments from the floor. Whether or not the practice of directing delegates was universal throughout the NU, it was strictly followed in the LSWS, whose executive would shortly formally censure two of its delegates for departing from instructions at the Council.[24]

The election of the NU executive, which took place during the Council, is even more significant, and has not previously been examined. Voting for candidates was not at the discretion of the delegates, so there is reason to accept the election results as a fair profile of opinion in the NU. The slate of candidates had gone out ahead, and their position on important issues had been laid out in their election addresses[25] as well as in public speaking, and in the *Common Cause*. Further, many of them had made themselves available during the previous weeks to speak to societies throughout the country.

The results decisively favoured those who were known by the wider membership to stand for the NU's taking a proactive role in discussion of the issues of peace and war. Of course, as was customary, most of the successful candidates were reappointments of familiar names. The four officers, Fawcett (president), Auerbach (treasurer), Courtney (honorary secretary), and Marshall (honorary parliamentary secretary), were returned unopposed, so no votes for them exist to be counted. Of the next seven names in order of number of votes received, only Lady Frances Balfour was in the 'patriot' faction. Oliver Strachey's candidature was successful, though not by a large margin; with 237 votes, he came in nineteenth of the twenty-one who achieved appointment.

Of the 21 candidates elected, ten can be firmly identified as favouring the peace position, as they later resigned over issues connected with the Hague Conference. To these ten can be added Macmillan, who did not resign but fully supported and helped organize the congress, and Margery Fry, who had said, inexplicably, in her election address that as a new candidate she felt she should not give her views; she had however expressed reservations about taking a pledge to put suffrage before party considerations, in case this should ever commit her to support a party favouring continuance of the war over 'a party standing for what seemed to be a just peace'. She came from a noted

Quaker family. Added to the peace tally, her 365 votes bring the total to 4190.[26]

Among other successful candidates, five can be identified as in the patriot faction; four of these were from the LSWS, the fifth from East Berkshire. These five polled 1539 votes and if we count the 'wasted' votes on five unsuccessful candidates known to be 'patriotic' (four from London and one from Oxford) the pro-war count rises to 2408.

The remaining four appointees, and Fry, were later seen by the internationalists as potentially 'progressive or at least not obstructive?'. Rackham headed the list with 473 votes; support for her was probably based as much on her position as Chair (reappointed by ballot within the executive every year) as on her views, which were officially impartial and personally ambivalent, since she favoured the peace work but held that it should be done outside the NU. Despite Marshall's hopes for them, the 730 votes polled by the remaining three have not been counted on either side.[27]

In summary, the peace faction, whose views were well known, won eleven of the twenty-one seats, and polled a significant majority of the votes cast. By chance, the four honorary officers were divided equally between the two sides. The election results indicate that many NU members might indeed have supported the kind of campaign that was wanted by many of the executive, and that they saw its feminist relevance and shared its vision. It is hard to know what to make of a scrap of paper, among the documents that later found their way to the Manchester Public Library, that indicates, in Millicent Fawcett's own handwriting, that she voted for (among others) every one of those who would soon resign. She did not vote for Oliver Strachey.

Post mortem: Interpreting the Council

The February NU Council had been the kind of occasion that participants play over and over in their minds and in their correspondence with each other for weeks afterwards.[28] But attempts to gauge how a narrow defeat – if it was one – might have been turned into a narrow victory by a slight change in wording, a better explanation, more persistence, or a Chair thought to be less closely identified with Fawcett's views, could not, in the long run, lead to any satisfaction.

Oliver Strachey, one of the most committed 'patriots', acknowledged that every so-called patriotic resolution had been given short shrift by the Council.[29] Strachey's reductive analysis, as presented a few weeks later at a meeting of the LSWS, was that there was an irreconcilable dichotomy in the NU, and particularly between the NU executive and that of the LSWS. The urgency of the war question, he said, had led all suffragists to take action, 'either 1) by joining pacifist societies, or 2) by strengthening our country in the fight against militarism.' Although the object might be the same, the different methods were 'apt to produce opposite results'. To take the first option was to hinder the second. While the 'Pacifist party', identified by Oliver with the NU executive, held that militarism at home was the most important target, the 'Patriotic party', represented by the LSWS executive, took 'the other side'. The goal of the pacifists, Oliver said, had been to capture the NU as an organ for pacifist propaganda, but they had found themselves opposed not only by a large patriotic party, but by 'a large section' of pacifists who feared the effect the move would have on the NU's effectiveness as a suffrage organization.[30]

When Marshall reran the Council meeting, and Oliver Strachey's comments, in her head and in scribbled comments, one of the most irritating features was, as it seemed to her, that the patriotic arguments had set up and knocked down a straw target, something that she had already feared and tried to forestall.[31] She wrote, 'there was no proposal of a "stop-the-war" or a "peace at any price" agitation; there was no expression of opinion with regard to the present war; no criticism of the way in which it is being conducted; no attempt to define detailed terms of a peace.'[32] Marshall's notes for a reply to Oliver Strachey embody some of the reasoned arguments she had given many times before. Her repeated use of the word 'unfair' also reveals something of her rising anger and frustration. It was unfair to use the labels 'patriotic' and 'pacifist', as unfair as it was to see one group as loyal to suffrage, the other as disloyal. It was unfair to accuse the 'pacifists' of trying to capture the organization for propaganda of their own, when they had in fact focussed on what they hoped would be common ground, and when they had exercised such 'extreme scrupulousness' in holding off from any action until the Council had had a full opportunity for discussion and decision. But within the LSWS, voices in support of Marshall's views were few and ill-heard; a solid phalanx of the London Society leaders stood with Oliver Strachey.[33]

The history of the LSWS and the role played by some of its members in crystallizing the 'patriotic' faction within the NU has not previously been described in detail. The Stracheys, of course, were not the sole authors of the opposition to the supposed 'pacifist party', but they had very general approval within the LSWS; leading members who were with them included Helen Ward (though she would later change her position), Ida O'Malley, Edith Palliser, Lady Frances Balfour, Clementina Black. Nor was the London Society the only one where the majority inclined naturally towards laying aside all else in favour of support for the war effort. Cambridge (city and county societies) had taken an important part at the Council, and in general, Oxfordshire and Berkshire seem to have been on the pro-war side, while Birmingham might go in either direction. Influential support for the 'patriots' also came from the Liverpool society, and specifically from Eleanor Rathbone, though her arguments relied much less on emotion than did Ray Strachey's; the Liverpool society as a whole stood behind her.[34] Societies particularly active in the peace faction included Manchester, Newcastle and Bristol. But whatever the prevailing view in a given society, there were doubtless dissidents to it.

The Annual Council of February had proved to be a watershed in the history of the NU, and yet our detailed look at what happened suggests that this need not have been so. Both those who wanted to work towards an enlightened peace and those who thought the role of the NU in wartime should be wholeheartedly behind the war effort had found some support in the Council. What had been lacking was any truly conciliatory spirit; the climate that had developed had been adversarial, with participants looking to win points rather than to find solutions all could live with. Worse still, the two sides had begun to demonize each other, with the self-styled 'patriots' condemning the peace women as traitors, and the peace women hearing only the words of attack and unable to recognize the degree of support they might command throughout the country, or to see that the door remained open, if not as wide open as they would have wished, to a worthwhile peace education campaign. The emotionally charged atmosphere of a country and a class suffering huge losses of life, and the personalities of some among the NU's leaders had made any outcome acceptable to all unlikely if not impossible.

5
Disaffection and New Directions

Planning The Hague Conference for April 1915

Less than a week after the February 1915 NU Council meeting, a handful of British women – Courtney, Marshall, Macmillan, Leaf, and Theodora Wilson Wilson (a Quaker suffragist and writer,[1] who like Marshall had roots in Cumberland) were in Amsterdam, where they met with women from Belgium, Holland, and Germany. Three days later they were back in Britain with close-to-complete plans and draft resolutions for an ambitious international women's congress to be held at The Hague in April.

Eight weeks was a short enough time for the work of explaining and publicizing the conference and setting up a new organization, let alone for making the necessary practical arrangements for women to go to Holland. While the peace work of the new group is not our focus, the political width of the network to which they reached out is relevant, since it was in fact the network created by these same women before the war on behalf of the NU.

Within a week of their return from Amsterdam, the English women who had been there called a meeting of delegates from various organizations to be held at the Caxton Hall on 26 February. Response to their call resulted in a large, representative and enthusiastic gathering. Chrystal Macmillan took the Chair. Margaret Bondfield was the first speaker and Marshall the other main speaker. Not just a propaganda meeting, the gathering formed an official 'British Committee of the International Women's Congress' (BCIWC) to carry the work forward. A small executive was appointed from among those already involved, and provision was made to co-opt ten more from women's organizations across the country.

Among those who took on prominent roles were the five who had been in Amsterdam; others include Margaret Bondfield, Isabella Ford, Ada Salter (a Quaker, member of the Women's Labour League, and wife of the humanitarian east-end doctor, Albert Salter), Lillian Harris (Women's Cooperative Guild), and Sophia Sanger. Mary Sheepshanks' name appears in early lists, though she was experiencing increasing difficulty with Fawcett over her position as secretary of the IWSA and editor of *Jus Suffragii*.[2] In addition, a large general committee was named (an early list shows about 150 names), representative of a wide range of dissidence; included are, of course, well-known NU members, and also some from other suffrage bodies (Mrs Despard, WFL, Sylvia Pankhurst, ELFS); many Quakers; women trade union leaders (notably Eva Gore-Booth, Esther Roper); Margaret Llewelyn Davies of the Women's Cooperative Guild; Lilla Brockway, wife of Fenner Brockway, the editor of the *Labour Leader*, and like him, already concerned about the possibility of conscription; writers (Olive Schreiner, Violet Paget, Caroline Playne); Lady Courtney of Penwith and Lady Ottoline Morrell; and a rather large number who, in accordance with current custom, are identified by their husbands' names, which does however enable us to recognize several of them as the wives of discontented Liberals: for example, Mrs Charles Buxton, Mrs Arthur Ponsonby, Mrs Charles Trevelyan, Mrs R.C. Trevelyan. Money came in well, starting with about £300 pledged at this first Caxton Hall meeting; within a short time the committee had premises and letterhead. Local committees were soon formed in Dublin, Liverpool, and Manchester, followed by Birmingham, Edinburgh, and Glasgow.[3]

A great deal of interest was shown as soon as the plans for the Congress became known. Inquiries from women interested in going to The Hague, or in supporting the enterprise, poured in, and before the list closed there were 180 firm applications. Sybil Oldfield's careful research into the women behind the 275 names of those who wanted to go and those who offered financial and moral support confirms some expectations, and also reveals some surprises. Not all were pacifists or non-militants. Many were suffragists, but there were also many Quaker women (most of whom were also suffrage supporters), and some active Labour women, together with individuals of various or no affiliation. Understandably, the great majority were women of some means, since only these could afford the cost; it is also probable that the 75 names for whom Oldfield could find no information included a higher proportion of less well-off women. The Women's Labour League actively encouraged all branches to send a member, and expected to be able to find funds to assist with expenses. Significantly, the great majority of the 200 identified by Oldfield worked as volunteers or for pay in some form of public service or social work; if they were themselves privileged, they had a consciousness extending beyond their own fortunate circumstances.[4]

NU executive resignations begin

Some executive members had foreseen the possible need to resign their positions even before the Council met, and had their minds almost made up as soon as the Council ended, in particular following Millicent Fawcett's provocative public speech. Maude Royden resigned as editor of the *Common Cause* at the next executive meeting after the Council, giving as her reason that she felt her work for peace could be more effectively carried on elsewhere, especially as the Council had given her no clear mandate.[5] For the time being she remained on the executive.

For Courtney and Marshall it was not quite so simple. A number of their supporters thought that, over all, the Council decisions left plenty of room for hope, and begged them not to resign. Some friends, including Marshall's own ever-supportive parents, thought indeed that they had given up too easily: Caroline Marshall told her daughter very directly that 'at the Council neither you nor Miss C. put up a fight for life. You were the patients who did not want to live'. Frank Marshall, who had been present, wrote to his daughter 'that the feeling of the majority of the Council was with you. But not being sufficiently alert and intelligent to see through to the meaning of things they were not quick enough to shew it and overpower the organised efforts of London, Birmingham, Oxford and Co.'[6] But the two officers had their minds made up by mid-February, and they announced their resignations at the executive committee meeting of 4 March.[7] Both declared that they were resigning from their posts not as a protest but because the work they did for the NU took all their time, and so they could not continue if they were not authorized to direct it towards what had become for them the most important objective. Both were willing to continue on the executive, though there was a snag here since officers were not drawn from the elected members of the executive but served *ex officio*; hence, they continued only by courtesy of the executive, and, importantly, were not allowed to vote.

With an uncharacteristic lack of tact, Marshall mishandled the way in which she offered her resignation, using the occasion to criticize the speech made by Fawcett at the public meeting of February 5, which she (justifiably) saw as contravening the agreement just reached by the Council to refrain from the expression of personal opinions when speaking on behalf of the NU. To make matters worse, Marshall discourteously failed to make sure that Fawcett was given her letter or notified of her decision ahead of the meeting.[8] Still angry, she wrote another more personal letter to Fawcett immediately after the executive meeting, using some inexcusably offensive terms.[9]

Marshall made a verbal apology to Fawcett the next day for the late delivery of the resignation letter, and her formal apology, given at the next meeting of the executive, was close to abject. But there is no doubt that immense damage had been done, and Fawcett's unforgiving nature fed on such a hurt, adding to the real injury of the loss of two of her most valuable officers. In accepting the resignations on 4 March she had paid tribute to the work of the two honorary secretaries with some generosity; but although she accepted Marshall's apologies on 5 and 18 March, she did so with little grace.

Fawcett was reluctant to recognize that the gulf between her attitude to the war and that of Marshall and her closest colleagues was now too wide to bridge; in her letter of 6 March, she was still at pains to explain how close her hopes at the Council had been to those of the peace education advocates. But once the bridge was out, the 'pacifists' were free to go further than they had, and the 'patriots' could also take a more extreme position.

After the resignations of Marshall and Courtney, the executive moved to clarify the official NU attitude. At the meeting of 18 March, Fawcett brought in a motion 'that it was undesirable for the National Union to take part officially in the International Congress of Women to be held in Holland in April.' The discussion that followed was heated and personally wounding; clearly decisions of the February Council had done little to promote clarity, much less charity. The breach between Fawcett and Marshall widened when Fawcett argued that 'the time for agitating for peace was so inopportune that to do so was almost treachery', words which Marshall in her turn would find hard to forget. Lady Frances Balfour was even more virulent, declaring roundly that 'participation in such a Congress would cast dishonour on our sons who were fighting at the Front' and threatening to resign and 'head a campaign ... against the women who acted in this way'. Swanwick and Royden took a position that seems to have been the equivalent of throwing up their hands in something near ridicule at what was happening. Although protesting at the accusations levelled by Fawcett and Balfour, Swanwick concluded that 'Having taken a course which entailed the resignation of Miss Courtney and Miss Marshall, it would be absurd for the Executive now to take another line which would entail the resignation of Mrs Fawcett and Mrs Auerbach'. Fawcett's resolution carried by 11 votes to 5, with Swanwick and Royden voting in favour. Although the minutes do not specifically say so, Fawcett must have made it clear that she would not stay on if her resolution did not pass. And she did not scruple to make use of the windfall of unexpected support; an unusual footnote to the minutes names (only) Swanwick and Royden, and in July, Fawcett would tell Catt that those two had 'acted with me' in voting against sending delegates, without mentioning the circumstances or their expressed reason.[10]

For Swanwick, the March executive meeting clearly marked her abandonment of all faith in the NU. She wrote to Marshall: 'As I see things now, there is no use whatever in making a prolonged misery of staying on the Executive. ... to stay on would result in futile and embittered wranglings. Mrs Fawcett *can* not see reason. Mrs Auerbach will be as difficult as stupid people always are and Mrs Rackham will exercise her power [as Chair] to suppress all objectors.'[11]

Determined to put an end to confusion, the dominant officers (presumably Fawcett) gave orders to the Secretary, immediately following the executive meeting, to send out a letter to all the NU societies and federations, spelling out that societies were not free to appoint delegates to the Congress, though individuals might go, and reiterating that the same applied to joining the UDC and to attending a National Conference of Women called by the UDC; and societies should not consider themselves free to express any opinion on the war.[12]

Millicent Fawcett's distress at the way things were turning out was real, but she remained unwilling to face how much of it was of her making. She even tried to have the minutes altered to reflect what she wished she had said rather than what she had in fact said, and was only prevented by the fact that she received them at the same time as other members. Courtney's disillusion was completed: 'What I think so black about this affair is that she is evidently ashamed of her speech but won't say so to those of us who were attacked. I think it is ... mean to try to get the minutes altered and not to write a word of apology in reply to my letter to her'.[13]

Fawcett went to tea with Helena Swanwick, who gave Marshall a vivid account of the conversation:

I was absolutely blunt with her and told her that though we didn't retaliate, she couldn't expect us to sit through speeches like those she and Lady Frances had been lately dealing out to us – I tried to make her see that she couldn't decently call her colleagues traitors and lunatics; but she just flushed and blinked and rambled away over all sorts of quite irrelevant things – I couldn't keep her to anything at all. Just before she went I told her I intended to resign from the Executive and she implored me not to – 'There is so much to be done! We must get into better relations with the London Society and you must help.' I said I was the last person to help there, as they deeply distrusted me and for my part I regarded the Society as the great stumbling block of the N.U.! ... I foresee a period of stagnation for the N.U. under its new Hon. Sec., and a rapprochement with London.[14]

The distance Fawcett maintained from her colleagues – and could not bridge when, as here, she tried – masked, in my view, a dependence on, and enjoyment of her close association with her hardworking colleagues, the more so if they were (comparatively) young and eager. The bitter criticism coming from her previous colleagues made her the more open to return to old friends in the LSWS, such as Lady Frances Balfour, and even more to accept the new close supporters, among whom the Strachey family featured largely.

Many individuals wrote personal letters regretting the resignations of Courtney and Marshall, as did at least twenty branches; a few others forwarded copies to the executive of resolutions passed in the same sense; even London sent in a resolution appreciating their work – although this one, honestly enough, lacked any expression of regret over the resignations.[15]

Democratic suffragists leave the field

While Marshall and Courtney were occupied with arrangements for the Hague Congress, heavy fallout from that event further decimated the NU executive. The loss of Marshall and Courtney as officers in February removed a very significant presence from the NU office, and their departure from the executive not only did the same but actually may have tipped the voting balance against the peace position. At best, the controversy over the interpretation of the resolutions passed at the February Council took place at executive meetings where the sides were very evenly balanced. From 18 March on, following their resignations as officers, Courtney and Marshall were no longer able to vote, even on occasions when they were permitted to be present, and this may have made a significant contribution to the consistency with which interpretation came down on the side of the pro-war faction.

Following the refusal of the executive to sanction delegates, the meeting of 15 April had before it letters of resignation from the executive from almost all the remaining Hague supporters, as well as a storm of correspondence from branches approving, disapproving, or raising questions about the decisions made by the executive, and about the resignations that had already been accepted. These many resignations from the NU executive may have been inevitable following the decision not to send delegates to The Hague, but strategically they were a disaster. The timing of the Hague Congress had nothing to do with the British situation, but was unfortunate in that it forced the issue in the NU. Among a total of ten new executive resignations were those of Swanwick, Royden, Ashton, Ford, Alice Clark, and Cary Schuster.[16] Leaf's resignation as press secretary followed in April over difficulty in interpreting what line she was or was not required or permitted by the Council decisions to pursue.[17]

In addition to the direct issue of support for the Hague Congress, the tentative emergence of an alternative feminist structure, single-minded on the issue of war, made it easier for leading suffragists to leave the NU executive, whether, like Swanwick, they were already anxious to be quit of the restraints and half-measures incumbent on their membership, or whether, like Alice Clark, they had hoped to hold the NU together by acting as a leaven.

Chrystal Macmillan, as ever, took an idiosyncratic position. She later wrote that although she had voted to send delegates to the Hague, the majority executive decision not to do so seemed to her no reason to resign; indeed, seeing members of the executive as responsible to the Council which had elected them, she considered that voting in the minority was one of the strongest reasons not to resign, but to remain in order to fight for her point of view.[18] Macmillan's argument makes a good deal of sense.

Marshall and Courtney in March and the remaining ten in April may indeed have acted with less than the patience and strategic skill these same women had shown in the previous four or five years when they had quietly revolutionized the geographic basis, the demographic makeup, and the political outlook of the NU. It is arguable that had they been willing to keep up the struggle in the executive, and at the same time build on what limited mandate had been granted by the February Council to conduct courses for membership and public on international relations and structures, the NU's impressive network could in fact have contributed something towards moderating the wartime and postwar climate of hatred between the peoples of the opposing nations so evident later when peace terms were under discussion. The Women's International League (WIL), as BCIWC soon became, would attempt the same, but as an identifiable peace group, it would largely preach to the converted, whereas within the NU the peace educators might have reached a large audience of the genuinely interested but uncertain, as well as many who were in sympathy but needed more knowledge.

All this is speculation, and much may also be said in defence of the resigners. Within the NU executive itself, convictions were strong on both sides. Ill will and distortion escalated. From a personal point of view, the seceders were doubtless withdrawing from a situation of constant frustration: from a public viewpoint, they had reason to doubt how effective education for peace could be in that climate. And while they lost the resources and to some extent the constituency provided by the NU, work through the WIL was free of many constraints inevitable within the NU.

The opponents of the Hague conference and of a peace education programme had no reason to be particularly satisfied with the resolutions passed in February, but had ample cause to take heart from the resignations. Those who had been uneasy before the war at the direction the NU was taking saw an opportunity, and were not slow to take it. Leadership and resources, especially from among the members of the LSWS, were not lacking. Fawcett was confused and distressed, but obdurate; she may well have been the one insuperable stumbling-block to any high-profile peace work on the part of the NU, but she had not opposed the education campaign.

Yet Fawcett continued to profess herself puzzled by what had occurred, and a few weeks later wrote to Carrie Chapman Catt: 'I entirely fail even now to guess the real causes of the *coup d'état* in our N.U. com^{ee} in April when 11 members resigned. ... In my opinion a great deal was due to nerves and overwork.'[19] But her use of the term 'coup d'état' is revealing. It is not those who are driven out of power who bring off a coup, but those who remain or take their places. Ray Strachey, prominent among the latter, does not use the term, but her private correspondence suggests that that was exactly how she saw the triumph of the 'patriots'. At the time, she was on the Riviera (presumably for health reasons), but Oliver Strachey kept her closely informed. After the débacle of 15 April, Ray wrote exultantly to her mother: 'A great cataclysm has happened in the Suffrage world and we have succeeded in driving all the pacifists out. They wanted us to send a delegate to the Womens Peace Conference at the Hague, and we refused. Then they resigned in a body – and they included the majority of our officers and Committee! It is a marvellous triumph that it was they who had to go and not us – and shows that there's some advantage in internal democracy, for we only did it by having the bulk of the stodgy members behind us'. All very well, but even Oliver Strachey characterized the remaining rump as 'very silly and bad'.[20]

The vacuum on the executive caused by the resignations, and particularly by those of Marshall and Courtney, was very large, but was matched by the vacuum immediately around Fawcett. Although Helena Auerbach, the NU treasurer, was closer personally to Fawcett than any of the younger members had ever been or would be, and commented on NU developments very frankly in her letters, she was neither an initiator nor a politician within the Union, and did not offer the stimulus and support that Fawcett took from working with dynamic younger women.

Ray Strachey was ready to step into the space at Fawcett's right hand, supported by Oliver, and by others in the LSWS and elsewhere. Whatever the deficiencies of her new advisers, with them Fawcett would no longer have to attempt the agonizing balancing act of the last few months – at which she had, in the long run, proved so inept. Ray Strachey meanwhile rejoiced in the defeat of those she dubbed 'the wild women of theory'.[21]

Just off centre stage, and little noted by historians, the LSWS had also undergone significant changes. Following the February NU Council, there had been several resignations from the LSWS executive and a few from the LSWS itself; at least two constituent London societies had also withdrawn from the LSWS in favour of direct affiliation with the NU.[22] While these defections are another indication of support for the peace faction, in practice they enabled the LSWS executive to speak more confidently with one voice – the voice of the faction led by the Stracheys.

Women's International League begins work

Meanwhile, the women's international conference took place at The Hague at the end of April 1915 as planned. The saga of the British women who wanted to attend, and who were prevented, is to be found elsewhere, as is the record of the conference itself.[23] The failure of all except the smallest handful of British women to get to The Hague detracted remarkably little from the interest and the eager participation in the follow-up which were soon demonstrated. The British wing of the International Conference of Women for Permanent Peace (ICWPP), which had been formed as the British Committee of the International Women's Congress (BCIWC) before the Hague conference, set to work to form branches.

Not surprisingly, those who had resigned from the NU executive and those who had been active in planning the Hague conference formed the core of the new British organization. But we also find among the officers Emmeline Pethick Lawrence and Margaret Bondfield, and on the executive were Sylvia Pankhurst, Lady Courtney, Charlotte Despard (of the Women's Freedom League), Mrs Barton (president of the Women's Cooperative Guild), Eva Macnaghten (a YWCA leader), Katharine Bruce Glasier (Labour speaker and novelist), Helen Ward (who had resigned from the LSWS executive in April), Ada Salter and Ethel Snowden (both active in the Women's Labour League), Marian Ellis (a Leicester Quaker), and the Hon. Mrs Rollo Russell.

Jane Addams of the United States, who had presided over the Hague conference, and who was one of the envoys to heads of government appointed by that conference, visited Britain in May 1915 and again in June, greatly helping the British internationalists to gain attention and firm up their organization.

Although so much of their time and attention was focussed on the new organization, those who had left the NU executive in order to be free to work on internationalism saw themselves as still very much part of the NU, and still held hopes of challenging the new leadership and re-establishing their position on the executive.

6
No Way Back

After the April resignations the rump of the NU executive had settled down to consolidate its position and to work, doubtless more comfortably, on other matters of concern to them. But in order to lay the matter of attitude to the war finally to rest, and to fill the vacant positions, a Special Council was called for June 1915, to meet in Birmingham.

The peace women hope to climb back on board

For those who had resigned, the Special Council offered a last hope of finding some way of working within the NU. Those who had left the executive, as well as the bulk of countrywide support for the Hague Congress, were still members of the NU, and some were still active on sub-committees. But if any relationship was to continue between the women's peace movement and the NU, there would have to be important developments. First, of course, some assessment had to be made of what position would be supported by the membership throughout the country, and some foothold regained in the NU executive. Cary Schuster commented with insight that, in her view, the division was 'roughly' between the anti-militarist north and the pro-war south.

The resigners had no power base from which to develop their strategy, but some were finding it desperately difficult to give up all hope of working within the Society which had been their life for so long, and of making use of the machinery they themselves had done so much to develop, in order to air questions which seemed to them so relevant to the political position and future of women. When it became known that a Special Council was planned, and before the date was known, Margaret Ashton of the Manchester WSS convened a meeting of those who had resigned and their supporters, at which their efforts could be coordinated, some clear resolutions drafted for the Council, and some plan put in place should the Council prove to be 'progressive' enough in its tone for it to be worth trying for re-election. Ashton herself would be willing to stand given certain conditions, as would Isabella Ford and probably some others, including Marshall. Courtney, she knew, would not.[1]

The meeting took place at the Sesame Club in London on 9 May and was very well attended by the invited group.[2] Helena Swanwick agreed to chair the meeting, although she herself was far along the road to separating her hopes completely from the NU. Two main themes were under discussion: the development of strategy for the Council, and the larger and closely related question of the future working of the NU.

Marshall brought to the Sesame Club gathering a plan by which the NU would divide into two sections, 'one section confining itself to direct support of women's claim to enfranchisement, and the other section extending its scope so as to include the advocacy of the fundamental principles which underlie that claim, and all work for the general advancement of women's position, socially, industrially, economically, and politically'. The suffrage section would retain the name and organization of the NU, the second section those of the EFF, plus the work of the Women's Interests Committee; funds would be divided according to membership at the time of division. Marshall had long toyed with the idea of a Women's Independent Party – of which this was a version – but was well advised (by Swanwick, among others) to avoid the use of that name.[3] Marshall's hope was that in moving away from the dispute over which faction should dominate in a single NU and instead allowing members a personal choice between the two courses, the necessity to overpower those who held the other view would disappear; they could, in effect, agree to differ in emphasis. The scheme had more logic than practicality and had no realistic chance of acceptance in the highly-charged emotional context of the NU at the time; it was quickly dismissed. Marshall herself does not seem to have pursued it at any length.

Catherine and Frank Marshall had toyed with the idea of mounting a direct challenge to the national executive by bringing forward a 'direct vote of censure ... for not acting in the spirit of the Res[olution]s' of the February Council,[4] but had seen this as very unlikely to succeed, and came to the 9 May meeting ready to support draft resolutions from Manchester and from the North East Federation.[5]

After lengthy discussion the resolution brought by Manchester was adopted to be forwarded to the Special Council. Although direct attack on the executive was avoided, it was, in effect, a retrial of the whole question of the interpretation of the February Council resolutions. Reaffirming, in words accepted in February, that 'the women's suffrage movement is based on the principle that social relations should be governed not by physical force but by the recognition of mutual rights', it went on to commit the NU not only to continue to demand the vote for women, but also 'By co-operation with other organizations working for these objects, and in discussion with women of other nations to promote the establishment of a stable system of international law and mutual understanding, upheld by the common will of men and women.'[6] Challenging as these words were in the context of the time, they fall far short of the radical stop-the-war campaign with which opponents constantly identified the resigners.

If the Manchester resolution should pass, restoring the possibility of the NU acting as a whole on a limited internationalist programme, most of those who had resigned would stand again for election. If it was not carried, the resolution brought by the North-East Federation was seen as a 'second string'; if this passed, the constituent societies would be free to work for better international relations, and to co-operate with other organizations for this purpose. But, as Marshall noted, some of resigners would not go back on the strength of this alone.

In planning for the Council, Marshall had also worked on precise tactics and alternatives for this or that outcome of this or that resolution or election. The exercise led to gloomy conclusions: if the 'forwards' lost the policy resolutions and the election, they would have to resign and leave the NU under the control of the 'backwards ... to rush rapidly and inevitably to oblivion'; if they won substantially, passing a vote of censure on the executive for not fulfilling the spirit of the February Council resolutions, they might 'recapture command of the N.U.W.S.S.' but only at the cost of losing Mrs Fawcett.[7] It is not hard to see what a heavy price that would have been, and how near to impossible effective work would have become even for the victors.

George Armstrong (one of those specially invited), however, believed that the 'desire for unity is the strongest thing in the Union, even stronger than loyalty to Mrs F.' Ethel Williams thought that it might be possible to set the constituent societies free to make their own policy decisions, to elect a majority of progressives to the executive, and still to retain Mrs Fawcett until the war was over, when it might be expected that she would retire from public life 'and the Union can then go ahead'.[8]

Getting down to strategy, the meeting at the Sesame Club carefully – and if anything over optimistically – counted numbers of those on either side on the rump executive and among the officers, spelling out those who were 'obstructive', as opposed to 'Progressive, or at least not obstructive?'.[9] They drew up a slate of those present willing to stand – nearly all were – if one of the two proposed resolutions were passed, and added to it a sufficient number of others who might be asked to stand, in an attempt to ensure a progressive majority. It was however, only too clear that, if the election were limited to filling the eleven vacancies, as the executive had decreed, it would only be necessary for 'London and Co.' to get one or two of their supporters in among the vacant seats to give them a majority, against which the peace women would be powerless.[10]

Williams would write to Rackham notifying her of the proposed resolutions, and the order in which they should be taken, and in a last attempt, would ask formally for an urgency resolution to permit the holding of an election of all the executive.

George Armstrong made an urgent plea that those present should refuse to 'throw up the sponge' but rather should 'rally *all* our forces, and put every ounce of effort' into turning things around, and probably the majority of those at the Sesame Club left invigorated and fully determined to do so. They knew from the response to the Hague initiative, and from letters from branches following the resignations, that they had substantial support in many parts of the country, and yet in their hearts they had reason to doubt their chance of success.

If the peace women had known in how many ways the LSWS was working to buttress its position, they would have had even more reason to doubt.

The LSWS directs the rump's plans

On 20 May Ray Strachey wrote to her mother:

> As far as activities go I am swallowed up for the moment in the effort to beat the pacifists out of the suffrage society. There is a small group of them which wants to capture the name and funds of the whole organization, and to use them 'to promote a just settlement after the war'. It really means a vague and visionary propaganda, and would obviously be the ruin of suffrage. I think we shall cer-

tainly beat them and drive them out. It seems a great waste of effort when such very important things are being done, but it's a job I can do, and nothing else seems even remotely useful. And in a way I enjoy it, and so does Oliver. He is even more in the thick of it than I.[11]

For the Stracheys, the Special Council would merely be an opportunity to consolidate the victory; they had no more wish for reconciliation than had been expressed by those on the other side who had gathered at the Sesame Club. Not all of the rump felt the same. Notably, Mrs Rackham, Chair of the executive, and sometimes considered by the resigners to be biased against them, continued to be puzzled and distressed by the extent of the rift; 'on questions of war and peace she agreed to a great extent', as she said, with the resigners, 'but she was going to work for them outside the National Union', a claim made good by her willingness to speak out at a suffrage summer school in Cambridge in tones which caused her to be pilloried as a pacifist, and her appearance on a list of those organizing a women's conference for the UDC in April 1915. Even those who had resigned came to number her among the 'progressives' in the rump.[12]

The LSWS executive was in a strong position. It was free of almost all dissenting voices and what few dissident branches there were had no ready machinery through which to express their views. The London executive was disproportionately represented on the NU rump executive, and so benefited from insider knowledge of any information coming from the branches. Leading London members now basked in the place close to Fawcett previously occupied by the democratic suffragists. The London executive members had in effect a two-stage pump, preparing material as a constituent society – with minutes that did not circulate beyond themselves, as far as I have been able to tell – and then putting on their other hats as members of the NU executive to move it along.

The most important business was to make sure the peace educators did not regain influence within the NU; here, the election was crucial. With neither precedent nor constitutional provision for responding to such a mass exodus, and understandably rejecting the generous democratic option of submitting the decision to the Council, the NU executive, prompted by the LSWS, easily decided to exercise its prerogative. Newcastle's plea to hold an election of the whole executive, made with substantial support, was rejected.

Even with the head start provided by its strength on the rump, the London executive was taking no chances. Learning that Manchester

WSS would nominate a number of people who had supported the Hague conference, they, like their opponents at the Sesame Club meeting, carefully counted heads. The eleven-member rump consisted of three officers (no parliamentary secretary had yet been appointed), three who served on both the London and the national executives, two more southerners who could be counted on, and the officially impartial Rackham from Cambridge; only Osler from Birmingham and Macmillan from Edinburgh might not be wholeheartedly behind the LSWS policies.

The LSWS executive exercised its right to nominate several more candidates, and took another step, probably not outside the rules but certainly not common practice; they enlisted the cooperation of several of the societies known to be in sympathy with their views to support what amounted to a joint slate, ensuring them a share of the London vote for their own (suitable) candidates in return for support for LSWS nominees and for Ray Strachey, who was standing for the position of Parliamentary Secretary against Chrystal Macmillan and Catherine Marshall.[13]

A general meeting of the LSWS, called as part of the preparation for the Special Council, was held on 17 May – coincidentally an eventful day on a wider stage, since it was on that date that the Liberal government gave way to pressure and the first coalition government was formed. This kind of one-off meeting, called at the discretion of the LSWS executive and organized by them, seems to have taken the place in the LSWS federation of the mandatory regular meetings of the other federations. Held in the Caxton Hall to accommodate the large membership, it provided the first open opportunity for the wider membership of the LSWS to express its views on what had happened since the NU's February Council; some bitter exchanges took place, with members taking sides on personalities as well as on issues. But the outcome was predictable, particularly as the LSWS executive agreed to ask 'independent' London branches (presumably those branches which had chosen to affiliate directly to the NU, rather than to the LSWS) to refrain from voting. The success of the LSWS executive in carrying support for the policies of the NU rump was never in doubt; resolutions were passed endorsing the refusal of the NU executive to send delegates to The Hague, pronouncing propaganda for anything other than suffrage to be unacceptable, and declaring affection for Fawcett and confidence in her leadership.[14]

An effort was also made to enlist the support of the smaller NU branches nationwide. A letter went out to all the societies with less than a hundred members, over the signatures of Clementina Black and Frances Sterling, both long-time LSWS members. They did not use LSWS letterhead or claim authorization from any group, but they backed their statement with the endorsement of eight distinguished suffrage supporters, including Lord Robert Cecil, Miss B.A. Clough (vice-principal of Newnham, who would herself be a successful candidate for one of the vacant positions), and Lady Strachey, matriarch both of the LSWS and of the Strachey family. The letter urged the importance of defeating the attempt of the resigners to be reelected, categorizing them as 'unwittingly decreeing the destruction of the National Union' by affirming 'the resolution that we should devote ourselves to other political issues in addition to Women's Suffrage'. Not sent just for open propaganda purposes, the writers asked recipient societies to let them know whether they would be sending delegates to the Council, and whether there was more they would like to know about 'the serious questions to be debated'. What response came in, and what use was made of it is not known, but it seems likely that receptive societies were urged to put their votes behind the LSWS slate.

Approach to the Council

The NU executive set 17 and 18 June as the date for the Special Council, a date on which it was impossible for at least six of the resigners to attend, as the executive of the BCIWC was to meet at that time, and Jane Addams would also be visiting from the United States. Curiously, the dissidents do not seem to have been aware, at their 9 May meeting, of the date which had been chosen, although it was minuted at the executive on 6 May; and Fawcett later said that the date had been planned as early as 30 April subject to confirmation of Birmingham's invitation. Although there is no evidence that the executive acted with malice in the matter, and altering the date would doubtless have been inconvenient, it is noteworthy that, when the resigners let it be known that they could not attend on that date, it was Oliver Strachey who moved that the date not be altered; others, including Fawcett, concurred, but expressed their regret.[15]

Pessimism among those who had resigned was further justified by developments in the Manchester society. Ashton had come to the 9 May meeting confident of her long held position as a spokesperson for the Manchester Society – she was its honorary secretary – but after her return to Manchester she ran into unexpected difficulties with her executive, and had to water down the resolution she had taken to

London.[16] The challenge to Ashton's role in the Manchester executive was a foreshadowing of a far more serious development in the Manchester Society at large, where a major crisis occurred just before the Special Council met, adding more discouragement and invalidating much of the planning done on 9 May. The Manchester WSS in effect suffered a palace revolution. A member named Margaret Conway succeeded in getting a specially called General Meeting of the Manchester society on 8 June to discuss the resolution to be forwarded in Manchester's name to the Special Council. At this meeting a complete turn-around of Manchester's traditional support for the radical side took place. The resolution was defeated by a substantial majority and the notice of motion for the Council withdrawn. Ashton and her supporters resigned from the Manchester executive the following morning, and the executive co-opted others *pro tem* to fill vacant offices, Conway becoming Acting Honorary Secretary. New delegates to the Council were appointed, and the new Manchester executive let it be known that no Manchester votes would be given to candidates for the national executive but those who would endorse Fawcett's policy, even if they had previously been expecting to stand.[17]

Fawcett and the LSWS cannot be proven to have been behind the Manchester coup, but certainly they watched it with keen interest and a suspect lack of surprise; Fawcett was 'greatly delighted and cheered by [Conway's] telegram received at 8.30' on the morning after the General Meeting, and thanked her 'very much for [her] vigorous action and for letting me know so promptly'. Pippa Strachey, Chair of the LSWS and sister of Oliver Strachey, also wrote to congratulate Conway on the move taken in the Manchester WSS, which, she felt, had saved the NU from losing whole Societies or Federations rather than individuals.[18]

Vigorous debate continued in the *Common Cause.* In preparation for the Special Council, the issue of 4 June 1915 carried statements both from the executive and from the resigning members and their supporters on 'The Future Policy of the National Union', as well as election addresses from most of those who planned to stand for the executive. In the main, the statements just reiterated the old arguments, with the executive laying stress on the danger of opening the door by a promise of cooperation with any and every group that might include peace in its objectives, and the resigners declaring that the cleavage lay between those who wanted to work for the vote 'simply as a political tool' and those who thought the demand should be linked 'with the deeper principles which underlie it'. As for the argument that the NU should

stick strictly to suffrage, the dissidents pointed out with some justification that, since the war began, the NU had extended its mandate to
undertake relief work and social service, which was not always non-
controversial, and which was carried out in varying ways by different
constituent societies.

Marshall and her colleagues on the executive committee of the
BCIWC, unable to be at the Council, wrote to the Chair, Mrs Rackham,
purportedly to counter misrepresentations regarding the Hague Congress,
which might come up in discussion. They pointed out that the Hague
Congress had never been intended to be representative; its planned
constitution, however, would be more representative than that of the
IWSA, and not subject to the same confusion of interests as the IWSA
had been when 'one of the three British members' (Fawcett) voted contrary to the decision of the NU. They also drew attention to the general
accord reached, contrary to (Fawcett's) prediction that only bitter
feeling would come out of the Congress. Copies of the Congress report
would be available at the Council. The signatories, in addition to
Marshall, were Courtney, Leaf, Royden, Swanwick, and Ford, although
in the event, Ford did attend and speak at the Council.[19] The thinly-
veiled attack on Fawcett, who was known to be responsible for the
'misrepresentations', was probably poor strategy.

The Special Council: 17 June 1915

The Special Council that convened on 17 June was almost an anti-
climax, so completely had power passed into the hands of the London-
dominated anti-Hague group. The passing of the first resolution,
congratulating the Danish women who had just obtained an equal
franchise with men, marked the beginning and end of unity in the
gathering. The rest of the meeting saw a rearguard action fought by
those few – including Frank Marshall, Ethel Williams, Armstrong, Ford,
and Ashton (all northerners) – who were there in support of the Hague
initiative. The resolution withdrawn by Manchester was allowed to go
forward in the name of Macclesfield, but was lost, and the executive
also carried its resolution pronouncing it impracticable to free constituent societies to act on controversial questions.

Even then the unpleasantness was still not quite all over. An attempt
was made to put forward a resolution expressing 'unabated loyalty to
Mrs Henry Fawcett, and ... firm trust and confidence in her wisdom',
but this extremely loaded wording was ruled out of order, a credit to
the integrity of the Chair. As Marshall later commented, it would have

been very unfair to try to force those who did not agree with Fawcett's position to appear to express personal censure. Instead the Council passed by acclamation 'their affectionate and grateful thanks [to Fawcett] ... for all her splendid work for the Suffrage Cause', wording which enabled George Armstrong to speak in favour of the resolution and avoided what could have been a very ugly division. Another resolution carried by acclamation regretted the retirements, thanked the retirees, and (though only by an amendment) directly mentioned in particular the work of Courtney and Marshall.[20]

The Council was experienced by the victorious LSWS leaders as a complete triumph for their pro-war stand. 'I have spent 3 days in Birmingham sweeping away pacifists', reported Pippa Strachey,

> They were like straws in a whirlwind which was satisfactory but boring. I found myself forced to my annoyance to figure several times as a sort of Christian Knight in armour to defend them at the expense of my cherished schemes and I had the revolting experience of seeing my lifelong foe licking my boots with a face black with emotion.[21]

Strachey does not identify her opponent, but it was probably the unfortunate Ashton, who was surely emotionally vulnerable in the aftermath of the Manchester coup, and who had been put in the humiliating position of having to accept Miss Strachey as a seconder to what had become the Macclesfield resolution. Fawcett shortly claimed that Miss Ashton 'now understands that some of her assertions were wholly unfounded and a misconception of facts'; later still, however, Fawcett said that although Ashton had withdrawn what she saw as personal insults, she was, said Fawcett, still accusing the NU executive of '*artfully* misinterpreting the wishes of the [February 1915] Council'.[22] Ashton remained one of those against whom Fawcett continued in unremitting bitterness.

The rump expands to fill the space available

The crux of the Council was the election for the vacant executive positions, and indeed it was the election that completed the rout of the democratic suffragists and put an end to wide geographic representation as well as to any significant political diversity. The voting cannot be compared with that of the February election, since the peace group withdrew their candidacy in June, but the makeup of the two executives tells the story.

The four officers acclaimed in February had been Fawcett (from London), Auerbach (from Reigate, Surrey, close to London) and Marshall and Courtney. I have counted the last two as representing northern interests: Marshall had long lived in Keswick, and Courtney, although from London had served her suffrage apprenticeship as secretary to the North of England Suffrage Society in Manchester with Helena Swanwick. Among the elected executive members, London was understandably the most strongly represented society with at least six members, including three who were also on the LSWS executive. Six came from widely dispersed southern locations, including Bristol, Street (Somerset), Cambridge, North Hertfordshire, Berkshire and Maidenhead. Two others were from the Midlands (Birmingham and Shropshire), and six from farther to the north (Leeds, Liverpool, Edinburgh and two from Manchester).[23]

Following the April resignations the rump executive, taking officers and members together, had been left quite comfortably homogeneous and southern, with only Osler and Macmillan from anywhere north of Cambridge. The June election added four more from London, including two from the London executive, seven others from the south, and Eleanor Rathbone from Liverpool.

When I first counted these figures, I was startled by the radical change they indicate. The LSWS executive minutes provide the answer. Of the eleven new members and one new officer appointed in June, all but one were either nominated by the LSWS or named on the 'cooperative' slate promoted by the LSWS in the lead-up to the Council. All come from or are connected with the relatively few societies which had never been comfortable with the EFF policy, let alone the Hague initiative. In addition to Rathbone, there were five from London, two from Cambridge, one from Oxford, one from South Wales, one from Salisbury (but nominated by Cardiff and Liverpool), and one from Brighton and Hove (nominated by London). The count is completed by Margery Corbett Ashby, a southerner with a strong Liverpool connection, who had resigned with Rathbone in early 1914 over the EFF policy; she was nominated by Liverpool and Falmouth.[24]

For all its new loyalty to Fawcett, Manchester no longer had a member on the executive after June. Could this mean that those who rallied to overthrow Ashton and her colleagues were not able to marshall any interest in the appointment of replacements for them? We do not know who voted, or how, in the difficult circumstances of the last moment withdrawal of the leading peace women who may have been the chosen candidates, for instance, of many of the northern members or societies.

Very few of the new appointees were women well known nationally for their suffrage activity. The societies involved in the electoral cooperation carried a sufficient vote count between them to leave little chance to the many candidates who relied mainly on the support of their own local societies, and with the elimination of the peace candidates, most of whom indeed did have a national profile and had commanded wide respect, the cooperative policy paid off with a one hundred percent success rate; the only unsuccessful candidates among those they backed were two or three for whom there simply was not room.

Contemporaries and historians assess the effect

Ray Strachey later summed up her view of the 1915 events in the NU in a few words in *The Cause*, claiming that after 'the resignation of several of the officers and half the members of the executive ... Mrs Fawcett was left with a small remnant at headquarters, but in the country at large, and among the rank and file of the members, her course was overwhelmingly approved.'[25]

Brian Harrison argues that Fawcett's success (with, as he says, the 'timely aid' of Eleanor Rathbone) in driving out 'the champions of the Labour connection', was 'crucial ... to preserving the Union as a broad church for feminists of many types'.[26] Rathbone may have been the first to use the term 'broad church' to describe what she thought had been saved, and what she saw as having been threatened by the Labour connection even before the issue of peace education surfaced, but unlike Strachey, Rathbone viewed the breakup as a great tragedy, despite her support for the LSWS position.[27] Certainly, the pre-war executive had turned the NU's non-party policy into something of a tightrope along which they had had to walk with great care. The electoral arrangement with the Labour Party had offended a good many Liberal members, and none more than Rathbone, but many other Liberal women had been disillusioned with the party rather than with the NU's new direction. The pre-war executive had contained members of all political sympathies, and its officers, notably Marshall as parliamentary secretary, had mounted an impressive all-party political pressure campaign, albeit largely behind the scenes, playing off one party's interest against another until quite strong groups in all three major parties were convinced of the need to sponsor some measure of franchise reform; as a corollary, NU executive members of all political stripes had had a role to play.

More simply, the claim that the June 1915 debacle kept the NU on a broad basis is rendered indefensible by its failure to take into account class and geographical factors. The pre-war leaders had found common ground with working people, including voteless men, and had actively involved great numbers of northern supporters, as well as drawing in some from southern regions (such as Bristol) which were very different from central and suburban London. The upheaval of 1915 returned the NU to the control of a small group of middle- and upper-class Londoners, of whom some were Liberal sympathizers, some were Unionist, but few if any would have dared say they favoured Labour (much less ILP), and none of whom could speak for the wide constituency of working women and men touched by the pre-war campaign. After June 1916 local societies to some extent continued to go their own way, but at the centre there was little ongoing debate and virtually no representation of the industrial north, and therefore little willingness or need to listen to the critical communications that still came in from some affiliated societies. Executives in the pre-war years had been leaning increasingly to the left, but there had still been representation of all sides on the executive, and sufficient balance to temper any more extreme notions.

Historians have largely accepted the view of Fawcett and Strachey as representing the fore-ordained direction of the NU and of the pre-war political work of the democratic suffragists as narrowing its basis, and have also maintained that the suggested work for peace education and the development and maintenance of international links was almost universally unacceptable. I have challenged this view on both points, first by drawing on election evidence from the February Council to indicate that at this point the more broadly based constituency which had developed in the pre-war years may indeed have been ready to turn some attention towards study of war and peace, and second by showing concretely how it came about that the June Special Council saw the NU shrink back to a very narrow base.

Even historians sympathetic to the peace women have accepted that the sweeping victory of the pro-war faction came about because 'the majority of the active members of the union were as unable to resist the patriotic appeal of the war as the majority of their fellow citizens', and that the June Council represented the true state of opinion in the Union.[28] Certainly, four horrendous months of casualty lists since the February Council, it was harder than ever to put forward the case for examining the way to lasting peace without being heard as disloyal to the soldiers in – and in increasing numbers under – the field of battle.

There is no doubt that the climate at the June Council was considerably less receptive to the peace women than it had been in February, and indeed than the latter had hoped. But I believe my analysis shows the importance of the role of NU internal politics in the June débacle. Factors taken into account must include: the disproportionate influence of the LSWS and the use they made of it; Fawcett's personal influence, and more particularly the 'patriots' exploitation of the loyalty known to be felt for her; the weak strategic position of the democratic suffrage leaders and their inability to attend the Council in person; the disfranchisement of those who would have voted for the progressive candidates by the withdrawal of their names from the ballot; the very existence of the new WIL organization, ironically lending weight to the thinking of a good many women whose inclination was towards work for peace that this work lay outside the role of the NU.

Ray Strachey also claims in *The Cause* that 'the union, recovering quickly from the trouble, went on its way unchanged.'[29] Marshall's view was very different. Reporting to Jane Addams on the progress of the BCIWC shortly after the June Council, she wrote:

> Mrs. Fawcett's name carries great weight with official people and with the Press. They do not know that the work of the N.U.W.S.S. during the last few years (since it reorganized itself and became an effective political force) has not been done by her, but by the group of progressive and energetic people (Miss Ashton, Mrs. Swanwick, Miss Royden, etc, and especially Miss Courtney) who are now being driven by Mrs. Fawcett's attitude to transfer their work elsewhere.
>
> For some time to come the N.U. will probably run on its present momentum, though the driving power has been so much reduced. The actions of the officers and Executive Com[ee] will continue to carry the same weight as heretofore, because it will not at first be discovered that they no longer represent the force in the country that they have represented during the past few years. Therefore their attitude towards us is bound to do us harm. The irony of the situation is that it is *our* work, and the effective machine which we have left in their hands, which enables them to do the harm! The retiring officers have always been thoroughly democratic in their methods, speaking always as the mouthpiece of the Union as a whole. The new officers will be supposed to be speaking for the same body of opinion, though the voice will really be the voice of Esau.[30]

No matter how much bitterness underlies Marshall's account of the pre-war development of the NU, it is accurate except in her almost irritatingly modest omission of her own leading role. Her claim that the NU no longer represented the same body of opinion in the country was based not only on a sense that an unverifiable number of supporters was no longer active in the NU, but on the nature and breadth of the support which had been lost, both within the organization and outside it.

7
Cutting Down the Election Fighting Fund

Policy at the centre

As the democratic suffragists foresaw, the change in the nature of the NU after June 1915 had to play out painfully in the erosion of the Labour and working class connection. The change manifested itself in two areas: in the EFF policy and more subtly in attitudes to women's work in wartime, which will be considered in Chapter 8.

Widespread as support had been, those who had initiated the EFF had had to steer a fine line between on one side significant minority opposition in the NU, and on the other the scepticism of some Labour Party leaders who feared that should one of the other parties declare its commitment to a women's suffrage measure, the NU would leave Labour candidates in the lurch. Support from Labour had come most firmly from the ILP, the left wing of the party. Opposition within the NU had included most of those now in control of the NU executive, who came from London and from those regions most uneasy with the policy. Fawcett had been fully convinced of the value of the EFF policy, and would defend it strongly even in her later writings, but in mid-1915 her support was not to be counted on.[1]

The Glasgow agreement of January 1914 now became the centre of controversy. The intent of the agreement had been to enable selected Labour candidates (mainstream and ILP) to accept help from the EFF in full confidence that the help would be continued through by-elections and the general election, whatever political change might take place. The NU also had promised not to work against Labour candidates anywhere. The Labour Party, on its side, was pledged to oppose any franchise reform that did not include women.

At the outset of the war, the NU's decision to suspend political work had been made easily but without detailed definition. Despite the suspension, the EFF, the by-elections sub-committee, and the 1914 executive had been anxious to leave a crack open for suffrage work at any contested by-elections, or in the event of a general election or the end of the war. They had carried a resolution, against some opposition, at the February 1915 Council, allowing the NU 'to take political action on the lines of the existing election policy ... should the Executive Committee deem it desirable'. Accordingly EFF work had continued in certain constituencies, keeping in touch with the plans of the Labour Party to run candidates, and making sure that EFF organizers were available where needed.

By the summer of 1915, the political landscape had changed. At the outbreak of war all parties except the ILP had offered a measure of support to the ruling Liberal government in its prosecution of the conflict. In May 1915, when Asquith formed the first coalition government, the lone standout was again the ILP. But the ILP included in its number many of the very men who had taken up the suffrage cause with energy and had helped the NU bring the Labour Party to the committed position it now held. Much argument now turned on whether the political changes brought about by the war should be regarded as covered by the Glasgow agreement, or whether indeed the war and the formation of the coalition government nullified the agreement altogether.

The relationship of Marshall to the NU executive had remained anomalous, and had to come to a final resolution after the débacle at the Special Council. Before their resignations she and Courtney had served on the executive *ex officio*, as parliamentary secretary and honorary secretary respectively. Marshall had also offered her resignation as EFF honorary secretary, though admitting to Fawcett, 'I cannot tell you what a grief it is to give up this work. It is the hardest wrench of all'. At that time, however, Fawcett had moved that she be asked to stay on.[2]

The post of parliamentary secretary was left vacant until the June Special Council, when Ray Strachey took on the work. Telling her mother of her appointment, she wrote, 'You will laugh, but there is as a matter of fact nothing to do, and I am just filling a breach and keeping out some poisonous pacifists'. Ironically, a very proper and exceedingly polite correspondence took place between Marshall and Strachey when the latter took over, in which Marshall offered every help and Strachey expressed the deepest gratitude and some humility in filling Marshall's shoes. Barely a week later Strachey confessed privately that she was finding the new job 'rather disagreeable'.[3]

After the Special Council in June the reconstituted executive refused to have Marshall's role as honorary secretary of the EFF serve as an entitlement to attend executive meetings regularly, and ruled that she would be invited to come only when necessary to present her reports and to take part in ensuing discussion. Marshall asked whether she could at least be present for the report of the parliamentary secretary, but the executive denied her this too. When this was followed by a decision that she would not receive the confidential minutes circulated only to the executive, but rather the less full ones as sent to the societies, her position as EFF secretary became virtually untenable, although once more, believing she might be able to prevent an irrevocable breach with the Labour Party, she agreed to stay on temporarily, 'under conditions', as she later said, 'which were an insult'.[4]

The EFF committee had included people who were not necessarily members of the NU and had in practice co-opted some members, though submitting the names to the executive for approval. Now the NU executive assumed the right to make appointments to the EFF committee from among NU executive members, exactly as it did for regular 'sub-committees', and the members appointed were not those who might be expected to be in sympathy with the EFF work. Some of the former members also stayed on, so now there was a mixture of those who believed in the work of the committee and those whose only wish was to see it buried. Marshall again submitted her resignation as honorary secretary to the EFF, and this time it was accepted, but she was asked to continue to serve as an ordinary member of the committee, and shortly after that was asked to stand in as EFF Secretary until Mary Stocks, the NU appointee, was free to take over. So she remained throughout the summer and autumn of 1915 taking part in difficult meetings within the EFF, within the NU executive, between the two, and between NU representatives and Labour Party leaders.

Differing views of the value and future of the agreement with Labour were sharply apparent at the first meeting of the new oil-and-water committee following the June Council. As Marshall acknowledged, there had always been three views of the EFF among NU members: some had been wholly supportive, some had seen it as only a device to put pressure on the government, with questionable ramifications, and some had disliked it from the outset.

Fawcett, in the Chair, opened by saying 'that the political situation was so changed by the fusion of the Parties that she thought the EFF work should remain in abeyance. The EFF Policy had been initiated as a whip to beat the Liberal Government with, and the Liberal Government no longer existed.' Marshall had prepared a report, but Fawcett's description of the policy goaded her into responding immediately. The attack on the Liberals was for her far less important than the goals of strengthening the Labour Party as the only party which had put women's suffrage in its platform, and of building further support within the Labour Party. It was vital to bring the movement 'into friendly relations with the Democratic movement in the country'. She spoke of the way in which support had been steadily built up in the trade unions, and of how the NU's wartime activities in relief work and in monitoring women's interests continued to affect relations with the Labour Party.

Marshall feared (and others hoped) that wholehearted supporters of the EFF policy were now in a minority in the NU, as they clearly were in the executive. Policy could only be set by the Council, but, said Marshall, if the executive thought the Council 'might wish to go back on its commitments, it would be best to tell the Labour Party so now'. Accordingly, the EFF and the NU were faced with questions and decisions to be made at several levels. What needed to be said to the Labour Party? and what irrevocable responsibilities had already been incurred in targeted constituencies? What action was called for?

Marshall read out the list of constituencies where EFF help had already been offered before the war. The list still makes impressive reading, identifying twenty-two constituencies in which support was committed to a Labour candidate. Seventeen candidates had the approval of the Labour Party or the ILP, and of the NU; five constituencies had yet to name candidates, who would be supported provided their personal views on suffrage measured up. Running down the list, Marshall showed that although little direct political work was being done currently, except for voter registration in two constituencies, continuing contact with worker organizations was provided by work related to the war and particularly where the remaining EFF organizers were active.

Sterling asked the question that must have been in the minds of all those who wanted to turn away from the EFF policy: was the NU 'absolutely bound to these men whatever arose'? Marshall replied that as things stood, yes, they were, and reiterated that if the policy was likely to change, it was essential to let the Labour Party know at once. A resolution was brought forward affirming that 'the continuance on present lines of any work in EFF Constituencies forms an obligation to support the Labour Candidates in those Constituencies at the next contested election, and that any withdrawal from that position at a later date would probably be disastrous to Women's Suffrage'. The motley committee approved it unanimously, but perhaps only because different factions interpreted it differently, some seeing it as an acknowledgement of commitments already made, others as a warning that it was time to drop those commitments.[5]

Early in August, working on communication with Labour about the general policy, Marshall and Fawcett met with John Hodge, Acting Chairman of the Parliamentary Labour Party (PLP) and separately with W.C. Anderson in his dual role as Chair of the national Labour Party and a member of the National Administrative Council (NAC) of the ILP. According to the reports of these meetings, Mrs Fawcett, in a statement more supportive of the EFF policy than would have been made by most of her new colleagues, explained that the coming of the coalition government had made action by the EFF impractical for the time being, but that there was no change in the NU's support for the policy itself, which would be picked up again at the war's end; meanwhile the organizers were working with the Labour Party on relief work in some constituencies, and a decision had been made to do registration work in support of Labour candidates where needed. Hodge showed himself ill informed about the relationship with the NU, but he affirmed that 'so far as the Labour Party was concerned, every member of it was a confirmed believer in Women's Suffrage' and indeed in adult suffrage. He said he looked forward to the resumption of party politics after the war, but seemed comfortable with the idea that both the Labour Party and the NU would have to set policy then according to circumstances. Marshall pressed him on whether 'the Labour Party could be relied upon to insist on the inclusion of women in any Franchise Bill and to make it clear that their support depended on keeping the women in?', and had to be content with an answer that was affirmative but couched in vague general terms.

Anderson, who had always been ambivalent about the EFF but had helped broker the Glasgow agreement, also claimed that all ILP members were women's suffrage supporters, but went out of his way to emphasize almost contemptuously that they would be whether or not the EFF supported them; financial support in fact, he said, had been at times an embarrassment; he did not mention that once an indirect channel for funding and practical help had been contrived, few candidates had been coy about accepting it.[6] But he conceded that EFF speakers had been educative, and that the policy had 'certainly gained you [the NU] much driving power amongst the working classes'. He shrugged off any idea of mutual dependence between the NU and the ILP, and said it was up to the NU to decide 'what policy they thought most advantageous' to the suffrage cause.[7]

Despite this well-meant effort to clarify the position about general policy and reassure the Labour Party, it would soon become apparent that there was no common understanding regarding the current level of commitment in the targeted constituencies.

In the constituencies

By the autumn of 1915 there was some stirring among the political parties. Despite the coalition, the party leaders assumed that the end of the war would mark a return to roughly the pre-war political party system, and low-key preparations for an election were beginning. The extent and limits of the NU's commitments had to be addressed. Voter registration was quietly under way in some constituencies, and in some EFF constituencies the Labour Party was assuming that it could call on the expected EFF support.

Initially, Marshall appears to have assumed that the warning given to the Labour Party applied only to the possibility that a future NU Council might alter its policy, and that help would continue, even through a general election, for candidates to whom it had been pledged. The issue had in effect become the familiar political dilemma of the extent to which an incoming administration is bound by promises made by an outgoing one. For whatever reason, by mid-September Marshall had lost all faith in the NU's commitment, and may have tried to force the NU's hand by making plain the effect on relations with Labour. It was now she who urged that work in the constituencies be stopped right away rather than dropped at a more crucial time.

Marshall acted in an unusual alliance with Mrs Coombe Tennant, a new executive and EFF member – one of those supported by the LSWS in the June election – who came from South Wales where opposition to the EFF had always been strong. Marshall's proposal to stop constituency work came up in an EFF meeting of which notice had not been sent to all members and for which no minutes are extant. Other evidence suggests that because the attendance was so small those present agreed not to forward the proposal for further action by the NU executive. Courtney, the only other 'old' EFF member present, who was in the Chair, was against the move, but her opposition was not on record as no vote was taken. Courtney understood that the issue would be held over until a later EFF meeting where they could hope to have the input of Ashton, Ford and others of the 'old' members.[8] However, the NU executive treated the proposal as a recommendation and at once went ahead, passing a resolution ordering the immediate cessation of EFF work.[9] When the EFF met again the executive decision was a *fait accompli* and some active branches had already been notified.

When the full EFF committee met on 5 October, the resolution to suspend work was again proposed by Marshall and seconded by Coombe Tennant. Marshall said that she herself had not wanted any change in the EFF policy or practice; she claimed that she had acted only to clarify the situation because she saw the change coming about unannounced. Margaret Ashton proposed an amendment to allow rare exceptions to the suspension where, 'in one or two cases it is impossible to cease work already in progress' without betraying 'the honour of the National Union'. The amendment carried, but Marshall was adamant that the NU executive must explicitly acknowledge that any support continued now (for example, in East Bristol) committed the EFF irrevocably to support at the next general election. If the executive would not make this clear, the EFF should withdraw Ashton's amendment and revert to the original stark suspension. The EFF committee forwarded this proviso to the executive with its amended resolution.[10]

Ray Strachey went to some trouble to look into each situation, as Marshall already had in July. The places where the EFF organizers were still engaged in what could only be described as active political work were, in particular, Accrington, West Bradford, and East Bristol; there were other locations where help might have reasonably been expected when the election came.

But once the executive resolution circulated, some felt the damage had already been done. Margaret Ashton wrote unhappily that it would be impossible to undo 'the harm that this action ... is bound to do. I wish I thought it only pusillanimous – I *do* think it dishonest. I don't think the reason is that they believe all party activities are stopped – they are not. But that they think it a good moment to throw over a policy which many of them never liked and only passively tolerated because they saw a passing advantage in it. I am very sore and sad.'[11]

The Accrington case ultimately came to a technical resolution later when the candidate, Bell, fortuitously decided to stand for a different constituency, releasing the EFF from commitment. Jowett, the MP and expected candidate in West Bradford, was interviewed by members of the NU executive on 12 October 1915. In answer to questions he made it plain that suspension of EFF help would be a substantial loss, but he accepted the situation with dignity; Marshall felt that he had 'supposed that I wanted him to be friendly to the National Union, so he said less than was in his mind and he did not intend to give the impression that he was hurt.'[12]

When it came down to the wire, suffragists in only one constituency actively contested the NU's withdrawal of support for their Labour candidate, although unmeasured bitterness remained elsewhere. East Bristol, where the relationship between the Labour candidate and the EFF – acting through the local WSS – was particularly strong and symbiotic, and currently dynamic, became the battleground.

East Bristol was an industrial area centred in the active dockland of this large southwestern port city. As the seat held by Charles Hobhouse, a notorious antisuffragist cabinet minister, it was a chosen suffragist target, and had been shaping up before the war as a model EFF constituency. Once some initial reluctance had been overcome, East Bristol WSS had become enthusiastic, and had been directly instrumental in the decision of Walter Ayles to stand for the ILP; the formal choice had been confirmed by the Labour Party executive in early spring of 1915.[13] On Ayles's part, the assurance of EFF backing was what had made it financially possible for him to get into the race.

By 1915 Annie Townley, the EFF organizer, was acting as president of the local Labour League and was an active member of the ILP. Although local plans to use her in peace education had been ruled out following the June Special Council no objection had yet been raised to her continuing to spend time in the ILP office, helping in particular with voter registration.[14] As soon as word reached East Bristol that the NU no longer sanctioned the work she was doing, Townley rushed to London to explain the local situation and to seek explanations from the NU. Talking to Marshall, she praised Ayles highly.[15] Ironically, although his opposition to conscription does not seem to have come up, the qualities Townley lauded in him may not have been much more to the executive's liking; she spoke of his competence, his high standing with the trade unions, and his good work for the Dockers Union on the Docks Committee of the city council. He was constantly consulted by the trade unions and would, she was sure, 'leap into popularity at the end of the war over industrial questions'. As for registration work, the Labour Party was lagging behind the other parties, and now wanted to make sure all the trade unionists were placed on the electoral roll. Townley was appalled at the idea of dropping her work; if she refused to carry on now she would never be able to pick up the threads again. All that she had done in three years to build trust would be lost, and Labour supporters would say it was no more than they expected: 'you just make use of us and will turn against us when it suits you'. In Townley's view the NU had an absolute obligation to continue what it had begun, and she told Ray Strachey that a breach with the Labour Party in East Bristol now would be final; she herself would resign 'rather than appear not to have been genuine to the Labour Party'.[16]

An EFF meeting was held on 20 October, at a time when few of the old members were able to attend (which happened so often that ill will was suspected).[17] When the discussion turned again to the special constituencies, and particularly to East Bristol, the minutes show Marshall struggling in a hostile environment to speak for those not present. Interestingly, they also show Fawcett once more as defensive. Rather than focussing on the extent to which the NU was pledged to Ayles, Fawcett claimed that helping him to be a candidate had surely been no injury to him; Marshall disagreed, pointing out that he was now being denied the aid he had counted on to support his candidacy. The committee had before it Isabella Ford's resignation (although this was later delayed), and Marshall also spoke again of the effect on Labour opinion of the resignations of precisely those members who had had the confidence of the Labour Party.[18]

At this time, the executive made no change, and now had to explain its decision to East Bristol. Marshall was not invited to be part of the group to meet with the representatives from East Bristol. When the full confidential report of the interview came to her, she angrily scribbled her comments in the margins. Ayles, supported by Tothill (president, East Bristol NU) and Townley, had been outspoken and acerbic, repeatedly stressing the breach of faith, and the impression that would be made locally and on the ILP. The ILP had done much to bring around hostile elements in the Labour Party, overcoming distrust of the middle class and the belief that 'the N.U. was not sincere, and would not keep its pledges'. Now they would have to explain that the NU were doing exactly what the doubters had expected; whatever name they put on the arrangement made at Glasgow, would the NU have seen no breach of faith if a Labour candidate had later said that he could no longer be bothered to support women's suffrage? Marshall repeatedly marked in the margin beside Ayles's comments, 'I said this', and 'I said this over and over again'.

Fawcett was obviously uncomfortable at the suggestion of bad faith. She reiterated more than once that the NU had always been 'straightforward' and 'above board'. Marshall wrote nastily in the margin 'It is 'above board' to repudiate a pledge, but it is not honourable.' Indeed, 'the whole question' for Marshall was whether or not the NU regarded itself as pledged; she was frustrated by the amount of time spent arguing with Ayles as to what part of Townley's work was or was not 'political' in nature. Yet when Ayles explained with clarity how his preparation for the election would be crippled by the loss of Townley's help and asked that a distinction might be made between this and any public political work, it was Fawcett who weakened to the extent of suggesting that the NU executive might reconsider the point. But Townley left 'feeling awfully sick of the N.U. and Mrs Fawcett was hopeless'.[19] Fawcett again evokes some pity; she did not share Strachey's single-mindedness on the issue, and her uneasiness may be to her credit.

Marshall wrote to Ray Strachey criticizing every aspect of the meeting with Ayles, from how it had been rushed into without further time for consideration by the EFF and the executive to the way in which it had been conducted. She asked for a chance to come to the executive and 'attempt once more to make it clear' what the consequences would be, adding, 'or a better plan would be to hold a joint meeting of the Ex: and the E.F.F. Committees'.[20]

Whether or not Strachey found Marshall's letter to her liking, she took at least part of it, together with others from Courtney and from Ethel Williams, to the next executive. The majority of the executive were now persuaded that the war had so changed things that commitments made before the outbreak need not concern them, so they focussed on what had happened since, which involved looking into details of what had been said and decided at different times since war began by both the EFF and the executive, and into how and to what extent decisions had been communicated to the Societies and the organizers. It was, on the whole, bound to be an unsatisfactory exercise. However, although Strachey understandably held that to make any exceptions now would serve only to dig themselves a deeper hole, Rathbone and several others reluctantly concluded that indeed the NU had renewed its commitment at least in East Bristol. To back out completely would dishonour the NU, and the consequent resignations from the EFF would make cooperation with the Labour Party impossible, 'and would to that extent tie the hands of the Council'. The executive then partially reversed its decision, agreeing to make an exception in East Bristol, allowing registration and office work for Ayles to continue, but informing him that this 'does not necessarily commit the

N.U. to give active support at the Election to the Labour candidate', and that the organizer and the local WSS should not take part in public meetings on his behalf.[21]

The EFF committee received this slightly wilted olive branch with some show of grace, but – as the executive had more than half expected – the old members such as Marshall found it still unacceptable because it treated East Bristol and Accrington as exceptions, not as two places among others where an irrevocable pledge had been made. The only agreement that emerged was to wrestle the whole question out again, this time, as Marshall had suggested, at a joint meeting of the EFF and executive committees. East Bristol would be notified that no decision had been made.[22]

The meeting on 18 November was a long drawn out affair. Rather than a realistic attempt to reach agreement, it was a last opportunity to present the opposing points of view, and to back them up with whatever pressure was available – such as threats of resignation from the old members most respected by Labour; all of this was set down almost verbatim in an 84-page report.[23] What was ultimately adopted (and approved by the executive on 2 December) was that work could be continued only in those constituencies where the executive 'is satisfied that suspension of work now would nullify the value of that which was previously done and where there are special conditions which justify exceptional treatment'. In these selected constituencies it should be explained to the Labour candidate that because of the altered circumstances of the war and the coalition government, the bearing of which had not yet been considered by the Council, the executive 'is obliged to ask them to consider that the support now given them does not inevitably commit the Union to give them support at the time of the General Election.' Very few of the old members were there when the executive resolution came to the EFF. Marshall proposed and Ashton seconded a motion declaring that in the opinion of the EFF, the decision 'will make further cooperation between the NU and the Labour Party impossible', but they were the only two there to vote for it; three on the other side voted it down.[24]

The agreement to continue support in, as it turned out, only East Bristol was small in the scheme of things except to those involved locally. The majority in the NU executive was more than sufficient to impose its will, and very few had any wish to support the EFF policy – let alone Ayles – in any shape or form; the concession was inconvenient and too small to reassure the Labour Party or to satisfy the dissident EFF members. Toleration of this thorn in the flesh came about mainly through the integrity of Eleanor Rathbone and a few others of the new executive, supported perhaps by the nostalgia of Fawcett for the heady days of pre-war politics. Fawcett justly described herself as having been 'a strong supporter of the E.F.F. from its very inception';[25] now she hated to be part of its dismantlement.

Although Rathbone's high-sounding claim that 'the fact that the Executive Committee contains members who have been disposed to be critical of the EFF has no effect on the mind of any one of us' strains credulity, she did her best to act as if it were so; indeed the statement may have been intended as an admonition to some of her colleagues, who were comfortably aware that 'the war offers an excuse to escape from a policy we have disliked'.[26] NU constituency work for Ayles was reluctantly continued even though he spent many months in prison as a conscientious objector.[27] He was not elected in 1918 but was a Member of Parliament for many years between 1923 and 1953.

The democratic suffragists had lost the battle to hold the NU to its pre-war pledges. The focus on East Bristol had overshadowed the more important question as to obligations in other constituencies where commitments for the general election had been made but no essential work was being done at that time. Marshall's best hope had been that the work could be suspended now and the policy left intact for future revival: the opposite had happened – the work in East Bristol continued but the policy was laid wide open for evisceration. Marshall was unable to extract any statement from the executive as to what advice they would give to the Council as to 'whether and to what extent they consider the Union bound by the pledges that have been given to the Labour Party and to individual candidates'.[28]

Marshall was constantly irritated with Ray Strachey at this time, not only over the EFF but over the question of women's war work and the relation with the trade unions. The veneer of courtesy in their exchanges grew thin, particularly on Marshall's side, perhaps because she was more engaged with the issue. At about this time, someone – probably Philippa Strachey – wrote on the back of one of Ray's private letters, 'This will explain what Ray is doing. The Labour-Pacifist people on the Election Fighting Fund Committee want to put the National Suffrage Union in the wrong by saying we have broken our pledges, and they are justified in breaking up our Union to form a Suffrage *Labour* Party instead. Ray's gigantic efforts are to put *them* in the wrong. I hope she will succeed! How they hate her! They write her awfully insulting letters but she keeps calm. Her good temper is a great asset.'[29]

The persistent rumour that Marshall in particular had sinister plans to hijack the EFF and incorporate it into the UDC or the WIL may have owed something to Marshall's earlier plan to divide the NU into two wings, but it owed more to ignorance and a general belief that opponents of the war were up to no good. Writing to Strachey, Marshall said that she would consider such a plan both dishonourable and silly. 'To anyone who knows the facts', she wrote, 'the idea that I should want to "capture" the E.F.F. for the U.D.C. would be grotesquely comic, were it not insulting.' As for WIL, that organization had no election policy, and certainly would not benefit from association with the NU. There was little of value left of the EFF, whereas WIL, Marshall claimed optimistically, was well set up with its own personnel and fund-raising capability had it wanted to enter the field.[30]

Others besides Marshall were appalled at the NU's abandonment of the EFF policy and the consequent loss of the carefully built relationship of trust and mutual support with the Labour Party. Ethel Williams wrote to Strachey that although there was no immediate ongoing work in the North Eastern Federation, so much damage had been done by what had happened in Accrington and East Bristol that when, as she expected, the NU tried to resume the Labour connection as a general election drew near, the Labour Party would reject them, and might only be kept in support of women's suffrage if a large number of women dropped the NU and joined the Labour Party instead.[31]

The focus of the EFF policy had been on preparation for the crucial general election which was already overdue. In the event an unexpected and even more important hurdle had to be cleared. Rather than supporting this or that candidate or party in a general election, suffragists would find themselves campaigning to influence major franchise legislation which had to be put through before such an election could even be held. But in this campaign too they would need to know who were their friends.

8
Relations with Labour: Women's War Work

The LSWS in control

The political content of the EFF controversy is obvious, but the dispute over the EFF was only the outward and visible manifestation of a more profound difference between the two feminisms represented in the NU, already defined by the split over peace talk. Women and war work provided another field of confrontation; on this issue the struggle took the form of a series of skirmishes rather than a pitched battle like the one over the EFF, but it sheds further light on what separated the two feminist views.

Women's work had been a major concern of the NU since the outbreak of war, and we have noted the sharp difference in approach of the 1914 executive from that of the LSWS. Now that the LSWS dominated the national executive what had been its policy became that of the NU, and this just at the time when the demand for women's labour was escalating. The government – still hoping to avoid introducing conscription – wanted women to move into traditionally male occupations to release men to volunteer for the army, and in particular to provide the bulk of the labour for the burgeoning munitions industry.

Angela Woollacott's fine study of women's work during the First World War shows the variety of occupations spawned by the armaments industry and the heterogeneity of the workers who responded. There was a place for women of every class and background, and Woollacott demonstrates that with rare exceptions women chose, fell into, or were assigned to positions that were seen as appropriate to their class. The outcome was to exacerbate class distinction rather than to lower it. What emerges is a picture of a new proletarian female work force, poorly organized but to a large extent relishing somewhat better pay and greater freedom than before the war – when many, for instance, had been domestic workers – but still subject to oversight and admonition from those who thought themselves their betters and who now served in monitorial roles as supervisors, policewomen, hostel matrons, and on occasion strikebreakers.[1] The work of the Women's Service Bureau fits exactly into this picture, supplying women for both the spadework and the oversight, and may indeed have helped paint it.

What Ray Strachey enjoyed doing she did very well indeed. In February 1916, she resigned as parliamentary secretary to the NU – to her credit since she was giving less and less of her attention to the NU's political concerns, and more and more to the LSWS's Women's Service Bureau. Several months earlier, she had been given a special tour of the new Park Royal Arsenal, and wrote ecstatically to her mother: 'The head of the place is asking us to supply 4000 women in the near future: and in the immediate future a certain number of Supervisors and Overlookers'. A visit from the head of Woolwich Arsenal followed, looking for the Bureau's help in increasing his work force from 23,000 to 34,000. 'We have to send him,' she went on, 'forty educated women for Supervisors day after tomorrow, forty next week and so on. It is thrilling! And the best of it is that we can do it.'[2]

The Bureau served the war effort in a number of ways, and supported women's interests in some important areas. Angela K. Smith draws attention to its function as an employment exchange, and to the remarkable extent and variety of training that it came to provide, in everything from acetylene welding, through driving and maintenance of automobiles, to glass blowing and dental mechanics. Unquestionably many women found openings and new opportunities during the war that they might not have found so readily without the aid of the Bureau.[3] To do Strachey justice, she tried also to obtain fair wages and reasonable conditions for women, but her interest in this often came in a poor second to supplying the bodies, except when her indignation was aroused, as it was later, for example, when women Strachey had found to fill military support positions were put under the command of a colonel.[4]

Both Woollacott and A.K. Smith admit to some difficulty in explaining the lack of evidence for suffragist interest in the conditions and pay of women in war work, and Woollacott suggests that the strength of the pacifist view in the NU may have had a part in this. Ironically, the opposite is probably true; it was the democratic 'pacifist' suffragists, now disempowered, who cared about labour conditions and had previously had the background knowledge and connections to work on them. In July 1915 Ray Strachey, indeed, found some inconsistency and doubtless a source of irritation in the interest taken by Marshall and her 'pacifist' friends in seeking to have women appointed to a committee overseeing the distasteful work of munitions manufacture. 'Quite so', said Marshall, but pointed out that her concern was with obtaining good conditions for women's work.[5]

Attitude to the trade unions

Trade unions were a major player as industry moved to a wartime footing, and the traditional skilled trades were particularly wary of 'dilution' – the introduction of unskilled workers, including women, into the expanding engineering shops. Although the Treasury Agreement negotiated by Lloyd George in spring of 1915 went some distance towards gaining the cooperation of the trade unions, tension between the government interest (production), the employers' interest (profit), and the trade union interest (wages and workers' rights) remained. The Munitions Act of July 1915, restricting the mobility of munitions workers and hence affecting their ability to negotiate higher pay, further increased the tension.

Women's advocates – in effect representing a fourth interest – found themselves struggling for the ground between the trade unions, the government, and the employers, and were thrown back, as far as the first two were concerned, into more or less the same arena where the EFF had been built and was now being fought over. Marshall took advantage of the meeting with W.C. Anderson about the future of the EFF to ask some pointed questions about women's war work, hoping perhaps that Ray Strachey would learn from his answers. Marshall asked Anderson whether the NU's work in defence of women's interests, women's war service and war relief was likely to cause conflict with the Workers' National Committee and with the trade unions, which might in turn 'put difficulties in the way of future co-operation on E.F.F. lines after the war'. Anderson said bluntly that joint action had always been difficult and that after the war the only uniting factor would be the women's suffrage demand. He made it plain that he thought 'sections of the Women's Movement' were pushing to get women into industry on any terms, even at the risk of undermining the work of the trade unions.

As far as her concern for working conditions went, Strachey might have favoured a more confrontational stance – for instance, sending delegations to certain trade unions or offering amendments to resolutions before the TU Congress – whereas Marshall, like Anderson, was clear that 'it was essential that the initiative in any matter of this kind should come from within the Trade Union Movement itself'. Asked (by Auerbach) 'whether it would not safeguard the interests of the men to admit women to the Unions', Anderson said that it would, but that it would not happen easily, and he added a warning: 'It must be done from the inside and from the workers themselves. If middle-class women were to start an agitation on these lines it would be regarded by the workers with great suspicion.'[6] Marshall will have remembered the hard work and months of behind-the-scenes lobbying that had gone into pre-war successes in bringing the trade unions one by one to a strong pro-suffrage stand, and holding them to it at the TUC, and remembered too that she herself had been warned on one occasion by Margaret Robertson Hills to keep her distance.[7] Hills was now no longer working for the NU; gone, too, were the northern executive members with understanding of the trade union movement.

At the Special EFF committee meeting that followed the interviews with the Labour Party leaders, Ray raised some questions but did not oppose Marshall's recommendations regarding an indirect approach to the issue of unionizing women in industry and to the need to enlist Ben Turner's help in keeping the women's suffrage cause alive at the coming TUC. Turner, of the textile union, was an old friend and ally of Isabella Ford in organizing women in Leeds, and of Robertson Hills in the campaign to win over the TUC to suffrage.[8] Strachey failed, however, to follow through on the recommendations – in fact forgot that they had been made – and failed to have anything concrete brought to the TUC. She then denied that there had been firm recommendations from the EFF until the minutes proved her wrong; perhaps a genuine (but nonetheless significant) lapse of memory.[9]

A small but telling incident on the related issue of the conditions for women in munitions factories (both pay and amenities) illustrates the difference between Marshall's and Ray's priorities. In August 1915, as honorary parliamentary secretary, Strachey brought forward with her own ostensible support a letter from Marshall to the NU executive, urging the NU to follow up on proposals made at a national conference on women's war service and to approach Lloyd George with a request for a representative committee of women with real powers to watch over the introduction of women into munitions. Although she does not seem to have told Strachey, Marshall had already discussed the proposal at some length with Lloyd George, then Minister of Munitions; she was now hoping to get the backing of the NU behind shaping it in a way that would serve women's interests.[10] By October Marshall realized that the demand had suffered a sea change. What she had sought was a committee to advise on proper conditions of women's employment; in the executive minutes the NU was agreeing to ask for a committee 'to facilitate the introduction of women into war work'. A very different thing, and for Marshall, much the same as what Mrs Pankhurst was doing.[11]

Brian Harrison accurately describes Strachey's wartime work for women's employment as unlikely 'to endear her either to trade unions or to the Labour Party'.[12] She wanted women admitted to the unions, but did little to reassure the unions, seeing them mainly as an obstacle in her way – as indeed they often were – rather than as possibly the essential means to real equality. Under the leadership of such as Marshall, Ashton, Courtney and Isabella Ford, the NU would surely have attempted to build on the pre-war foundation and the respect of the WNC to work with the trade unions to make visible the extent to which the interests of both could be best served by voluntarily opening the doors to women, a close analogy to the pre-war campaign to fuse the interests of women and working men on the suffrage issue.

For women's advocates the issue was complex. There was active competition within women's organizations for the hearts and minds of women – as well as for their working bodies – in reference to war work. Emmeline and Christabel Pankhurst had become such vocal hun-haters that the Ministry of Munitions subsidized the WSPU to put on a parade promoting women's 'right to serve',[13] and they continued to urge women to support the war effort, showing little concern with efforts for just conditions. In this, they were close to the position taken by Mrs Humphry Ward, the leading woman anti-suffragist; both Emmeline Pankhurst and Mrs Humphry Ward also ardently recruited men for the forces, and later did what they could to counter industrial unrest.[14]

Emmeline Pethick Lawrence, a former (disowned) colleague of the Pankhursts in the WSPU, now a leader in the WIL, sounded the alarm when she heard 'in confidence', she told Marshall, of a 'rumour of [an] Albert Hall meeting of Duchesses etc. on the same lines as Mrs Pankhurst's demand – to back up the Gov't without conditions, asking simply to be used.' She suggested countering with an alternative 'Great Patriotic Rally', emphasizing the other side of patriotism, which would stress the value of maintaining health and efficiency, and the patriotism implicit in safeguarding liberties. Marshall went to a couple of Pethick-Lawrence's meetings, though she does not appear to have worked actively on the scheme, but nothing seems to have come of it. Although Margaret Bondfield, Evelyn Sharp, and Margaret Llewelyn Davies had attended early planning meetings, Pethick-Lawrence had difficulty holding on to support from the Women's Cooperative Guild and from women's labour organizations.[15] The women's labour leaders may well have decided that something so reminiscent of a militant demonstration was less likely to be effective than the steady pressure they were putting on behind the scenes – with trade unions and with what government committees they had found their way on to – and might indeed be counter-productive. On the extreme left Sylvia Pankhurst and her transformed and solidly working-class East London Federation of Suffragettes campaigned uncompromisingly for better conditions for women and against the capitalist war; they were all but shunned as allies.[16]

Nominally, the NU was of course still on the side of good pay and conditions for women. A number of those who had resigned from the executive, including Marshall, had remained on the NU Women's Interests Committee, providing themselves with a certain right to continue to monitor issues of women's work and to comment on NU policy. Writing frequently and critically to Strachey, Marshall surely made more use of this toehold than was appropriate from someone newly out of office, and although most of her comments had some legitimate basis, her view that Strachey was blundering badly comes through. In truth, it was not always that Strachey was blundering; she was following a different agenda.

The climate within the WIC was more congenial than that in the new EFF, but any substantive action could only proceed by means of recommendations to the NU executive. From the outset, the WIC had tried to accompany any help it gave in opening up new fields for women's work, for instance in agriculture (where conditions were notoriously poor), with 'an effort ... to educate [women's] minds on the question of combining and standing out for proper wages and conditions.'[17] But the committee's achievements after mid-1915 were minimal except in a few areas where there was still a fundamental feminist accord between the views of both NU factions; lip service might be paid, but action was harder to come by. Yet the WIC had value in keeping communication open with some of those now without representation on the executive.

Women's interests at the periphery

Although for the political work of the EFF, policy effectively came down from the NU executive, there is evidence that in some places things were rather different as regards women's interests and labour relations. In the areas where the EFF connection had been most active the same NU people, with the same EFF organizers, continued to work with the same Labour women and sometimes men on projects that arose spontaneously from war conditions. The NU had given its blessing to the continuing involvement by authorizing organizers in a number of places to work first for relief and later for women's interests; the new executive may have been rather naive about the political connotations. East Bristol was not the only place where this had led to an almost symbiotic relationship with local Labour groups. Some of the issues that the WIC attempted to address at the centre were playing out in a microcosm in Manchester.

Mrs Tomlinson, a leading Manchester suffragist, kept Marshall informed from time to time, and a series of her letters in August 1915 reflects the many-sided controversy taking place over women's war work. The Manchester Women's War Interests Committee (MWIC) was not a sub-committee of the NU but an independent larger body on which the NU had two representatives,[18] and which had established a good relationship with the local branch of the Amalgamated Society of Engineers (ASE). Rather surprisingly, both the MWIC and the ASE regarded Mary Mcarthur's Federation of Women Workers (FWW) with suspicion, and when the FWW claimed to represent women in the area, the local ASE instead accepted the MWIC as the women's representative.

Well aware as she was of the political colour of the NU executive since the June Council, Tomlinson found it ironic that the NU had lent the radical Annot Robinson to the Manchester WIC, writing '... but they cant say afterwards they have not been clear about the position as I have again written to point out that we are an entirely independent comtee and outlined the kind of work we are doing – it is really a comical situation, no one can consider our work non-controversial.'

Tomlinson told Marshall that the MWIC had just met with what she called the employers' Armaments Output Committee[19] and had two hours of intense argument. Three trade union men were present 'and were most helpful. ... Without them we should have been squashed.' The majority of the Armaments committee (the employers) had been absolutely hostile to the idea of a guaranteed wage, asking 'Would Lloyd George guarantee their profits?' and accusing the women of 'using a national emergency to make a bargain for women and force up wages'. When Tomlinson countered by asking whether the committee thought wages and conditions were outside its scope, at least one man present said yes, that output was their only concern. That set the TU men going, and they referred the committee to the Munitions Act, pointing out that the purpose of the TU section was to deal with difficulties arising from the suspension of normal TU rules, and that adequate wages for women were part of the agreement with the government. This silenced the committee, at least momentarily.

Tomlinson had come away feeling much reassured: 'If the Trade Union men will only back us all along as they did Friday, I feel we shall be in a strong position.'[20] Later Tomlinson learnt that the argument with the TU men had continued heatedly after the women left; the employers, she told Marshall, would not be so afraid of the minimum wage for munition workers 'were it not that they fear such a raising of the standard would affect the women who have been employed for some time in engineering'. The TU group, she said, were making a complaint to the Munitions Advisory Committee; she and Annot Robinson felt that the Manchester trade unions were identifying with the work of the women's interests committee in a completely new way.

Such local success was cheering, but Mrs Tomlinson had also to report that she had been told in confidence that 'the Gov't has appointed four *men* (T.U. we presume) to go into the question of the minimum wage for women.'[21] However, the Manchester glimpse leaves us with a picture of alliances that the democratic suffragists had they still had power would have liked to strengthen at the national level. In October when the MWIC was trying to get support for the inclusion of women on the local Munitions Committee and for the minimum wage, Tomlinson made it plain that she no longer felt any real connection to NU headquarters, nor expected any help from them: '... we will call in at the N.U. offices if we are in London', she wrote, 'and be quite amiable ... we certainly have no intention of being tied up by the London Committee'.[22]

As long as some of the old guard remained active on the WIC of the NU, efforts to look after the interests of women working in munitions continued. In September 1915 Marshall urged the Home Office to appoint more women factory inspectors; she was not impressed by their boast that they were appointing three additional inspectors to meet the need of the thousands of women newly employed in factory work. She kept in touch not only with the MWIC but with WICs in a number of places, and found what they reported about women's health in the factories disturbing; the ill effects could easily be prevented by the use of special knowledge and a little imagination, and she begged that women doctors should be consulted.[23] Rathbone promised detailed information on conditions in Liverpool, where she believed women's wages – being kept down by the small demand for women's work in the trades – were probably worse than in any other comparable town. Rathbone was honorary secretary of the Liverpool Women's Industrial Council, an umbrella group for about a dozen organizations, and also of the Liverpool Soldiers and Sailors Families Association.[24]

By mid-1915 women were being taken into the Civil Service in larger numbers than ever before, but often at bargain rates, and this too was of concern to the WIC. In October 1915 Marshall had a letter from Mabel Crookenden, the former principal secretary of the NU, who had left in the aftermath of the April resignations. Their working relationship had been one of mutual respect and affection; Crookenden signed her letter 'Yours with much love' and Marshall addressed her as 'Dear Crookie'. Now Crookenden was bitterly angry both with the government and with women who accepted posts at pay well below their qualifications – or at no pay. The position of getting women into higher posts was worsening, she claimed, because women would take anything; she had been asked if she knew of volunteers to help in translation at the Admiralty – they must be '*fully qualified and trained* and willing to work from 10 am to 7 pm'. The Admiralty already had two such volunteers and needed more. Crookenden appealed to the NU to urge women not to volunteer and not to accept posts below their qualifications. To Marshall she wrote, 'Can you pull strings and get this shewn up? ... I'd like to take every farthing from these monied women and let them see what it is to be dependent on your earnings and find the market closed against you because the work is being done voluntarily! It fairly makes me boil!' She was also looking for work, and asked Marshall to put in a word for her.[25]

Marshall took the issue to the NU Women's Interests Committee, which passed strong recommendations on to the NU executive; and she put Crookenden's name forward for a post at the Ministry of Munitions. The post was offered to her – initially at a salary of thirty shillings a week (£78 a year) and then at £150 a year; after Marshall intervened directly with Lloyd George, Crookenden finally accepted it at £175, £25 less than she had received as NU Secretary. Marshall's letter to Lloyd George had been read out to the staff board and, according to Crookenden, had certainly been 'the turning of the scale', resulting in her winning out over well-qualified women who would have accepted less money.[26] Marshall had been glad to combine her personal concern for Crookenden with the political cause, although it is unlikely that her success in Crookenden's case was reflected in any government policy change. In effect, she had drawn on her personal capital, rather than having the moral force of the NU behind her, and she had achieved a personal rather than a public victory.

The complete dominance of the LSWS in the NU executive had in effect brought about a failure in the NU's decision-making process, which until the outbreak of war had managed, albeit not always easily, to accommodate a wide variety of views, in part through a carefully limited flexibility allowed to branches. Strongly opposed convictions and the high emotions surrounding the war had first eroded and then had swept away the will to compromise: by June 1915 there were only winners and losers. At the centre, while the newer democratic suffragists had held a majority on the executive before the war, other interests had also had representation and had been able to make themselves heard in policy-making; now only one view prevailed. What had followed was a major change in policy, especially in relations with the Labour Party and with working women and men.

9
Separate Ways

Founding the Women's International League

Throughout the summer of 1915 the leading democratic suffragists tried and failed to recover an effective position in the NU executive; tried and failed to save the essence of the EFF; continued to try with only limited success to bring the influence of the NU to bear through the Women's Interests Committee on concerns they thought important. The emotional toll taken by the events of the spring was heavy; Swanwick, Courtney, Marshall, and Royden had taken intermittent holidays in Cornwall, separately and together, but for some even this break was laden with correspondence and concerns. Fortunately, even before the June débacle, they had found other outlets for their energies, other directions in which to pursue their vision.

All of course were interested in what had come out of the Hague Congress. The British Committee of the International Women's Congress (BCIWC) took off to a very good start throughout the late spring and summer of 1915. Visibility was higher perhaps than could have been hoped for. Even the failure of those who had hoped to attend the Congress to reach Holland had attracted attention, not all of it hostile. The two hundred women who had wanted to attend included many who were well known, if not all nationally at least within one or other feminist or peace circle, so that a substantial focussed audience was eager for news. Further, after having been left in disarray and all but voiceless for the first few months of the war, those who opposed the war for any reason or who wanted to address internationalist issues were regrouping, finding each other, and forming a loose kind of dissident sub-culture. They were hungry for hope and for any promising initiative, and for some the drama of the Hague conference and the work of the envoys was more appealing than endless intellectual discussion.[1]

The *Labour Leader* reported faithfully on peace issues, as it had from the outbreak of war, and so now did the *Manchester Guardian*, which was also open to correspondence. The *Common Cause*, to the credit of the NU and in conscious fulfilment of at least part of the commitment made in February, kept its columns open to reports and to correspondence on both sides of the peace issue. In addition to the two visits of Jane Addams, the published reports of the Congress became available, and there was continuing news of the journeys of the envoys appointed there to visit heads of state in both belligerent and neutral countries, carrying the plan for continuous mediation which had been accepted by the Congress. Remarkably, the envoys succeeded in meeting with heads of state, senior officials, or both in almost all of the countries they visited, and were received 'gravely, kindly, perhaps gladly' in the words of Emily Balch (a United States feminist pacifist, and later a Nobel Peace laureate) 'by twenty-one ministers, the presidents of two republics, a king, and the Pope'.[2]

The British section (BCIWC) attracted substantial support, and not only from among disillusioned NU members. The impressive lists of politicians, peers, pressmen (editors and journalists), writers, academics and bishops who were eager to meet with Addams during her two short visits are a tribute to her remarkable stamina (in spite of poor health) and also reflect a fairly substantial and widespread undercurrent running in favour of seeking some way towards a lasting peace. The interest shown is also a credit to the high profile and respect gained before the war by leading suffragists; Marshall and Swanwick in particular played a big role in facilitating Addams's meetings. But Addams's official meetings with Lord Robert Cecil, Lord Crewe and Lloyd George (all cabinet ministers, and the last just appointed Minister of Munitions) were sobering, and perhaps diminished her hope for a good outcome; while many sought her out the politicians in power in Britain met with her reluctantly and gave her scant encouragement.[3]

BCIWC kept the office it had taken before the Congress, continuing to hold well attended meetings and to encourage new branches. Swanwick, who had pulled her roots out of the NU almost completely, gave the work her full time attention. Marshall and Courtney also put a great deal of energy into it, but both were, as we have seen, still struggling against the fate of the EFF, and Marshall in particular was temperamentally unable to leave the NU to work out its own salvation or damnation under new leaders. Emily Leaf helped put together

Towards Permanent Peace, the official report of the Hague Congress – and, incidentally, missed the good staff, the information files, and the telephone that had been taken for granted at the old NU office. Margaret Ashton was particularly active in setting up a Manchester branch.

Macmillan's role was again singular; she remained on the NU executive, but after a short return to Britain, left once more to serve as an envoy to the northern capitals, accompanying Rosika Schwimmer, and stayed away to work with Aletta Jacobs. Considerable difficulty, complicated by interpersonal tensions, attended the work of the ICWPP, exacerbated by the division of its leadership between New York and Amsterdam. Courtney and Marshall were anxious about the extent of the work being carried out by individuals (including Schwimmer and Macmillan) before any structure, clear plans for funding, formal reporting mechanism, or democratic constitution were in place, but this is outside our present focus; the ICWPP did not wash its dirty linen in public, and Macmillan kept the BCIWC usefully informed of her mission.[4]

Finally, with the groundwork laid, the planned meeting of the British Committee, open only to subscribers, was held on 30 September and 1 October 1915 at the Caxton Hall. Officers and a new executive were elected, objectives were agreed upon, an appeal approved to go to the women of the British Dominions to join in the international venture, a new name – Women's International League (WIL) – adopted, and a structure put in place. On the first evening of the conference, Lady Brassey held an At Home for two hundred of those attending, at which the speaker was Madame Duchêne, the leading French proponent of the ICWPP.

By mid-October WIL had an office at 12 College Street in Westminster and letterhead showing Catherine Marshall as honorary secretary, Emmeline Pethick Lawrence as treasurer, and Helena Swanwick as Chair. Bondfield, Courtney, and Ashton were Vice-Chairs. Five to represent WIL on the international committee had also to be named, but the election of these was left to the executive, which made its decision on 21 October; those chosen were Bondfield, Courtney, Marshall, Swanwick, to whom was soon added Louie Bennett, elected by the Irish group to honour a decision made to ensure one Irish member among the five, pending a ruling by the ICWPP regarding separate representation of minority groups within nations, a conscious effort to avoid falling into a colonial pattern.[5] The elected executive continued to be broadly representative of a number of different women's organizations that had supported the Hague initiative.

WIL's overall objective was defined as to establish the principle of right rather than might, of co-operation rather than conflict in national and international affairs, first by working for 'the development of the ideals underlying modern democracy in the interests of constructive peace' and secondly for 'the emancipation of women and the protection of their interests'.[6]

The role of the new organization in relation to the second part of the programme, the suffrage question, exercised some of the internationalists. Should its suffrage work be limited 'to the bare demand for the political enfranchisement of women'? or should the new organization link that demand to what Marshall saw as 'the fundamental principles from which it draws its life, and stand for a broadly democratic, feminist and pacifist programme'?[7] Meanwhile the centre of the ICWPP and WIL work clearly would initially be peace and internationalism; the nature of its possible suffrage involvement remained largely academic throughout 1915.

If WIL was focussed on work for peace, the NU was equally focussed on support for the war effort. Throughout the debate that had divided the NU down to the June Council much of the rhetoric on both sides had been couched in terms of the nature of suffragism. Opposition to NU participation in the Hague Congress, and to having the NU work for a peaceful settlement after the war, had made use of the argument that such work was outside the mandate of the NU as a suffragist organization while the peace women had emphasized the fundamental connection between peace and women's rights. But to read the minutes of the NU executive after the departure of the internationalists is to find the NU focussing more and more of its attention on matters whose connection with suffrage principles is at least equally questionable; supporting war work may have won some government and public approval, but is in itself neither inherently feminist nor anti-feminist. In any event, in 1915 suffrage remained on the back burner, although the NU was able to keep up its parliamentary connection. Neither organization had forgotten the dormant franchise issue but neither had spare energy to put into it.

Individual choices and directions

Loyal as they were to WIL, a number of the suffrage internationalists formerly of the NU were restlessly seeking additional outlets, and to some extent went their separate ways. At the beginning of the war Maude Royden's radical Christian pacifism had alienated her from most of her professing fellow Christians especially within her own Anglican community; she had been shocked and deeply distressed but had not followed along when one after another of the leading clergy publicly supported what they saw as a righteous war. At the end of 1914 she had found support, to her great relief, in the Fellowship of Reconciliation, of which she became a founding member. In July 1915 she campaigned with the Women's Peace Crusade, courageously confronting violent crowds with non-violence, but the experience was terrifying and she found it hard to see it as effective. Unfortunately Royden and the rationalist Swanwick, however much they both stood for peace, had almost incompatible personalities and at times barely shared a common vocabulary; before the end of 1915, Royden gave up her work in WIL and concentrated mainly on another aspect of her Christian feminist vision, working towards a full role for women within the church.[8]

Kathleen Courtney, too, took a leave of absence from WIL at the end of 1915, going to the eastern Mediterranean to work with the Friends' War Victims Relief Committee, motivated it seems by an urge to get involved in hands-on work, and as she had earlier told Macmillan 'suffering from an utter disgust with organisation of all kinds ... the prospect of constitution making is distasteful in the extreme'.[9] Macmillan herself resigned from the BCIWP executive in August because her work for ICWPP was keeping her out of the country.

Isabella Ford and Margaret Ashton continued active in WIL as speakers and organizers; both were also much occupied with building the movement in their local bases of Leeds and Manchester. Others actively taking part in their own areas included working women such as Hannah Mitchell.

As Chair of WIL, Swanwick worked well with the diverse elements represented on the executive. But her closest colleague was Marshall; they understood and trusted each other, and communicated well by letter or in person. Swanwick was devastated when Marshall chose to give a major part of her peace work to another organization, the No Conscription Fellowship (NCF). Towards the end of 1915 it became clear that conscription was imminent. On 16 December 1915, WIL sponsored a public meeting 'To present the Women's Case against Conscription' at the Portman Rooms in London; Marshall shared the platform with old and newer colleagues, including Margaret Bondfield, Charlotte Despard, Emmeline Pethick-Lawrence, and Maude Royden. While the Military Service Bill was before Parliament, WIL committed itself to opposing it and gave its blessing to Marshall to give 'her whole time to this work during the present crisis'.[10] But some WIL leaders were understandably distressed when, the Bill having passed, the NCF took over Marshall's life. Swanwick in particular, always fiercely protective of the resources of the women's movement, bitterly regretted the loss of Marshall's genius to a (primarily) men's cause, however worthy in itself and strongly as she herself believed in the promotion of peace and the conversion of men to peaceful means as essential groundwork for the advancement of women. It was not without a struggle that she came to accept the loss.[11]

Marshall herself was much exercised over the decision as to where to devote her energies – and characteristically too much inclined to believe that she need give nothing up, but could stretch herself just that bit more to cover everything that needed doing. She did indeed continue to serve on the WIL executive, but she was no longer available on a day by day basis to give her attention to WIL's work and her support to Swanwick.

Lingering regrets and a continuing friendship

The erosion of the EFF had brought home to the democratic suffragists the extent to which they were now without significant influence within the organization they had built. Some of those now in control within the NU also experienced a sense of loss. Late in 1915 a frank and friendly exchange took place between Eleanor Rathbone – now back on the NU executive – and Catherine Marshall. Close in age and both originally strongly Liberal in outlook, a respectful affection existed between them. Rathbone had earlier written bitterly in the *Common Cause* against the actions of the peace faction, an attack which had probably been at least in part because she found herself disinherited as a believer in promoting peace by the clear line drawn between the peace cause and the NU – although she herself had helped draw that line. But now she and Marshall were willing to rebuild personal bridges.

Rathbone followed the fortunes of WIL almost wistfully and read the founding principles with interest. Rathbone 'felt so strongly in sympathy with the first of [these] two objects' ('the development of the ideals underlying modern democracy in the interests of constructive peace') that she sent a donation. She gave only qualified support to the second – work for the emancipation of women – acknowledging that it 'sounds unexceptionable' but adding that in light of previous statements made by Marshall she could not help reading into it 'a Regan and Goneril-like intention to treat the N.U.W.S.S. as in its dotage, which you will supercede if you can', a not altogether unjustified accusation.

She told Marshall that she was glad that the latter thought cooperation possible between 'those who think as you do and the rest of the N.U. ... it has been taken too much for granted that those who could not support your proposal that the N.U. should adopt your aims officially are necessarily not in sympathy with your aims or only in sympathy with them in a half-hearted and academic fashion. One may want the utmost vigour of action without feeling that that action can be suitably undertaken by a particular organization'. She would not join WIL, but offered to help where possible with 'your gallant international adventure'.[12] She let down her guard and good-humouredly acknowledged her ambivalence about the war; like many women, she felt shut out of the national action, writing, 'I find it quite aggravating enough to be [a] woman and for the first time in my life, would give the world to be able to migrate into a man's skin – the vulgarest little cockney Tommy Atkins would do. But I suppose that sentiment will only make you more than ever think me a lukewarm sort of Pacifist.'[13]

Indeed Rathbone gave both personal and executive support where she could, attending a WIL meeting in Liverpool that was addressed by Marshall and trying to make sure that a meeting of the NU executive in September (to part of which Marshall might come in her continuing role as EFF Secretary) was not set at a time which would conflict with a speech Marshall was to give to the annual conference of the National Union of Women Workers on women's share in the work of political reconstruction after the war.[14] The mistrust had gone from their relationship, and they had some useful correspondence about conditions of women working in munitions.

Mrs Fawcett addresses internationalism

In quite a different way, Mrs Fawcett found her leading role in international suffrage slipping and did her best to try to regain the initiative. She was placed in an odd position by Jane Addams' visits in May and June 1915. Here was a distinguished suffragist, a colleague and fellow officer in the IWSA, visiting Britain and attracting a great deal of public attention. But Addams was on a mission towards which Fawcett had expressed strong disapproval, which she had made sure did not receive official suffragist blessing, and the participants in which she had publicly categorized as traitors. When it became clear that she was not on the list of those to be met with during Addams' first visit,

Fawcett wrote – probably in some hurt – welcoming her, expressing relief that Addams had not been on the Lusitania (which was sunk by torpedo the day she landed), and saying she was sorry to hear she was leaving so soon as she had hoped to have a little party of friends to meet her. She also invited Addams to a hastily convened meeting of the Headquarters Committee of the IWSA, saying that she wanted to bring forward a proposal from Sweden.[15]

The proposal Fawcett referred to was a plan emanating from the Swedish suffrage affiliate and now circulating in IWSA branches to hold a women's conference at the end of the war, when and where the statesmen should meet to formulate peace terms. Fawcett may still have been within herself not wholly convinced that she was on the side of the angels over the Hague Congress (particularly as her prophecies of disaster had not been fulfilled); at best, the continuing attention paid to the envoys, and Macmillan's role as an envoy, must have rankled. She gladly pursued the plan of a postwar suffrage conference, hoping to see it adopted by the IWSA and by opponents of the Hague Congress, rather than having the IWSA throw its support behind the conference already determined on by the ICWPP. Fawcett had had friendly responses from the presidents of the German, French and Danish Societies. With some ambivalence, she said she hoped it would be an occasion for cooperation.[16]

When Carrie Chapman Catt suggested that the ICWPP should be invited to send representatives to the projected postwar conference, Fawcett sent for Marshall (just days after the June Council) 'and was very anxious to know' what the attitude of the new group would be. Marshall told her that she expected they would be happy to send delegates 'as the I.W.S.A. wd. be pressing for one of the points of our programme, viz. the enfranchisement of women in all countries.'[17] Although she did not spell it out, Marshall foresaw already that the IWSA agenda would be narrower than that of the ICWPP, whereas Fawcett continued to hope that the objectives of the latter could be subsumed into those of the IWSA or at least controlled by it. To Catt, she described herself and Adela Coit as 'strongly opposed' to withdrawing and leaving the field to the ICWPP, willing to agree to unite with them '*but only on the basis that the I.W.S.A. call the congress*', and only willing to support the idea of two separate congresses if every effort at union – on her terms – had failed.[18]

The IWSA was not quite in Fawcett's pocket and was in danger of becoming another battleground. The BCIWC had been disappointed in the IWSA official response to the Hague initiative, but the Congress nevertheless had been the child of the suffrage movement, drawing most of its support from constitutional suffragists. The peace women had kept up a comfortable enough relationship with the IWSA to see it as a potential force for good on the international scene, particularly with Mary Sheepshanks staffing the London headquarters. But Fawcett was now seriously at odds with Sheepshanks, who had the misfortune to be in a sense her employee. From the start of the war, Sheepshanks had seen it as right to maintain neutrality, refraining from allocating blame to one nation more than another, but as her biographer says, her editorship of *Jus Suffragii* 'was quite the opposite of neutral as regards the wicked lunacy of the Great War itself', and she had made it plain that for her the role of the IWSA would be better fulfilled in promoting internationalism than in according any virtue to rampant patriotism.[19]

In mid-1915 it almost seemed as if Fawcett, having purged the NUWSS of pacifism, was now bent on cleansing the IWSA, and early in June Sheepshanks indeed resigned both her positions (as international secretary and editor of *Jus Suffragii*), as a result of Fawcett 'making it quite impossible for her',[20] as Emily Leaf wrote to Marshall and Courtney (who were trying to relax in Cornwall). Sheepshanks had attended a Whitsun weekend Fabian school in Keswick, where, she later wrote, 'Pacifist and patriotic views were synthesised to some extent, and everyone enjoyed blowing off steam'. The older Marshalls had afterwards 'captured' her, 'rowing her home in perfect moonlight on a glassy lake'.[21] After an idyllic interlude of three or four days at Hawse End, the Marshalls' home on Derwentwater, Sheepshanks returned to troublesome times in London.

Apologizing for bringing such disturbing news, Leaf told Marshall and Courtney 'I saw Mary Sheepshanks last night and she was in great distress ... Mrs Fawcett ... is furious because she went to the Keswick Conference ... [and] scolded her as if she were a child – and she resigned on the spot'. Fawcett, Leaf added, 'is also very angry with Chrystal [still travelling as one of the Hague envoys] – and Mary says the Committee with only Mrs Fawcett and Mrs Coit is quite impossible.' Leaf feared that Fawcett and Coit would appoint a new editor before Macmillan got back, which would be a calamity. Someone, she wrote, should get Mrs Chapman Catt 'to put her foot down – and request Mary to withdraw her resignation. I believe Mary would do this – as she really wants to go on with the work if the conditions are possible – but they aren't at present. ... You see until Miss Macmillan comes back – Mary is quite helpless. She is frightfully depressed about it – and would I think be glad of help from some of us – if we could do anything.'[22]

Whether Catt (who liked to see the IWSA as a force for peace) intervened, or Macmillan became involved, or Leaf found some tactful conciliator, or Fawcett and Sheepshanks worked it out on their own, the crisis was resolved by some means, and Sheepshanks resumed her work, though never in a situation of great comfort. In September Adela Coit professed to account for Sheepshanks's 'strange behaviour' towards Fawcett and herself by suggesting that she was ill – and had been for some time.[23] Sensible and balanced letters from Sheepshanks about the difficulties of editing *Jus Suffragii*, written around this time, suggest otherwise.

Sheepshanks continued throughout the war to publish news in *Jus Suffragii* that 'would present the human face of the "enemy" to all women readers whatever their nationality'.[24] But to some any hint of 'pacifism' was unacceptable. In October 1915 the president of the French Union for Women's Suffrage came in person to the IWSA's board to complain that there was too much talk of peace in *Jus Suffragii*. The NU executive took up the complaint, agreeing to write a letter to Sheepshanks, endorsing the position of the French society and 'protesting against the indentification [sic] of the paper with pacifist propaganda'. They strongly condemned the October issue, asserting that it contained 'no less than 5 articles, all dealing with and advocating pacifism'. Osler, who was not present at the time, read the minute 'with very great surprise' and then 're-read very carefully and critically' the five articles and brought her analysis back to the NU executive. She found 'in no single one ... any suggestion of immediate peace or of terms of immediate peace.' To Osler, with so little of suffrage news to report it seemed 'a suicidal policy ... to exclude speculative and general philosophical articles on the questions of war and peace'. Fawcett showed no interest in Osler's description of the articles, which she brushed off as 'not good articles ... fluffy stuff ... appeals for peace', saying that if she wanted articles in favour of peace she could read more thoughtful ones elsewhere; the French position obviously reflected her own and she backed her argument with angry references to the prominence *Jus Suffragii* had given to the Hague Congress, together with emotional references to the French 'with the Germans on their soil and the noise of their guns within earshot of the gates of Paris'.[25] From then on, Sheepshanks gave in to the extent of no longer including articles by well-known opponents of war; she maintained that the omission caused a drop in subscriptions.

Losses and gains

The events of April and June 1915 had brought major change to the British feminist scene, though probably only those most closely involved had any clear picture of what had happened. The NUWSS still boasted a substantial membership; funds, though somewhat diminished, still came in; and the executive was no longer riven by dissent (even if Osler spoke out once in a while). Its nationwide organization and communication network were still in place, and some of its trained organizers were working in various capacities across the country. Dissatisfied branches were an irritant but not a threat. The contribution the NU had made to enrolling women in war work, both as hands and as supervisors, had added to its credibility with the government. That the EFF had been effectively dismantled was a cause of satisfaction to the NU leaders; the loss of the relationship with Labour and with the working class that went with the political break was intangible and not a matter for concern to those now in control.

What the democratic suffragists had lost was very evident. Although they had created a new organization in WIL, the structure still needed work; as for the international body, the ICWPP, it had good visibility but virtually no structure, and some thoughtful internationalists feared for its ability to maintain any kind of unity. Those who had left the NU executive no longer had access to the machinery they had built up, either for political work or for outreach. What visibility they had was for their peace work; they themselves saw the connection with suffrage, but it was not widely noticed. They were committed to the same vision as before, but were to some extent scattered in the work they were doing. WIL lacked the political currency with which to build connections with any party, yet in another sense it had broadened the catchment, drawing in democratic suffragists who had previously been active in a wide range of different fields, other suffrage organizations, trade union work. And, like the new NU, it had clarity of purpose.

As we have seen, Fawcett expressed some hope that the end of the war would see the women's movement drawing together again on international issues. Before that time came, the challenge would be whether they could act unitedly on the franchise.

10
Back to the Franchise

Suffrage sidles into view again

The changed conditions of wartime government led to the franchise issue coming up in a new form. No government would have chosen to address the contentious question of major electoral change at the height of a war, and even the suffrage organizations had not expected that they would.[1] Within the NU, the heat of the controversy around the Election Fighting Fund reflects the expectation that there would still be a crucial election before the franchise question was again addressed.

The precipitating factor was that, inconveniently, a general election had been due in 1915. Faced with a perceived need to delay the election, unable to agree on a new registration formula, and anxious to avoid controversy over either the abolition of plural voting or women's suffrage, the government, after toying with several proposals, had simply extended the life of parliament by one year and validated the old register. The problem accordingly had to be addressed again early in 1916.

Initially the problem was seen as relating to the registration of voters. The franchise was hedged about with a variety of residence and property qualifications, and the difficulty of compiling a new register in wartime conditions – without disfranchising soldiers – was overwhelming. When suffragists realized that the government was going to be obliged to make changes many thought that the party truce implicit in Asquith's coalition government formed in May 1915 presented 'a unique opportunity for a settlement by consent'.[2] But although the Coalition under Asquith worked well enough to further the prosecution of the war for some months, suffragists were over-optimistic in their hope that political amity extended to other areas. In a cabinet that now included every shade of opinion from the leading anti-suffragist Lord Curzon to the publicly committed adultist Arthur Henderson, agreement was hard to find on so political an issue as registration, let alone the larger question of franchise reform.³

Suffragist anxieties

However busy suffrage women were with other issues, all organizations followed what they could learn of the registration question intently. While most suffragists had their early discussions mainly behind closed doors and approached public action with care Sylvia Pankhurst, as ever, was radical, proactive, visible – and was regarded with extreme caution by most suffrage bodies. In December 1915, she convened an informal conference of women's suffrage societies, which the NU did not attend but which was useful in providing a stepping-stone to a more broadly representative conference in late January 1916, this time attended by members of the NU as well as of the United Suffragists, the WFL, WIL and some smaller bodies. Here Sylvia moved a resolution demanding adult suffrage. Marshall, Swanwick, Royden, and Emmeline Pethick Lawrence all spoke in support; Evelyn Sharp, despite her association with Sylvia in the United Suffragists and her agreement in principle, urged a less demanding tone in stating so radical an aim. An amended resolution proposed by WIL simply urged the suffrage societies 'to demand a Government measure of Women's Suffrage now', and finally passed, although Ray Strachey spoke against even this on the surprising ground that if a new parliament were called before the end of the war it would be 'unwise to press the question of Women's Suffrage at such an election'. Despite the effort to paper over the cracks it was apparent, as the WIL annual report would say, that suffrage organizations were not prepared to take a common stand.⁴

In part the disunity resulted from distrust between organizations going a long way back – between militants and non-militants, for an obvious example. In part it came from distrust between individuals; Fawcett, reinforced by others from the LSWS, not only shared the rather general distrust of Sylvia Pankhurst but remained bitter against the cohort who had gone from being her closest advisers in the NU to being the founders of WIL.

The democratic suffragists carried with them into WIL a belief in the value of a broad franchise and much of the socialist idealism they had found before the war. In addition the pre-war work of individual leaders had given them more than a nodding acquaintance with a number of political figures across the whole political spectrum. WIL however lacked the power to deliver the funding, organizational support, national network, and political credibility which had been vested in the NU before the outbreak of war, and what resources it had had so far been exercised in its major role of peace education and action.

Although the NU still had resources and credibility in high places far outweighing those of WIL it was evident that these were unlikely to be set behind a truly democratic franchise. From the outset of the renewed suffrage concern the NU executive refused to put their name to any demand for adult suffrage although some members and in particular some northern NU societies called for them to do so, or alternatively to allow them to work for adult suffrage on their own.[5]

In some other regions branch societies that responded to the changed NU by falling in line with what was going on at headquarters may in consequence have lost working-class support. A letter from Marshall's mother provides a – subjective – glimpse of what she saw happening in the Northwest Federation (NWF). After a meeting of the Keswick society on 8 May 1916 and of the NWF at the beginning of June at which Caroline Marshall had pushed with limited success for a more forceful suffrage resolution than that sent out by the national executive, she wrote in disgust to her daughter that 'the N.U. is in a backwater and likely to remain so,' and described her efforts to convince the local leadership that the Cumberland industrial towns (mentioning Workington, Whitehaven, Cleator Moor, Maryport, Barrow): 'all have working class who would be with us, [but] all have quite the wrong comm*ees*. ... We lose immensely by this genteel Liberal, *stupid, slack*, membership. We shall always stick. We want another society in each town.'[6]

New suffrage coalitions

Two groupings of suffrage bodies emerged during the summer of 1916 in response to continuing rumours about what was going on behind government's closed doors and to the growing awareness that more than a mere updating of registration must come. In March, at Rathbone's urging, the NU began work on setting up a Consultative Committee of Constitutional Women's Suffrage Societies (CCCWSS), which took form in May. Against Rathbone's wishes the NU executive refused to include WIL and women's labour organizations.[7]

Meanwhile – also in March – the WIL executive on its part resolved 'to cooperate with any organization working for Adult Suffrage and opposing the extension of the franchise to men if women are not included, provided that there can be general agreement as to methods and policy',[8] but for some weeks did not follow this up actively. Marshall's situation may have contributed to WIL's initial slowness to take action. She of all the former NU suffragists was uniquely qualified by talent and experience to give leadership in the political campaign. But throughout the spring and summer of 1916 her work for the No Conscription Fellowship was intensely demanding. After the passage of the Military Service Acts in January and May 1916 crisis followed crisis. Marshall was constantly in the thick of following the work of the tribunals, publicizing cases of injustice and illegal abuse, visiting prisoners in military custody, informing senior government members that conscientious objectors had been illegally taken to France and were in danger of being shot, and trying in a largely hostile climate to effect change in the conscience clause that would make it more consonant with its purpose – all of this in an organization whose committee members disappeared one after another into jail and where she herself was falling in love (perhaps for the first and last time in her life) with the charismatic chairman, Clifford Allen.[9]

Despite all this, Marshall maintained a role in WIL and once she became fully conscious of the emerging suffrage issue she began to act. Arthur Henderson had written to WIL in March inviting them to send a memorandum to the Labour Party Committee on Electoral Reform, but – as Marshall rationalized in a letter to him at the end of May – WIL had postponed acting on it 'as the matter did not at that moment seem urgent and there were so many other claims on your time and ours.' Marshall's excuse seems rather specious, with more truth in the second than in the first part; Henderson, leader of the Labour Party and now a member of Asquith's coalition cabinet, could surely have been trusted to have a notion of what was upcoming and urgent. Indeed, by the time Marshall wrote asking whether WIL might send a deputation to present such a memorandum she was told that the Labour Party had already 'sent its report to the Government and that it is therefore too late to make use of a memorandum from us, and that a deputation would consequently serve no useful purpose'. Henderson did however promise to 'give careful attention to any memorandum' they might send in. Marshall was reduced to asking humbly for a copy of the Labour Party committee's report, which she felt might make it unnecessary for WIL to draw up a memorandum.[10] The letter circulated by Henderson dated 12 May 1916 and presented to the Cabinet on the same date advocated adult suffrage but suggested that it was acceptable to the suffragists that women should not receive the vote until the age of twenty-five.[11] The idea of an age differential to address the irrational but prevalent fear of having women form the majority of voters had surely already been discussed informally, but it jars to find the concession being officially made so early by the most influential representative of the Labour Party, the very body that might have been expected to stand firm for full adult suffrage.

In the absence of any clear sense of what direction things might be taking the anxiety of the women's suffragists was increased by what appeared to be another serious threat. Both the Liberal War Committee and the Unionist War Committee passed resolutions in May 1916 in favour of the 'principle that every man in the fighting forces should have the vote', and *The Times* lent its support. Fawcett wrote to Asquith as early as 4 May acknowledging that 'the accidental disqualification of a large body of the best men in the country' by their absence from home was unacceptable, but pointing out that to go this route would be to place the franchise on an entirely new basis. Her letter and his reply, which merely said that legislation was not contemplated at that time, were both published in *The Times*.[12]

Fawcett's letter to the Prime Minister, couched in an almost fawning tone, dwelt extensively on the service of women in war work and on a more favourable public and political opinion. When Marshall wrote on behalf of the WIL executive she also referred to women's contribution but stressed the future rather than the past, drawing attention to postwar problems to come, including 'the maintenance of future peace' and urging the need for women to be part of the solution. 'The Nation,' she wrote, 'will need all the best brains at its command and cannot afford to set aside half of its people'. She concluded her letter with a reference to 'pledges ... unredeemed', a reference to Asquith's long-standing (if rather vague) promises that 'when a measure of franchise reform was introduced, the question of women's suffrage should not be left out of account'.[13] In effect, while Fawcett – for the NU – seemed almost to beg for the vote as a reward for good behaviour, Marshall – for WIL – claimed it as a right and a national necessity.

Inviting supposed supporters to a private conference of representative suffragists, Swanwick was blunter still. Referring to *The Times*'s approval of the principle of votes for fighting men she said no one wanted the fighting men to lose their vote, but to alter the qualification from a property basis to a military one would make an extension of the franchise to any who could not fight more difficult. She feared the influence of the Northcliffe press, which had proved 'its capacity for driving the Government to do what it has repeatedly declared it would not do'. Electoral questions must be addressed by a franchise bill to introduce adult suffrage not by tinkering with registration. 'To enfranchise every man in the fighting forces,' she pointed out, 'would be to introduce an entirely new and militarist qualification and to render immeasurably more difficult the task of securing the enfranchisement of those who can never fulfil this qualification.' Marshall, too, urged the need for meeting the threat of a military qualification which would be damaging to labour, to women, and to pacifism, 'by a vigorous and organized demand for adult suffrage and not by a mere negative opposition'.[14]

The WIL private conference in early June 1916 was limited to two representatives from each of a number of organizations and was followed by a public conference at which the resolutions passed supported the view of a military qualification as disastrous and a setback to the women's suffrage cause, affirmed that the best response was to push for adult suffrage and to oppose any measure altering the basis of the franchise that did not include women, and urged all democratic organizations, not just suffrage societies, to support the demand. A larger gathering again convened by WIL led to an organization calling itself Votes for All (VFA), which set to work to canvass and organize democratic opinion.[15]

Government dilemmas

While the suffrage organizations jockeyed for position on the outside, of far more immediate consequence was the jockeying going on inside the political arena, where suffrage formed only a part and women's suffrage an even smaller part of the concern which swirled around the registration issue, compounded by highly political questions of Irish discontent, party interests, the power of the House of Lords. All of these contributed to the failure of government attempts to formulate a viable franchise bill, resulting in the passage before the summer was out of another extension of the existing registration.

Throughout the summer of 1916 the Cabinet and the House of Commons laboured with the registration and franchise issue. More than anything else the process exposed the lack of trust and any long-term common interest between the different political groups making up the coalition government: when franchise reform is in the air all parties inevitably jump to guard or promote their own interests. It remained extremely difficult to determine terms of reference for any committee or conference to draw up proposals, let alone to decide who should sit on such a body or to whom it should report. Consequently, while the Cabinet wrestled unsuccessfully in private and in parliament throughout the summer of 1916, unable to find unity or any proposal acceptable to the Commons, the public immediacy faded for a few weeks.[16]

The women suffragists on the whole recognized that they needed to be alert and visible in order not to be wilfully and gladly forgotten, and that they had to do what they could to guard against having their interest traded off against the interest of some other group. Meanwhile wisdom dictated that they must not appear so aggressive as to provide an excuse for once more excluding them from the franchise, so they kept their channels of communication open, awaited developments with some discretion, and did not air their differences in public.

On 14 August Asquith introduced yet another interim proposal for procedure that would prove abortive but accompanied it with a speech which was hailed as a breakthrough; he announced his conversion to some form of women's suffrage, although without making any firm commitment to effective government support. Far from leading to any immediate advance in the women's cause, Asquith's speech was followed by renewed wrangling in government circles, but suffragists in and out of parliament took heart and began again to take a more proactive role. Within a week an informal conference was held at the House of Commons, where supporters from all parties under the leadership of Sir John Simon met with representatives of the women's suffragist societies.

Swanwick told WIL supporters that 'the enfranchisement of women has become a live issue with remarkable suddenness', and went on to forecast optimistically that the anticipated measure would be a democratic one, with cooperation from all parties. She named recent important converts – notably Walter Long, a Conservative Unionist, in the Cabinet as president of the Local Government Board – and remarked on the 'extraordinary fervour' with which much of the press had come over. She added 'We believe that there is overwhelming popular feeling for the complete enfranchisement of the whole people for the Parliament which will have the immensely difficult task of building up after the war. None but hopeless reactionaries or sectarians', she wrote, 'would try to keep up the miserable opposition of sex to sex, or class to class'. She cautioned that vigilance would be necessary and commented scathingly on a revival in *The Times* of the old idea of submitting the franchise question to a referendum, but she warned against any kind of agitation at the present time.[17]

What was not clear to the suffragists was the peculiar effect which the existence of the coalition would have and indeed was having on the suffrage issue. Swanwick had mentioned the continuing opposition of such men as the long-time leading anti-suffragist Lord Curzon (in the cabinet with the role of lord privy seal) and the conversion of others from antis to supporters. While the coalition in one sense freed individuals to depart from a party line, it also freed them to stick to their own opinions without consulting the broader party wisdom. Numbers might tell in the House of Commons, but in the cabinet the need to obtain unity was significant. Lord Curzon in particular was clearly a loose cannon whose dissent could embarrass the government seriously and whose influence in the House of Lords, where there was much sympathy with his position, could delay or effectively wreck a broad measure.

Finally the government's absolute need to find a way out of the dilemma led to the empowerment of a conference of members of both Houses of Parliament under the chairmanship of the Speaker, charged with bringing forward a proposal. The suggestion for the use of this method had come from Walter Long, and it was he who continued to press it forward.[18] Long had been a notorious anti-suffragist but was now seen as a supporter, though there was no reason to suppose that he thought the women's franchise of great importance.[19]

Differing hopes and expectations of suffragists

Chairing both the WIL and its offspring the Votes for All committee (VFA), Helena Swanwick took a leading role in pulling together the left-wing campaign for adult suffrage. She had already on the occasion in July of a proposed Select Committee (one of the aborted attempts at a process) collected signatures for a draft letter putting the case and urging that 'Anything less than womanhood suffrage would not give a fair representation to the women', and she had also written to Asquith on behalf of VFA, enclosing the draft letter and asking that the way should be cleared by giving the committee a mandate wide enough to enable it to consider 'the enfranchisement of all adult men and women.' In September the draft emerged in final form as 'The Claim for Adult Suffrage', and the signatories were invited to a conference on 22 September 1916, at which the VFA in effect transformed itself into the National Council for Adult Suffrage (NCAS). In all of this Swanwick had consulted J.S. Middleton, and kept in touch with the Workers National Committee (WNC).[20]

The gulf between the Fawcett coalition and the adult suffrage supporters is clearly illustrated by a comparison of the composition of the NCAS with that of Fawcett's group, the Consultative Committee of Constitutional Women's Suffrage Societies (CCCWSS). Made up largely of church suffrage societies, professional women's suffrage societies, and Liberal and Unionist groups, the CCCWSS was almost exactly what it might have been had it been constituted in 1910. Little trace can be found here of the radical transformation of the NUWSS between 1911 and 1913. The subject of adult suffrage was often raised but the CCCWSS steadfastly refused to adopt it despite protests from some northern NU societies.

The NCAS on the other hand was chaired by Henry Nevinson, with Emmeline Pethick Lawrence as treasurer and James Middleton of (but not representing) the Labour Party as honorary secretary, jointly with Kathleen Courtney (now back from her overseas work); named on its executive were among others Margaret Bondfield (Women's Trade Union League, Women's Labour League), Margaret Llewelyn Davies (Women's Cooperative Guild), George Lansbury (editor, *Herald*, former WSPU supporter), Mary Macarthur (WTUL, Workers' National Committee), Evelyn Sharp (United Suffragists), and Robert Smillie (Miners' Federation). The list of signatories to the manifesto of the nascent NCAS, 'The Claim for Adult Suffrage' represents an even wider spectrum.[21]

The formation of the adult suffrage coalition went well, but was not trouble-free. Past history and personality problems accounted for some of the difficulties. For instance, Sylvia Pankhurst was known to be in full support of adult suffrage but was feared unlikely to be careful in her choice of strategy. The NU, now free of any wish to court the left, could afford to be fastidious about the company it kept; but Sylvia and her constituency of East London workers and women belonged with the NCAS and were made welcome there, whatever private reservations there may have been. Already in early September 1916, Sylvia had caused unease at some gathering, but whatever she had done, the incident was followed by a much less characteristic one when she went to see Swanwick and 'very warmly expressed regret for having acted imperiously', even saying, 'One isn't always wise!'.[22] The Workers' Suffrage Federation (WSF), the descendant of the East London Federation of Suffragettes (ELFs), and of the Women's Suffrage Federation, all vehicles of Sylvia Pankhurst's leadership, remained affiliated to the NCAS until late in 1917.

Bitter memories remain

Swanwick and Marshall may have been willing to submerge their differences with Sylvia in the common cause, but they did not have to work closely with her; nor had they done in the past. Another matter altogether was the intimate working relationship and affection that had existed within the National Union and had been shattered by the controversy over response to the war. Kathleen Courtney evidently hoped that the time and the climate were propitious for healing the breach with Millicent Fawcett. Emily Leaf, who had somehow avoided becoming anathema to Fawcett – despite her resignation as press secretary and her friendship with those who had espoused the Hague conference – was encouraged by Fawcett's having called at her house (albeit while she was out) and wrote to tell her how much Kathleen Courtney would like to see her. 'I know,' Leaf wrote, 'she has felt the long absence from you – and many others – very much, and it would be a real happiness to her to see you. Could you spare the time to come here to lunch one day when you are at the N.U. It would be such a pleasure if you would.'[23]

Fawcett's response, though moving in its way, was unyielding: 'I thank you for your letter: but I think it better on both sides that things should remain as they are at present. When the crisis in the history of the NU executive took place in the spring of 1915, of all the resigning members three only (or more properly two only) addressed me in terms which were personally – and I cannot help feeling intentionally – wounding. Miss Courtney was one of these. ... I can do no more at present. I think it was George III who began a day in his diary with the words "Remember to forget" something. Perhaps the best thing I can do is try to remember to forget'. Fawcett's supporters understood and even praised her intransigence.[24]

But the sorrow of Courtney and her friends was real and Courtney made further efforts to heal the breach. After a 'chance meeting' later in the month Courtney herself tried writing directly to Fawcett saying that she had never intended to wound her and expressing her deep regret that she had done so. Fawcett formally accepted the apology, but rejected the olive branch, writing, 'I now accept your assurance that the wounding was not intentional. ... But I am sure that now the best course is to leave it all alone and let the details at any rate gradually fade from our remembrance'.[25]

In her letter to Leaf Fawcett had added 'I am quite ready of course to cooperate with [Miss Courtney] if our work should bring us together and I meet her in social intercourse if that should come about accidentally'. In this final stage of the suffrage campaign the two indeed sat down together more than once as part of a small group of leaders, and also appeared in larger gatherings. They doubtless behaved towards each other with meticulous correctness. But such underlying interpersonal tensions must have added to the political differences preventing trust and any measure of unity between the supporters of women's suffrage.

Any hope that one organization or even one coalition would represent all suffragists was now highly unlikely; Swanwick could pull in some left-wing organizations, particularly those representing substantial numbers of working class women; the NU for its part relied on its reputation and on the traditional middle class suffrage constituency.[26] However, as the government began at last to move forward the suffragists did not openly display their differences.

11
The Vote at Last

The Speaker's Conference

The Speaker's Conference, after some delay, began its meetings on 12 October 1916, and continued twice-weekly sittings throughout the autumn and winter. Its mandate was wide: to bring forward recommendations on everything relating to parliamentary elections and to the local government franchise. The need to prevent one or other interest group of political significance from refusing cooperation ensured that all would have some representation at the conference and all would have to be prepared for some measure of compromise; even so, the makeup of the conference was jealously watched by all factions. No one was chosen for a single reason; starting with a conventional formula based on party affiliation roughly in proportion to representation in Parliament, names were juggled to balance views on other concerns – the soldiers' vote, proportional representation, and women's enfranchisement among them. So the women's vote was only one among a number of possibly contentious issues, but it was given substantial consideration when appointees were selected. Specifically, Sir John Simon and W.H. Dickinson were known Liberal suffragists. The three Labour members were adultists, in accord with the approved policy of their party. Others, particularly among the Unionists, were committed anti-suffragists. No one could count heads with certainty, since the war had affected the opinions of many people, but Lowther, in whose hands the final choice rested, strove for a balance.[1]

The chairmanship of Lowther seems to have been generally well accepted, although suffragists did not at once recognize him as one 'whose impartiality was beyond question'.[2] Remembering his role in destroying the Reform Bill of January 1913 by his ruling that no women's suffrage amendment could be entertained despite previous government promises, Caroline Marshall described his appointment as 'rather ominous I fear for us', while the Women's Freedom League categorized 'the concatenation of Mr Long and Mr Lowther [as] of evil augury for women'.[3] But Lowther chaired the conference with patience and skill, evidently seeing as the desired outcome that he might help bring from the conference an agreed set of recommendations, not that his personal preferences should be met.

The work of the Speaker's Conference was carried on behind closed doors, and no official record of its deliberations was preserved, although a number of participants recorded their recollections sooner or later.[4] Initially, it seemed likely that the efforts of thirty-two men thrown together on the very basis of their known differences would break down in failure, but with some exceptions most seem to have accepted that some clear direction must emerge from their deliberations if a serious crisis were to be avoided.

Lowther knew from the start that women's suffrage might be the most difficult of the issues to be dealt with, and delayed discussion until agreement had been reached on a substantial number of other points, ensuring that the members already had a stake in the success of the conference and now had a predisposition to come to agreement rather than seeing the work already done go to waste.[5] Women's suffragists were encouraged in December 1916 when Lloyd George replaced Asquith as Prime Minister. Lloyd George had long been a declared if somewhat shifty friend of women's suffrage, and he was accessible in a way Asquith had never been. But suffragists had reason to know that he was a politician before he was a supporter of any cause, and hopes were tempered by the fact that his Cabinet had a substantial Conservative Unionist component.

Cabinet and parliament did not settle down quietly to await the conference report, but continued their anxious and sometimes angry wrangling meanwhile. Within the Speaker's Conference, four obdurate anti-suffrage Conservative Unionists resigned following Lloyd George's rise – one to take government office, the other three because they saw the conference as moving in too radical a direction and hoped that their resignations would wreck it. In the event the opposite occurred; agreement was easier to reach with more open-minded replacements chosen by Lowther.[6]

Meanwhile suffrage advocates necessarily engaged in a game of second-guessing the best chance for the women. Each organization and group evaluated strategies according to its own priorities, and all were forced to weigh the ideal (as each saw it) against the possible, the possible against the probable. Would a show of strength behind an uncompromising demand for adult suffrage convince the conference and ultimately parliament of its inevitability? Or would it prove fatal to the enactment of even a small concession? Was a readiness, on the other hand, to settle for a narrow female franchise the only way to obtain that vital breakthrough? Was a restricted female franchise, in fact, a satisfactory solution? Who would be the key players? How could they be influenced? And, crucial to the adultists, how much unity could be brought to bear behind a truly democratic suffrage?

If the more influential suffrage leaders were in agreement about anything, it was that care must be taken to avoid any militancy or aggressive demonstrations that would once more give lukewarm suffrage supporters an excuse to declare women unfit to exercise the franchise. The relative docility of Sylvia Pankhurst made this easier. The lack of interest shown by Emmeline and Christabel Pankhurst was also fortuitous. The former was in the USA from January to August 1916, and the latter in Paris until early 1917. More importantly, when in Britain both were now primarily occupied in whatever they saw as best furthering the war effort, whether by attacking Asquith for weak leadership or by rousing industrial workers to greater efforts. When Emmeline did first re-engage with the suffrage issue it was to have a supporter declare in the House of Commons that the WSPU would not press the women's vote at any risk to that of the serving men, a threat that she had chosen to read into Asquith's obscure statement of August 18 1916.[7]

While the Speaker's Conference did its work suffragists could only do their best – often with little but rumour to guide them – to canvass support among parliamentarians of both houses for what they hoped to see in the report and in ensuing legislation, consulting among themselves and their parliamentary sympathizers, and when possible with members of the conference. However decorous the renewed suffrage lobbying might be, a great deal of it went on. At times, the consultations brought together those bitterly estranged from each other. In December 1916 a small private meeting took place at Sir John Simon's house, attended by Simon and W.H. Dickinson (both members of the Speaker's conference). The gathering was small and informal but the four guests, Fawcett, Courtney, Mary Macarthur and Henry Nevinson could provide between them some sampling of opinion in the NU and the CCCWSS, the WIL and the NCAS, the WTUL and the WNC. The Speaker's conference was just about to take up the question of women's suffrage, but so far no details had yet been discussed and they wanted to be prepared. Fawcett's report, the only one we have, suggests that the discussion centred on how to give the vote to women – but not too many women. Fawcett thought there was 'a general agreement that raising the voting age for women was the least objectionable way of reducing the number of women.'[8] But the other guests are unlikely at this stage to have conceded that hope of an equal franchise should be given up.

Reaction to the conference report

The Speaker's Conference released its report early in January 1917. To the credit of the participants, what emerged was not a series of vague suggestions, but a set of concrete proposals, ready to be formed into legislation. Unanimity had been reached on registration, the male franchise, redistribution of seats, university representation, methods and costs of elections, the local government franchise, and the rights of soldiers and sailors. The women's vote was the most significant of the issues which had failed to gain unanimous support and so had had to be decided by a majority; the proposal approved was to allow the vote to any woman who was on the local government register or whose husband was on it, with a suggested minimum age of thirty or thirty-five.[9]

Was the glass half full or half empty? The conference report brought the gap between the traditional and the democratic suffragists into sharp focus. The NU executive and with it the CCCWSS rapidly made up their minds to accept the half full glass with gratitude; the NCAS continued to claim a longer draught. All knew that the glass was not yet placed firmly on the table.

Response of the adult suffragists

Before the Speaker's report was issued the NCAS, besides keeping in touch with politicians, had worked to educate its own constituency and raise women's awareness of the importance of the franchise – for instance issuing a series of leaflets drawing attention to the power of the vote to better conditions for women workers, trade unionists and families. They continued to work with their wide coalition of working women's groups and when the Speaker's Conference reported they paid attention to those who would be omitted under its proposals.

Initially the leaders of the CCCWSS and the NCAS hoped to find common ground in their response to the Speaker's report. Courtney and Marshall met separately with Ray Strachey during the first week of

February. Strachey, they found, 'deprecated [the] "extremist" line, [and was] inclined to take what was offered and not risk losing that by asking for more', but they agreed that it would be useful to have a joint meeting of suffrage and other women's organizations as soon as the bill was tabled; Marshall reported that Strachey even conceded 'that all possible pressure should be brought to bear *before the introduction of the bill* to improve on the Speaker's report.'[10]

The exchanges seem to have been cordial; Strachey shared with Marshall that she had learnt that McCallum Scott and Harcourt (both previously hard-line anti-suffragists) were no longer strongly opposed. She also reported that 'she had heard that the Conference had definitely endorsed 35 as the age for women to vote, and that the Speaker had added "or 30" on his own account, because when he saw it in type the 35 looked so ridiculous!'.[11] Marshall may have tried to interest Strachey in her thinking on the special role the NU might play in making a case for 'the patriotic claims of young war widows, young professional women (teachers, doctors, nurses, V.A.D.s) ... young Industrial women, who will be particularly affected by reconstructive legislation ... munition workers, and war workers generally', all categories largely excluded by the age clause, all categories which might be seen as within the NU's bailiwick.[12] Indeed, a day or two after her meeting with Marshall, Strachey wrote to Dickinson, pressing the need of the unmarried woman worker for the vote, and questioning the age clause.[13]

The WIL leaders were clear in their own minds that WIL was a suffrage organization. But they knew that its role in campaigning for peace might be a disadvantage in public relations. The pacifist focus, while drawing in many dissidents, caused the organization to be seen as a questionable ally by some politicians and some suffragists; WIL publicly kept a fairly low profile within the NCAS once it was established, although the WIL leaders conducted much of its work.

At a personal level Marshall in particular felt that she laboured under a similar disability in a more acute form. While the NCF was never an illegal organization, its activities were seen as subversive, some of its publications were seized, its premises were raided, and its members were repeatedly court-martialled and re-imprisoned for refusing to obey military orders. Fearful that her connection with conscientious objectors would be used to taint WIL's suffrage activity, Marshall resigned office in all suffrage organizations some time in January or early February 1917.[14] However, neither the fear of lessening the credibility of WIL and the NCAS nor her own excessively full schedule prevented her from throwing herself into the suffrage campaign in line with the policies and indeed on behalf of those two organizations. The respect she commanded – her personal political capital – remained remarkably high; even without the formal structure of such an organization as the NU had been, and despite the NCF connection, influential politicians would meet with her, sometimes at her request, sometimes at theirs.[15]

Although the NCAS had been founded on the clear-cut principle of full adult suffrage, the executive and constituent organizations were not agreed on whether this was still a realistic objective; some were understandably very reluctant to give it up, particularly in light of the franchise proposed for all men over 21 on a simple short residency. The NCAS executive discussed the need to decide whether to stand out for full adult suffrage or whether to move towards some compromise that would enable them to cooperate with other suffrage organizations; they gave thought to alternative solutions. They recognized the 'prejudice and fear' behind the felt need to keep down the number of women voters, seeing it as 'a real factor ... to be reckoned with' and looked at alternative ways of working around it.[16]

The NCAS leaders carried their message to politicians of all parties. During February and March Marshall met with (among others) Henderson, Dickinson, Lord Robert Cecil, Hugh Law (of the Irish Party), Lloyd George, Asquith, Bonar Law, Sir John Simon, and Lord Lytton. Marshall's notes show that a number of those she talked with believed that 'it was a question of take or leave the Speaker's Conf[erence] report' and that any attempt at change would open up all the old controversies and be fatal. The NCAS leaders nevertheless invited consideration of some change in the basis that might perhaps reduce the number of new voters instead of specifically the number of women.[17]

The decision to include women had carried in the Conference by fifteen to six, the decision not to enfranchise women equally with men had carried by twelve to ten, the proposal to enfranchise women 'occupiers' or the wives of occupiers by a bare nine to eight, leading to the further limitation of the proposal by the age clause. But the makeup of the Conference had been planned to balance opinion rather than to represent parliamentary views proportionately; there was no need to assume that voting in the Commons would follow the same pattern. Although many seem to have taken the close figures as a warning, Simon was prepared to advise suffragists that change could be hoped for.

Simon shows up as the most supportive of all the politicians. Despite his personal experience of the difficulties that had surrounded the women's franchise in the Speaker's Conference, he clearly thought and hoped that there was a real possibility of improving on the conference proposals. He would have liked to avoid the demeaning age inequality; he favoured setting a higher age than 21 for both men and women. Simon repeatedly affirmed his agreement 'with those who say "if this is such a great opportunity don't let's be cowardly about it, let us go forward with spirit"', and urged suffragists to 'take as courageous a course as you think wise', though he cautioned, on tactical grounds, against giving opportunity for criticism by suggesting too complicated a measure or by visible dissension among suffragists. He reminded his hearers that the choice between the proposals as they stood and full adult suffrage was not the only one; they could look for something better than the present plan but avoid raising the full force of opposition to adult suffrage.[18] It was he, too, who made sure that WIL and the NCAS were included in formal or informal consultations along with the more compliant NU and CCCWSS.

Response of the Labour Party

If Simon's response was almost more than could have been hoped for, Henderson's was the reverse. An interview with him on 9 February convinced Marshall that 'the Labour Party are in a great fright about ... jeopardizing the chances ... by raising any contentious issues ... of (a) getting a bill introduced (b) getting such a bill pressed through', and that they were not prepared to insist on any guarantee 'that we shall not be thrown overboard to lighten the ship'.[19] Henderson, distracted by many things, may have been – as we have seen – the first to offer the age discrimination solution to the cabinet and to the Speaker's conference, and he is not known to have given thought to the implications of the property clause. He now rushed to celebrate the conference report alongside the NU, with scant regard for the views of the NCAS, which represented many working women and might have been thought to be more representative of Labour's constituency.

Marshall was justified in her fear that the Labour Party might not come through for the adultists. The Parliamentary Labour Party, salivating at the breadth of manhood suffrage spread before them, fearful of having it snatched away from them, and (for those who gave it a second thought) absolved of any feeling of guilt by the NU's apparent gratitude for a place at the table – even if below the salt – quickly pledged their support. The leaders of the NU and of the Labour Party had already jointly held a celebratory 'Women Workers' Demonstration' at the Queens' Hall.

On 20 March 1917 the Labour Party held a special suffrage conference, attended by representatives of all sections of the party, by the
Women's Labour League (WLL) and by women's industrial organizations. The resolution approved affirmed that the conference, 'while
adhering to its repeated demands for complete adult suffrage ... wel-
comes the efforts made by the Speaker's Conference ... it is of opinion
that the Parliamentary Labour Party should support the recommendations of the Speaker's Conference, providing that the enfranchisement
of women is agreed to, and calls for immediate legislation on the general lines of the Report.' An addendum moved by the National Federation of Women Workers was approved, reading, 'This Conference
further requests the Parliamentary Labour Party to secure the inclusion
of women on the broadest possible basis, and especially to ensure that
the bulk of wage-earning women are not excluded from any Franchise
measure'.[20] The women's organizations had got their word in. Yet the
amended resolution was misleading and self-contradictory, and was
certainly read by the Parliamentary Labour Party as stopping short of
committing it to making a stand for anything more than the Speaker's
Conference proposals, which excluded most women wage-earners.

Robert Smillie for the Miners' Federation and Mary Macarthur of the
WTUL, the WNC, and the NCAS introduced an amendment to support
a new franchise only if women were included on the same terms as
men. The amendment was defeated 'after a long and animated discussion', and those casting their votes against it included the WLL, a body
whose mission from the outset (1906) had included working to widen
the franchise for men and for women. Since 1912 the WLL had
identified itself with full adult suffrage, but had now evidently allowed
itself to be persuaded that the proffered manhood suffrage, together
with an instalment of woman suffrage would be put at risk by maintaining their stand for adult suffrage.[21]

Response of the NUWSS

The willingness to examine the Speaker's recommendations critically
that Strachey had seemed to show in private meetings with NCAS
leaders in early February did not make its way into NU public policy.
As soon as the Speaker's Conference report was out, the NU officers –
like the NCAS – met with parliamentarians and government members.
Unlike the NCAS, they do not seem at this stage to have carried with
them any wish list from their constituency, but rather went to find out
what was likely to be acceptable. A subtle difference in style can be

seen between the WIL and the NU, underlying and effectively reinforcing the palpable difference in goals. Caroline Marshall had put her
finger on the difference in a letter to her daughter early on in the
renewed suffrage campaign. An officer of the Northwest Federation had
told Mrs Marshall complacently that 'The NU have Cabinet advice for
all they are doing', in response to which Caroline said she had 'asked
who had advised the Cabinet'? When meeting with politicians as the
NU's parliamentary secretary before the war, Catherine Marshall, though
seeking information and willing to receive advice, had also always
looked for a real dialogue in which she would make the hopes of her
constituency known and frequently would draw attention to the likely
political consequences of some contemplated action.[22]

Lloyd George had a great many other things on his mind besides
franchise reform, but it is hard to imagine that calling a general election on the old register, with no attempt made to follow up on the
Speaker's Conference report, would have been welcome except to
the most difficult of his new Unionist allies, and even they were torn
between their dislike of Lloyd George and their feeling that he was the
man who could win the war. However, Lloyd George did consider
the idea and meanwhile made good use of the carrot of the advances
suggested in the report and the stick of the threat of a general election,
hinting at the options to members of parliament, the government,
the public and even the press, all to help ensure that if a Bill were
introduced it would have the easiest ride possible both in and out of
parliament.

The officers of the NU were flattered by top-level secret consultations, frightened by the threat of losing the measure altogether, and
hustled on by a spurious urgency. Within two weeks they reported to
the NU societies. Taking advice from 'one of our best friends in the
House of Commons' Fawcett and Strachey had 'interviewed two members
of the War Council and seven members of the government', both suffragists and antis, as well as other MPs. The advice they received was
'practically unanimous'. The government, they were told, would not be
able to introduce a bill which did not include women, but would introduce no bill at all unless it was assured of 'practical unanimity in the
House and little opposition in the country', and would instead opt for
an immediate general election on the old register. Women's suffrage
on the lines proposed by the Speaker's Conference 'with a possible
modification of the age limit' was 'the only form likely to be acceptable
to all parties', including 'moderate anti-suffragists ... but it is quite
certain that the proposals embody the maximum measure which they

would support', while those who wanted a broader measure would be content to take this as an instalment.[23]

Decisions were easy to make in a body so close to homogeneous, and the executive's letter to branches in effect announced a major policy change, an abrogation of the commitment to work for the vote for women 'on the same terms as is or may be held by men', although it did not announce it in such terms. The executive's decision was made on government advice without consulting its constituency, and was followed up by immediately publicizing the policy – all this despite the fact that an annual council was scheduled for later in February. The process invites comparison with the scruples exhibited by the 1914 executive in responding to the war emergency.[24]

On 12 February the NU executive passed a resolution:

> That the Executive Committee of the N.U.W.S.S, recognising that a Bill based on the recommendations of the Speaker's Conference will confer the Suffrage upon women, even though not upon the terms for which they stand, determines that if no wider measure of Women's Suffrage can be secured they will support the proposals of the Speaker's Conference and they urge the Government to introduce a Bill embodying the general lines of those recommendations without delay.

The NU executive took the resolution forward to the CCCWSS the following day, where it was approved with the addition of a clause urging that the enfranchisement of women be an integral part of the Bill; it was agreed to send the resolution to the government and to members of both Houses. The letter to branches went on to emphasize that the account of what had happened 'is of a *most* private nature, as it embodies opinions received in strict confidence' (though the letter attaches no names to the opinions, and the NU officers were hardly the only people to know of the general election rumour), and concludes with an admonition to prepare deputations and representations to MPs but not to proceed with them until the Bill is introduced, since 'agitation of any widespread nature on ... Women's Suffrage is only likely to be harmful and to cause the opposition to crystalise [sic].' Added is a particular warning against approaching 'newly-converted or anti-suffragist members ... unless it can be done *through their personal friends.*'[25]

It was a curious letter, and some of the less compliant members did not receive it well. Rathbone had already objected because most of the women munitions workers would be shut out from the franchise.[26] Mrs Thoday, honorary secretary of the Manchester and District Federation of the NU, herself elected in 1916, and now one of the few dissenting members of the NU executive, held that nothing:

> short of immediate political necessity could have justified us passing such a resolution so near a Council. The political necessity we did believe existed but it transpired later that we were misinformed. ... I cannot see that we gained any *advantage* by passing it. We were told by Sir John Simon to be *sagacious and courageous* to welcome the affirmation of the principle and leave ourselves free to work for a wider measure. By saying that if we get nothing better we will *support* (not even *accept*) these recommendations we make the likelihood of a wider measure less. We *may* have secured a few Conservative votes ... I think we have turned our back on the Industrial women and by this have lost much support from Liberal and Labour.[27]

Action at the NU Council (21–23 February 1917) was confusing, but resulted in opening the door to a slightly more proactive stand by the NU. An executive resolution, not identical to the one previously circulated, was approved; the promise of support had been dropped out and the focus was to urge the government to introduce a Bill without delay, 'provided that it contain as an integral part provision for the enfranchisement of women'. An urgency resolution to broaden what was being asked for was moved by George Armstrong. Mrs Thoday and Courtney were among those who spoke in favour.[28] The Urgency Resolution which emerged and (after some amendment) was approved read:

> That this Council, while welcoming the finding of the Speaker's Conference on the principle of Women's Suffrage, notes that the age limit for women voters has not been definitely specified and records its opinion that in any legislation based on the recommendations of the Speaker's Conference the specified age should be such as to include the younger industrial women and the widows of sailors and soldiers left by the war, heads of unrepresented households, who are mainly excluded by the recommendations as they stand. Further, that the Executive Committee endeavour to obtain the best terms possible so far as seems consistent with not endangering the passing of the Bill.

This was a substantial improvement on the direction taken earlier by the executive, and reflects a lingering taste for democratic suffragism in the NU's wider constituency, but it was of course dependent on the executive for implementation, and they had already publicly and privately made known on behalf of the NU their willingness to support the Speaker's Conference proposals. In their public pronouncements more continued to be heard of support than of any effort towards a wider or revised basis for the franchise. Inexplicably, Fawcett began to claim from about this time that the NU was pledged to acceptance of the Bill and could not honourably promote any change, a position hard to find in the Council resolutions. In an article in the March *Contemporary Review*, Fawcett also wrote that there was a general feeling that women should accept the Speaker's Conference recommendations 'not with mere acquiescence, but with joy'.[29]

A Bill in sight

By the clarity of its proposals, the Speaker's Conference report had facilitated the introduction of legislation. But substantial Conservative resistance to broadening the franchise, and in particular to women's suffrage, delayed for two more months any decision even to introduce legislation. Although Conservative opinion was divided, numerically significant antagonism to the conference proposals was shown among Conservative MPs.[30] Within the Cabinet, the fact of coalition government ensured that a mere parliamentary majority would not suffice, since Cabinet unity behind a government bill was important, and anti-reformers were adamant in their opposition; the Cabinet in effect was deadlocked.

The impasse was finally broken by the device (at Asquith's initiative) of introducing a motion in the House of Commons in late March 1917 in support of the Speaker's Report, which would enable the bill to go forward as a House of Commons bill rather than a government bill. Learning of Asquith's decision, Marshall wrote:

> The fact that Mr Asquith is going to move a resolution, and that his group are so keen to get an electoral reform bill passed without delay, coupled with the fact that they all admit that no bill can pass without at least some women in it puts us in a strong position for pressing for something better than the Conference recommendations so far as women are concerned, – or rather would have put us in a strong position if the National Union and other bodies had not taken such a pusilanimous [sic] line from the first.

It remains to be seen how much harm they have done. I greatly fear that they on the one side, and the Adultists who want to oppose anything short of perfection on the other, will play into the hands of Bonar Law and company who are anxious for an excuse for doing nothing and having an election on the present register.[31]

Asquith was indeed playing an unexpected role and contributing positively to the women's cause; his motives may well have been questionable, but the result was critical. Marshall commented that he 'seems to have done really handsomely' and was pleased that he attributed his forward step to the need for women's participation in after-war reconstruction, 'and not to any newly established deserts owing to war work'.[32] And he seems to have credited Marshall with remarkable knowledge, rather bizarrely turning to her to provide him with 'figures showing the numbers of women who would be enfranchised if the age for enfranchisement were 35, 30, 25, and 21 respectively'. She did her best to comply, but since the figures would be based on a register that was not yet in existence, she had to tell him that she was unable to come up with any numbers she would consider valid.[33]

The government would be responsible for framing the legislation, and resistance to Asquith's plan within the Cabinet – which still ostensibly had the option of pressing Asquith into an immediate dissolution – continued until the last moment. The biggest concession to Cabinet anti-reform opinion came regarding the women's suffrage clause; the vote on this would not be backed by the government whips, and should it be defeated, the bill could go ahead without it. So the women's franchise remained vulnerable.[34]

Interlude: Greeting revolution in Russia

Into the middle of all this, while suffragists and politicians in Britain were mincing delicately around each other over the details of parliamentary reform, news came of the Russian Revolution, a dramatic and complete change of regime in one of Britain's allies.[35] As soon as the first news of events in Russia reached England, dissidents, from the opponents of war to the advocates of adult suffrage, reacted with enthusiasm, seeing it as the revolt of the people against militarism and believing briefly that a mass movement to lay down arms and bring power to the people would spread right across Europe. The first statement of the Russian Provisional Government declared, amongst other things, in favour of amnesty for all political and religious offences, freedom of speech and press, freedom to form unions and to strike, extension of these liberties to the army as far as possible, and the adoption of universal suffrage. Further – and of great importance to such as Marshall – the revolution so far had been accomplished by a simple non-violent uprising of the people.

There were ironies in the situation, especially in that the official response was perforce superficially almost as welcoming as that of the dissidents because the government was desperate to maintain the Russian alliance and keep the Russians fighting on Germany's eastern front. However much the Cabinet may have feared the outcome of the revolution they found it imperative to try to establish cordial relations with the new regime and dared do nothing to curb the exuberance with which the revolution was welcomed by a large segment of the British public, including the war weary and some who were genuinely pleased to be free of the embarrassing link with the Tzarist regime. The NUWSS sent restrained congratulations.[36]

Under her NCF hat rather than under her suffragist hat, though with the support of WIL leaders, Marshall took a major part in organizing the Charter of Freedom campaign to welcome the change in Russia and to demand that the British government emulate it. The climactic event was a sold-out mass public meeting at the Albert Hall, sponsored by a wide spectrum of left labour groups, and held on 31 March 1917. George Lansbury chaired the gathering; Lord Parmoor gave his support in money and words. Speakers included Nevinson, Smillie, Royden, Wedgwood, and Zangwill; Swanwick joined Marshall on the platform, as did Massingham and J.A. Hudson. Pelican Press produced an elegant 12 page programme which included the words of songs for the audience to join in, culminating in the singing of 'The Red Flag'.

Such a display of support was almost overwhelming to those swimming against the current as part of the anti-war movement, who now found themselves surrounded by a crowd cheering for everything they stood for: release of the conscientious objectors, universal suffrage, freedom for Ireland and for India, an end to war. Marshall 'felt simply intoxicated with a sense of freedom and joy and *fruition* – the fruition of all the heroism and sacrifice and suffering that has been preparing for this miracle in Russia.'[37] Positive public response to the Russian revolution may have had little to do with Russia, but it was an outlet for pent-up feelings of frustration with wartime restrictions, erosion of liberties, militarism, endless and increasing casualty lists. The extent and enthusiasm of the response sheds a brief flash of light on the width of unfocused disaffection among the British public after three and a half years of war, and on an unarticulated longing for something different.[38]

The idealistic revolutionary fervour of the early days never found a concrete channel to effect significant change in Britain, and had little direct impact on the suffrage campaign. But it may have increased the level of self discipline required from democratic suffragists to continue their efforts to win some improvement in the terms of the franchise Bill in a discouraging time.

Suffragists work for a limited objective

All this revolutionary fervour came just when most adultists were having to accept the need for compromise. Events since the middle of March had been in effect definitive. The Labour Party's decision to accept what was offered, together with the compliance of the NU, had drawn stark attention to WIL's lack of a power base, and showed that the many working women whose organizations made up the NCAS had no politically potent support behind them. Even earlier WIL and the NCAS had had to accept that the usefulness of campaigning for full adult suffrage might be at an end. The NCAS Council held at the beginning of March, while reaffirming that adult suffrage 'is the only ultimate solution of the franchise question' acknowledged both that the Speaker's Conference proposals were a real advance, and that a Bill would only pass if it commanded general agreement. The NCAS resolved to continue to press for a franchise to include working women and war widows, but tacitly acknowledged that adult suffrage might not be within its grasp. The WSF, represented by Sylvia Pankhurst, continued to stand out for nothing short of full suffrage and withdrew from the NCAS.

By the end of March WIL was ready to join with the NU in simply lobbying to make sure the women's clause stayed in the Bill and passed, while keeping alert for any opportunity to widen the franchise. By this time, too, the NU was ready to receive them back into the fold and although Fawcett would remain 'fearsome about pacifists',[39] we find the two groups gingerly working alongside each other. When WIL convened yet another 'Great Mass Meeting' for the night before the debate on Asquith's motion, the NU agreed to cooperate – although unofficially – in response to an invitation taken to the NU office in person by Isabella Ford. The gathering was advertised by flyers headed 'England Can Do Better' that read in part 'Russia in war time, by revolution, has enfranchised her people, and our Parliament, with the democracies of the whole world, acclaim her. Let England do better and grant immediately a popular franchise for her women as well as her men by constitutional reform.' The leaflet refers to the organizations which had presented the Memorial on 20 February (from the 17 February CCCWSS conference) and to the Labour Party Conference; its banner line reads 'All these support the General Lines of the Speaker's Conference Report, and call for Votes for Women on the widest possible basis'.[40]

The debate on Asquith's motion took place on 28 March, and its acceptance in the Commons was unequivocal, far beyond expectations. Henderson had told Ray Strachey a few days earlier that 'he thought that if there were a majority of fifty or sixty on Mr Asquith's resolution the Government would proceed with it'.[41] Clearly he hoped for at least that margin, but he was far from predicting that it would be approved by 341 votes to 62.

Now that the way was cleared to go ahead with legislation several politicians again took the initiative in meeting with suffragists, although often less in order to hear their hopes than to lecture them on the course they should follow. Lloyd George had already agreed to meet with a large deputation, and in part he dictated its makeup to the NU; he wanted to meet with representatives from all the women's suffrage societies at once, including the Scottish and Irish groups. He particularly named Mrs Pankhurst and although Fawcett and most of the participants disliked the idea, they accepted her presence – but not as part of the official delegation. Fawcett agreed to introduce the deputation. Ray Strachey, who arranged the details with Lloyd George's secretary, declined to include the Workers' Suffrage Federation (Sylvia Pankhurst's organization, the renamed East London Federation of Suffragettes), on the grounds that their objectives were different. She does not seem to have refused to include WIL, but apparently simply did not invite them. Swanwick, who had long had an intense dislike of Lloyd George, wrote to Marshall: 'I heard this morning that the deputation to Ll G was being arranged by the NU and that they didn't want us. Also that the little scoundrel had insisted that "Mrs Pankhurst should be present" !! Do you suppose she will sit at his right hand? It really is monstrous and I'm glad we are not invited.'[42] Lloyd George took the occasion to reinforce his message that the suffragists must accept the compromise embodied in the Speaker's conference report rather than risk defeat.

Now that a Bill was almost assured the NU executive watched events eagerly, and canvassed with energy and efficiency through its own branches and through the women's party organizations, doing its best to keep suffragist MPs up to the mark, to convert or disarm anti-suffragists, and to deepen public support. A pre-war practice was revived to good effect; branches surveyed the opinions of their local MPs, asking them to commit themselves to vote for the women's clause. Constituency pressure was invoked wherever it might prove useful. A Consultative Committee of women suffragists and MPs was set up, at the suggestion of the NU and with the help of Simon, who may again have been the one responsible for seeing that the NCAS and WIL were offered representation; the NU executive was anxious to keep as much control as possible over who would represent women on the Committee.[43]

Millicent Fawcett and Ray Strachey tirelessly met with politicians. Strachey particularly sought out conservative MPs and peers, also reaching some through their wives; on record are meetings with Steel Maitland, Lady Selborne, Runciman, Lady Brassey, and Lord Robert Cecil, among others. The Lords were feared as a stumbling block in the path to women's suffrage because of the preponderance of Unionists in the upper house and because of the presence there of some most vocal and active anti-suffragists, notably Lord Curzon. Nevertheless, women suffragists had always had a number of active and influential supporters among the peers, including some Unionists, and because it was part of so large a measure the clause in the new Bill presented a more complex issue than would have been seen in a simple female suffrage bill, and could not be dismissed by the Lords without consequence.[44]

Ironically, despite Fawcett's aversion to having anything to do with Mrs Pankhurst, Strachey and Fawcett apparently did not hesitate to use the threat of militancy (presumably to be, deplorably, committed by others) whenever they thought it might be effective.[45] The WSPU itself played a minimal role in the final stage of the campaign, and avoided any hint of renewed militancy. Emmeline Pankhurst had difficulty accepting that the hated Asquith could now be helping the cause; she was more supportive of Lloyd George, whom she saw as running the war more competently. The WSPU, however, held a rally on 18 April at which Mrs Pankhurst, said Rathbone, 'made a good women's suffrage speech and there was no indication that she contemplated resuming militant methods'.[46]

While the NU's lobbying was extensive, its objective remained circumscribed by caution and an almost superstitious devotion to the terms in the Speaker's Conference report, despite Simon's earlier repeated assurance that they were not set in stone. While the Bill was still being drafted George Armstrong requested that the Council resolution asking to have the age for women to vote set to include young women workers and war widows be forwarded to suffragist MPs. What came out was almost a reversal of the intent of the Council resolution – and of Armstrong – and in effect closed the door to any need for the drafters of the Bill to consider admitting younger women voters. Instead of sending the text of the resolution to MPs as Armstrong had asked a letter went to members of the Cabinet (on a motion from Strachey and Rathbone) saying that the executive 'understand that the proposals ... in the Electoral Reform Bill must necessarily contain the age limit of 30 or 35. They urge strongly that 30 rather than 35 should be inserted and desire to point out that otherwise the majority of industrial women and war widows will be excluded.'[47]

At the same executive meeting Rathbone took up another issue of particular interest to her – and in turn quickly found herself the victim of the NU's timidity. She drew attention to an anomaly in the Speaker's Conference recommendations regarding the local government franchise. The rather small group of women who qualified in their own right as occupiers of property had already gained the municipal vote before the war; now it was proposed to grant the parliamentary franchise to wives of occupiers, but the Speaker's conference did not propose also to extend the local vote to wives. Rathbone saw an immense potential for good in enabling married working women to influence municipal politics, which so closely affected their lives. She brought her concern to the NU executive after sounding out several parliamentarians. Dickinson had told her he had long had the need in mind and 'that women might begin to agitate for it at once' with a view to having the improvement made in the Bill or by amendment, though at that time he did not know what form the clause relating to local government might take. Sir George Cave (then in charge of the Bill for the government) had been firm that the Bill would be drafted on the lines of the Speaker's report. At Fawcett's suggestion Rathbone had also approached Mrs Humphry Ward, the leading woman anti-suffragist, who had always supported the women's franchise in municipal government (seeing it as an appropriate extension of women's domestic function) but Ward's response had suggested that she had some hope of trading a wider local vote against the women's parliamentary vote; Rathbone had quickly backed off. After discussion the executive came down again on the side of caution, resolving 'That, while appreciating the importance of the point raised, this Committee consider that it is for the present inadvisable to move in it.'[48]

The Bill before Parliament

The Reform Bill that was introduced in mid-May contained no surprises. It passed second reading that month by 329:40, and on 6 June went into Committee, the stage at which it was open to attack by clause by clause amendment, before it again came up for a vote on the whole.

The situation in the House of Commons was unusually complex and hard to read. The Unionists in the Cabinet reluctantly supported the Bill, the Unionist Parliamentary Party opposed it, seeing it as bringing them nothing but electoral disadvantage, but could not carry with them all their members; many Unionists would swallow the wider male suffrage in order to see the soldiers enfranchised. The Asquithian Liberals were divided and in disarray, lacking leadership since Asquith largely withdrew after his one effective action in making sure a Bill did reach parliament; they had little trust for Lloyd George. Lloyd George wanted the Bill to go through; he had some enemies and some followers in all parties. In particular many saw him as the man who could win the war. The Irish Nationalists had their own fish to fry, and were concerned mainly with the clauses directly affecting them. Their support for the women's suffrage clause was hoped for, but some suffragists (the NU among them) held back from pressing to have the government put its whips behind the women's clause because they feared that hostility to the government would cause Nationalists to vote against it just because it had government support.[49] Party leaders issued whips, but the rate of observance was lower than usual. The Labour Party showed scarcely any interest – except for some ILP faithfuls – especially after Henderson was forced out of the Cabinet in August; Labour expected good things from the new franchise, but was occupied with other matters of moment outside the Commons, especially with developing a new and challenging party programme. A significant number of MPs were absent on military service, particularly from among the Unionists, but also for several months including Sir John Simon.

Although these factors made accurate numerical predictions difficult and served to maintain the tension among suffragists, it is hard to see that the extent of their anxiety really had justification. Not only had voting on Asquith's motion and the second reading been highly favourable, but the Commons of 1917 was not an unfamiliar body. Part of the NU's stellar pre-war political groundwork had been the painstaking conversion of MPs, one by one, leading to a majority of declared suffragists among MPs. The parliament of 1917 may have been ragged and party structures somewhat disorganized, but it was still the parliament that had been elected in 1910. For many MPs their vote for the 1917 suffrage clause marked at least the second time they had so voted, and a considerable number had been part of a majority voting for one or other earlier bill that had not been given facilities to proceed.[50]

In 1917 reasons and rationalizations for supporting the women's clause abounded, ranging from the cessation of militancy and approval of women's war work, to the feeling that it was no longer an unfamiliar idea and should be settled. Even in the political context there were surely more not fewer reasons to support women's suffrage than there had been before the war. Concern over how the new electors would vote was present but once it was clear that some women would almost certainly get the vote that fear might be in part balanced, as it was in relation to the new male electorate, by the bandwagon effect, the wish not to be seen as hostile by the newly enfranchised.

Nevertheless hostile amendments were abundant during the committee stage, emanating mainly from a determined group among the Unionists; they met with a few successes and many failures. Fearing to open the door even a crack, the government routinely opposed amendments. Divisions were unpredictable, with kaleidoscopic changes in voting patterns from one amendment to another. Many, as Pugh says. 'were inclined to change sides without having altered their opinions'.[51] Such fluidity surely made lobbying worth while. Anti-suffragists made capital of the women's franchise, as if it was this of all issues that would make or break the Bill, but it was a small fish among many small fishes when the Bill was before the House. The clause was in the expected form, with the voting age set at thirty. The outcome was a triumph, with the clause approved by 387 votes to 57, with a majority of those present from every party, even the Unionists, voting for it.

No genuine attempt was made to widen the women's franchise in the direction advocated by the democratic suffragists, although there was one mischievous and embarrassing attempt by opponents to throw out the age specification altogether, in the hope of wrecking the Bill and making it unacceptable if not in the Commons then in the Lords. The attempt was defeated in a lunatic interlude in which confirmed suffragists argued against the amendment and confirmed antis defended the rights of women.

Rathbone, however, had not given up on the local government clause. Failing with the NU executive, she had unsuccessfully tackled the equally reluctant Women's Local Government Society, and more productively had enlisted the help of Sir Charles Roberts, a supportive Liberal MP who in his turn drew in other parliamentary suffragists. Finally, after the extent of cross-party support in the Commons for Roberts's amendment became apparent during the second reading of the Bill the NU came around – followed by the Women's Local Government Society – and brought suffrage societies across the country into the drive, strongly supported by working women's organizations. So overwhelming was 'the flood of letters and telegrams' sent to Cave that he went to the length of withdrawing, in this one instance, the government's formal opposition to any amendment and the amended clause was approved without a division.[52]

The Bill worked its way through the House of Commons through the rest of 1917, to some a ray of light in a gloomy year, to others doubtless an added aggravation. The war dragged on with no end in sight; the Irish independence issue remained unresolved; the US entry into the war in April had brought no immediate relief; shipping losses to German U-boat attacks escalated through the first half of the year (and then gradually diminished with the convoy system); food shortages became pressing and the government failed to implement effective controls; the British army bogged down in the mud and blood of the Passchendaele offensive with heavy casualties and no significant advance; serious discontent rumbled barely below the surface among workers and less visibly within the armed services. No wonder that even a major measure of parliamentary reform was not in the front and centre of everyone's attention, let alone that of the Cabinet. Finally, however, the amendments had all had their chance, and in December the Bill was approved and ready to go to the House of Lords.

All this may be seen as begging the crucial question: how much of the support was dependent on the retention of the narrow basis coming from the Speaker's conference proposals? Some especially among the Unionists doubtless accepted the limited women's vote in the hope that it would stave off a broader measure, even recognizing perhaps that what was offered was satisfactorily class based; respectable married women over thirty might even help balance off the enfranchisement of the unknown young male voters. But Lloyd George's attitude was of primary importance. His power came from the perception of him, widely shared among people and politicians – including some who did not like or trust him – as the only man for the job of saving the country at this time, so he had a great deal of weight to put behind any measure. Although often able to confuse others about the issues, Lloyd

George may have seen this one more clearly than most. What had come from the Speaker's Conference suited him well, sitting as he was on the fence between the Unionists and the tattered Liberal Party. Before the war, some Liberal supporters – notably Lloyd George himself – had favoured a wide measure since the limited extension implicit in granting women the vote 'as is held by men' as it was at that time would have increased the Conservative vote. Now here was a bill that would add a very large body of male voters. No need to add even more to the numbers by a wide enfranchisement of women, especially just at a time when the Labour Party might be in a position to capture much of the new and unpredictable male electorate and perhaps shake off its ties with the Liberals.

However, not all the government's commitment to the conference proposals was necessarily related to their content: what they wanted was to see it go through as easily as possible, and discouraging tinkering seemed the best route to this. Lloyd George and his closest supporters went out of their way to present the Bill as if it must stand or fall as a whole. We have seen how this artificial absolutism was used to bribe and scare both the Labour Party and the women suffragists, and it was effective in seeing the Bill through with minimum changes. But at each stage – Speaker's Conference report, Asquith's resolution, introduction of the Bill, passage of second reading – it had become less and less possible for the government to allow the Bill or even the women's clause to fail, engendering a great deal of ill will and dropping themselves back into the morass of unresolved issues around registration and the franchise. Had there been a drive for a wider women's franchise, it is hard to imagine that the Bill would have been abandoned to keep the women out. Most of the factors that helped carry the Bill through the House of Lords would still have been operative, though the majority might have been reduced. Now that the Bill was before the Lords some of the same reasons as affected the Commons were operative for individual Lords, particularly the more fluffy rationalizations, such as lip service paid to women's work in war time. But concrete factors also contributed to the Lords' acceptance of the Bill, and of the women's clause. Because the Bill had had so large a majority in the Lower House, it was clear that any serious attempt to tamper with it in the Upper House would not be tolerated.

Unionist opposition in both Houses was vitiated by the fact that although many Unionists were hostile on principle to the idea of franchise reform, many opposed this or that part of the Bill for a number of different reasons, and in the same way liked this or that provision.[53]

Parts of the proposed reform, indeed, were much to the taste of a number of peers and Unionists. Nicoletta Gullace has postulated that the war had caused a deep cultural change in gender perception, with service taking the place of actual maleness as the emblem of masculinity and hence of value.[54] While I see this as affecting only a sub-culture, and certainly not as the conclusive factor in women's enfranchisement, the climate of war, as Gullace says, provided a potent language for the claim for the vote, especially (I would suggest) precisely where it could be most useful in weakening opposition to women's enfranchisement, that is among Unionists and in particular Unionist Lords. Correspondingly, it certainly played a role in the lowering of the voting age for soldiers to nineteen, and in the mean-spirited disenfranchisement for five years of conscientious objectors.

Related and equally important perhaps in the acceptance of the whole Bill was a conviction, prevalent among those who had been long-term advocates of compulsory military training even in peace time, that the army experience of the young men conscripted under the Military Service Acts would turn them into well-disciplined conservatives, deferential (if of the working class) and ready for leadership roles (if of the officer class). This rose-coloured picture of the military owed much to pre-war and colonial experience when indeed career soldiers, and especially the officers best known to them (in many cases sitting on the parliamentary benches beside them), were likely to be conservative in thinking and politics. For them, conscription was an overdue and hopeful development,[55] and the acceptance into citizenship of these disciplined young men might, they hoped, offset the dangers of the broad male franchise which had somehow ridden in on the coattails of their original concern to ensure the soldiers' vote.[56]

Had the women's clause barely scraped through in the Commons, opponents in the Upper House might have tried to defeat the clause and retain the Bill; Curzon toyed with the idea of trying to force the government to agree to a referendum on the issue. But the Commons vote had been overwhelming; when the day came for the division in the Lords, Curzon spoke at length of his reasons for opposing women's suffrage, and then declared his intention to abstain, basing his capitulation on the need to avoid serious confrontation with the Commons, which he was well aware might lead to more Upper Chamber reform. The women's clause passed by 134 to 71 on 8 January 1918; the Bill was approved a month later, and became law in March 1918.

For the NU executive, composed much as it might have been eight years earlier, the winning of the vote on terms that would have looked good in 1910 was a cause of unalloyed rejoicing; they had few regrets for those left out. They were right that finally breaking the gender barrier was not a small thing. For the democratic suffragists the last stage of the campaign had brought disappointment and disillusionment; women who had given such leadership before the war had had to stand by without the power to speak for those they had taken as their constituency. Despite this, there were few suffragists who did not join in celebrating the achievement, if some did so with more reserve than others.

12
Conclusions

The story told here has been in many ways a new one, revealing fresh information that may change perceptions of suffrage activity during the war, and raising new questions – many of which we cannot hope to answer. In conclusion I shall examine the reasons for the narrowness of the enfranchisement won by women in 1918, and shall look more speculatively – and also more personally – at a broader view of what may have been lost. Finally, I shall return to the women whose story this has been, giving a brief account of how they pursued their disparate visions after the war was over.

Why did so few women win the vote in 1918?

Historians have increasingly come to recognize that well before the war broke out the time was ripe for some measure of women's suffrage to be enacted in Britain, as was indeed beginning to occur in one after another of the western democracies; New Zealand had set an example as long ago as 1893.[1] Only shifting and inevitably temporary party political considerations, together with the difficulty of enacting a law which had both support and opposition in all parties, were delaying the enactment of some measure. Further, the signs were all pointing to the likelihood that when it came the measure would be a broad one.

Yet by the time the franchise bill was introduced two things were assured. One was indeed that some women would get the vote, but the other was that the women's franchise would be a narrow one. I argue that there should be no surprise at the first of these developments but that the second should not be seen – as it long has been – as having been inevitable from the outset.[2] What should surprise us is not that a women's suffrage clause was included but that the franchise granted was so narrow.

The fact is that no effective attempt was made at any stage to win adult suffrage or even improvements in the women's clause. Yet Simon had encouraged the women to press for betterment and Rathbone had proved that it could be done; her mini-campaign had eventually tapped into the nation-wide networks available to the NU and into significant general goodwill – and had carried all before it. The impression left is that the suffrage societies had been only too glad to have an opportunity to take part in the action, and that a wide public was supportive. Yet no faint shadow of such a campaign was mounted to widen the women's parliamentary franchise.

Although there were significant numbers who cared enough to want a campaign, they had no power to put it in train. Such a movement might have been expected to begin as soon as reform was mooted, to involve democratic suffragists in the Labour Party and in women's organizations, and to put steady pressure on politicians and public to challenge the classist element in the measure as well as the exclusion of the younger women. Swanwick had indeed initiated a campaign through the NCAS – well before the Speaker's Conference was even formed – in some confidence that the democratic forces would rally behind the cause. With a campaign in full swing and drawing in substantial public support, adult suffrage might have been a visible and viable option at every stage from the Speaker's Conference through drafting, discussion, and final approval – and if not full adult suffrage then at least some improvement of the women's clause, reducing the voting age to twenty-five perhaps, or basing the vote on a residential or lodger's qualification, to enfranchise many unmarried women and the less well off.[3]

Between 1910 and 1914 democratic suffragism had become a strong coherent force. Important as was the EFF arrangement, the identity of interest between democratic suffragists in the NU and in the Labour Party had moved beyond an arrangement of mutual political benefit. The NU had reached out to both women and men in all parts of the country to foster a mass movement. Structurally, a highly effective democratic network had been developed, resulting in a lessening of class tension and a real increase of mutual respect between people of different backgrounds who had previously had only a shallow knowledge of each other's lives. Working women's organizations were healthy; although some held back from a close relationship with the NU – preferring to go where adult suffrage was the declared policy – women leaders had come to know and count on each other and together to bring a deepening feminist – but not anti-male – understanding to bear on political and social issues.

At the beginning of the war the depth and the health of the relationship between Labour and the NU had played out in the comfortable personal and organizational interchange shown in the response to the crisis, when common interests were assumed. Relief work had been just naturally carried out by the NU and the WNC with consultation and sharing. Labour had been able to work with proffered NU resources in confidence that NU leaders at the centre and workers at the periphery, whether themselves of the middle or working class, were aware of the care that needed to be taken to avoid classist errors such as thoughtless volunteering. On its side Labour had paid more attention than ever before to the strong and now consciously feminist women who headed up the various Labour and working-class women's organizations.

By the time that the suffrage issue emerged again in 1916 the close relationship between Labour and the democratic suffragists had completely dissipated. The internal transformation of the NU back into a London-based middle-class organization that has been a theme of this book left the NU unresponsive to its remaining northern and working-class members, and with no interest in a broad franchise – but still, as Marshall had predicted, conveniently seen as authorized to speak for a broad constituency.

Those omitted from the franchise by the 1917 Bill included the bulk of women war workers, young widows, and single women of any age (except for the few who owned property or earned enough money to rent unfurnished living accommodation) – groups that included many women who had formed the heart of the NU constituency as it had evolved down to April 1915. Some of these women had their own organizations to speak for them, and these bodies had turned to the NCAS as soon as it was formed, reassured by the familiar names and known politics of its leadership. They rightly recognized it as having inherited the mantle of democratic suffragism; they were joined by the more radical individuals and suffrage groups. But what the democratic suffragists proved manifestly not to have taken with them out of the NU was any share of the prestige and power which had accrued to the NU under their leadership between 1910 and 1914.

Meanwhile the working women and the working women's societies who had joined with the democratic suffragists in NCAS found – unpredictably – that the Labour Party was not there to stand by them. The fear of losing the chance of manhood suffrage by any generosity to the women was an immediate factor but surely the causes went deeper. The change in the relationship between the democratic suffragists and the Labour Party played a role; the pre-war understanding did not carry over when the women left the NU to form WIL. Once manhood suffrage was virtually assured the Labour Party had no need of suffragist support, nor – since the EFF débacle – did they have to acknowledge any debt. The severing of the connection with the NU's former democratic suffragist leaders enabled Labour leaders to avoid receiving unwanted advice; no effective suffrage body was on their backs urging them to help widen the franchise. Instead, the new NU – with whom they had no real affinity – danced with them in celebration of the compromise.

None of this satisfactorily explains the Labour Party's lack of support for the working women, a constituency which might have been expected to vote Labour. Indeed, there is evidence that the middle-class housewives who formed the bulk of the women who did get the vote under the new Act voted conservative in the 1920s – so the party's indifference may have done real harm to its electoral prospects.[4] The reasons for the Labour Party's failure are complicated and go beyond the mandate of this study, but some contributing factors can be suggested.

Not all Labour men wanted women to be altogether equal. Subtle influences which cannot be quantified were at work. Labour men were as subject as others to the irrational fear of the country being run by women, a fear exacerbated by the appalling death rate. Among trade unionists, so painstakingly won over towards the support of equality by the democratic suffragists of the pre-war NU, some had been embittered by wartime experiences with the encroachment of women into the workplace, the loss of jobs to dilution, the loss of protection from conscription by the training of women to fill their places, and even the psychological blow of seeing a new independent spirit in wives and daughters, some of whom were able to earn much better money than previously.

Although before the war the socialist ILP had always led support for women's suffrage within the Labour Party, socialist theory could be turned against the women's cause by enforcing a choice between combating class oppression and combating gender oppression. June Hannam and Karen Hunt's study of socialist women in Britain shows the enduring nature of the tension that peaked at times when it had something to feed on – as it did during the war. The many stresses in the relationship fostered and exacerbated by the war encouraged downright misogyny at some levels, and a return, on the part of some leaders, to an emphasis on the need to choose socialism over feminism. Along with this came a return to the classism implicit in a cultivated mistrust of middle-class women. Harold Smith and Pamela Graves have shown how this played out in the 1920s, when labour women again and again found themselves steered away from working with other feminists to protect or promote their own needs – for instance, in their demand for access to birth control.[5]

Many working women's groups that joined the NCAS were also affiliates of the Labour Party, and some large and potentially effective male Labour bodies were prepared to put their weight behind the women's cause, notably Robert Smillie and the Miners Federation. But women labour leaders were also becoming aware of fresh gender tension and did not choose to force a conflict they could not win. When first the Parliamentary Labour Party and then the special party congress called at the end of March 1917 pledged support for the limited measure, most of the women's groups too came in – how willingly we hardly know – behind Labour's support for the Speaker's Conference proposals. The NCAS and the women it stood for had to accept that there was no power base left to them. As we have seen, it was at this point that the democratic suffragists mostly went along reluctantly with the NU's limited objective of merely monitoring the passage of the limited measure through parliament.

Beyond the franchise

The loss went deeper than can be seen by simply depicting the failure of suffragists and labour to work together for a broad female franchise in 1917. After all, the full franchise was only withheld for another ten years, albeit a critical decade. I have drawn attention to the potential of the pre-war connection between the NU and not only the Labour Party but also working men and women, and shown how the deliberate destruction of this connection left a gap where there could have been a powerful alliance. It may be unrealistic to suppose that had they retained control of the NU the democratic suffragists could have prevented the growth of ill-feeling fed by so many factors, but had the suffragists been visibly positioned – and active – on the side of fair dealings for both women and men, and between women and men, they might have kept the door open a crack for the sense of trust and the vision that had been building before the war.

The Labour Party, which shows up rather poorly in my brief sketch of its indifference to the women's claim, was in fact in 1917 entering into what was in many ways a very positive stage of development. At the beginning of the war there had been serious disagreement within the party, with the ILP taking an anti-war stance and the rest of the party pledging support to the war effort, where of course workers' cooperation became ever more indispensable. The work of the War Emergency Workers' National Committee had helped prevent an irreparable split. By 1917 Labour could look forward with optimism, gaining strength internally, deriving power from the indispensability to the nation of trade union cooperation, increasing its membership, looking forward to fielding far more candidates in the coming election, and now welcoming the advent of manhood suffrage. One central thing was lacking; the Labour Party had not taken the steps needed to draw in the full participation of women, the very thing the democratic suffragists had been hoping to see in place during the era of reconstruction.

A new Labour Party constitution, a defined domestic policy, and an internationalist foreign policy were all developed in 1917 and 1918.[6] The last of these has particular interest for us. The Russian Revolution had opened up a new perspective, and although the nature of the revolution underwent radical change in Russia, it had helped democratic socialists to envisage a new role for themselves, nationally and internationally. War weariness was widespread. Although their inclusion in Lloyd George's coalition (where Barnes represented Labour after Henderson left) committed the party leadership to supporting the government's policy in relation to the growing industrial unrest, Labour leaders were well aware of growing dissatisfaction with the way the war dragged on and with the government's apparent resistance to any move towards peace.

You did not have to be a pacifist to long for peace in 1917, and Labour was ready to give thought to what would make for a just and lasting peace. Henderson's official contact with re-emerging international socialism had widened his perception of what might be attempted by a party with a claim to speak for the mass of ordinary people, and he and Ramsay Macdonald were able to work together on developing a vision for the future. The Liberal dissidents who had joined with anti-war Labour members to form the core of the UDC were now largely within the Labour fold, and the influence of the UDC charter points on the Labour programme is evident. Cardinal demands were for a League of Nations, an end to secret diplomacy, and disarmament.

The foreign policy programme developed by the Labour Party is full of echoes for a student of the women's attempts, at The Hague in 1915, to give an international voice to what they were sure was the inner will and wisdom of women, and of the common people of both genders who were the victims of wars made by rulers. Here, two years later, were the same things being said, the same programme put forward, although more specific to situations that had developed and more hedged about with caution. Historians have drawn attention to the extent to which the Labour programme anticipated the spirit of Woodrow Wilson's Fourteen Points.[7] Not only were the Fourteen Points even closer to the women's congress resolutions, but Wilson had seen and welcomed those resolutions. Sadly, the Labour Party made little use of the abilities and progressive thinking of the democratic suffragist leaders, many of whom remained in the party all their lives but were called on only for minor roles.

Although women working for peace have often been labelled as believing that their contribution stemmed from a claim of female moral superiority, I have not found this view prevalent among the democratic suffragists of the early Women's International League for Peace (WILPF). What they claimed was experience that differed in some ways from that of men and led to a perspective that was needed beside that of men at every level from municipal through national to international, not only to achieve justice for themselves but to bring the full spectrum of human resources to bear on the problems of living in the world. The Labour Party, for all its high ideals, lost an opportunity to encourage full equality for women in its counsels, and did little to break the male monopoly of decision-making in foreign policy and international affairs. A powerful example of differing male and female experience can be taken from May 1919; while allied statesmen argued about security and the spoils of victory in Paris, WILPF women personally saw not only the suffering of former enemies but more importantly the political opportunity Europe's tragic situation presented for cultivating a climate of peace by directing the resources of the nascent League of Nations towards the supplying of physical needs and the restoration of human rights and social justice.[8] If we accept that the objective of peace making was the declared one of promoting lasting peace, the proposals of the 'idealists' for international cooperation may well have been more realistic and more productive than the policies of statesmen.[9]

What became of the women we know?

This study has brought us close to the lives of some of the women involved on both sides, and will be rounded off by a brief look at what became of them.

Millicent Fawcett's contribution to the winning of the vote had been sustained and real. She had become something of a cult figure by 1915; the LSWS leaders, who knew her very well as an ordinary human being, had occasionally made use of loyalty to her to cut off discussion of issues. But even the democratic suffragists in the main recognized the passage of the women's clause as a legitimate day of triumph for Fawcett; many sent her warm messages. Fawcett's first vote, in the December 1918 election, was cast enthusiastically for Lloyd George's coalition, not only because she appreciated his role in the advent of women's suffrage, but also because she fully shared the view of him as the man who won the war. Along with the rest of the NU she continued to express appreciation to Henderson and to Labour.

Once the middle-class vote was comfortably in hand, the NU was more vocal in support of extending the vote to working women, but Fawcett did not think it right to make an issue of this immediately; disagreement over this may have contributed to her decision not to stand again as president in January 1919. To the end of her life she was never inactive. She joined with the Inter-Allied Suffragists to try to put the women's case to the treaty-makers at Versailles (see epilogue below), she travelled, she was appointed as one of the first women magistrates; she was in demand as a feminist champion. She wrote her reminiscences, endorsing again the value of the EFF policy but omitting all reference to the contribution of those with whom she had worked so closely from 1910 to 1914. *What I Remember* came out in serial form in 1924 in the *Women's Leader*: this first version finds Fawcett still viewing the women's conference at the Hague in 1915 as 'a bit of German propaganda intended to weaken our resistence [sic]';[10] the phrase was omitted when the book was published. International sisterhood did not come naturally to Fawcett; her refusal to join in appealing against the Allied blockade (while she was still president of the NU) is justly described by Rubinstein as 'harshly unfeeling'.[11]

Eleanor Rathbone succeeded Fawcett as president of what was now the National Union of Societies for Equal Citizenship. Her long career as a feminist and a political and social activist has been well detailed by her biographer, Susan Pedersen. She may be seen as sometimes right and sometimes mistaken in the causes she espoused, but she emerges always as a figure commanding respect and motivated by a profound sense of responsibility; Pedersen's subtitle 'the Politics of Conscience' is well chosen.[12]

Ray Strachey qualified for a vote, presumably by virtue of Oliver's status as a householder; later she herself was a property holder. Ironically, the dynamic, dominant Pippa, unmarried and living with her family, did not.[13] Both continued active in the LSWS, with a major interest in women's employment and economic standing. Ray stood three times – unsuccessfully – as an independent candidate for parliament, and later became secretary to Lady Astor, the first (conservative) MP. Although I have deplored her role during the war, both for its direction and for her methods, she stands out as an original and attractive character in many ways, particularly perhaps in the unselfconscious idiosyncrasies and determined independence of her private life.

Kathleen Courtney was re-elected to the NU executive in March 1918, where she worked congenially with Rathbone for a number of years especially in support of Rathbone's campaign for family endowment. Always preferring hands-on administrative work, she went to Vienna after the war to work with the Friends' Relief Commission. She played an important role in the international work of WILPF, and continued as a supporter of the League of Nations and later of the United Nations.

By the time the Bill was approved in the House of Lords years of stress and a long-standing inability to accept the need to pace herself had caught up with Catherine Marshall; she would not be fit for work again until early in 1919. Clifford Allen was released from prison early in December 1917, himself so ill that the authorities were anxious to avoid having him die in prison, and the two of them struggled through a difficult convalescence together, before they parted – at his wish. Marshall recovered sufficiently to attend WILPF's postwar conference in Zurich. Recurrent severe illness prevented her from reaching her potential, but the archive she left shows her still as a dynamic and powerful personality, working for WILPF in Geneva, attempting to gain nomination as a Labour candidate for parliament, trying to mediate in some conflict situations, and helping Jewish refugees in the 1930s.

Of all the peace women, no one had a sharper awareness of the dangers left by the peace settlement than Helena Swanwick. In herself, she exemplified the awareness and education which in 1915 the peace women had hoped to extend widely through the NU network, and which WIL had only been able to bring to a more limited audience. By the end of the war she had a profound knowledge of the working of international relations. Good will she knew was essential, but it had to be backed realistically with structures and actions that would lessen tensions and gradually lead to more stability. She believed deeply in the need for women to be heard on international issues, but she did not see this sentimentally; they must bring not only a fresh perspective but knowledge. The remarkable critique of peace terms and the League of Nations covenant arrived at by WILPF in 1919 owed much to Swanwick's work, and through the interwar years she continued to study, to speak, to write about the League, disarmament, and ways to move away from the balance of power system that she believed perpetuated hostilities. She remained active through WILPF at the League of Nations in Geneva and at home through the Labour Party and the Union of Democratic Control.

A number of years ago I was one of the first to have the privilege of using the archive of the international section of WILPF when it was transferred from Geneva to the University of Colorado. As I worked my way through the documents, I heard the women again and again putting forward workable correctives to just those very errors that exacerbated the bitterness that encouraged the rise of Nazism, that opened the way to a profit-making armaments race, that failed to solve colonial issues, that stood in the way of an effective League of Nations, that put narrow national self interest before even the minimum cooperation that might have helped move towards the peace that all statesmen professed to want and most common people genuinely desired. Knowing the outcome, I found the tragedy of their inability to make themselves heard where it counted almost unbearable.

Earlier still, I had been just old enough in 1939 and quite sufficiently aware to experience the last fading of the hope that international affairs could turn around towards a true peace without engulfing us in another war. As a teenager I attended a League of Nations Union Summer School in Geneva in August that year, hearing from speakers on all sides and earnestly discussing with idealism but little optimism what might yet be done. Afterwards a few of us spent a week walking in the French Alps with no access to news reports; when we came down from the mountains, we were met by terminal news. We barely reached home in Britain before the war broke out.

13
Epilogue

After some women had won the vote, and the war had come to an end, the story of the constitutional suffrage movement is generally seen as continuing almost seamlessly – although not without tension – in the transformation of the NUWSS into the National Union of Societies for Equal Citizenship (NUSEC). This view takes no account of the sharp change of direction that had taken place in 1915, and ignores the broader vision of democracy which had informed the NU for the years immediately before the outbreak of war; if the transition in 1917–18 was seamless, that in 1915 had marked a sharp break with the pre-war pattern and direction. While the reincarnation in NUSEC was a triumph for good sense and a tribute to the importance that the suffrage movement had had for many women, changed circumstances ensured that it would not become the locus for democratic suffragism.

Although the story of the Women's International League is also available, its continuity with democratic suffragism is seldom remarked. Clearly, WIL's inheritance was only partial; it was not a direct organizational successor to the pre-war NU in the same way as NUSEC was – and had indeed to start from scratch as far as funds and infrastructure went. More importantly it was formed from the beginning as a section of an international body, the Women's International League of Peace and Freedom (formerly the ICWPP), which enhanced its transnational role, but at the same time set limits to its effectiveness as a national feminist group, even, as Alberti has pointed out, preventing it from affiliating to NUSEC.[1] Yet it is a mistake to see democratic suffragism as having simply disappeared after its proponents lost out within the NU to the more conservative suffragism of the LSWS, and lost out in the wider political sphere to the sharp turn of the Labour Party away from the potential of an integrative feminism towards an exclusionary and even patriarchal emphasis on the class struggle.[2]

Feminists and the Peace Settlement

Democratic suffragism before the war had been characterized by two outstanding features. The first of these was the remarkable group of women who had comprised its leadership. After the war, suffragists were faced with the challenge of choice between a multiplicity of feminist causes. In common with others, those who had supported the Hague Conference now found themselves free to work on a variety of social and political issues from postwar relief to party political work. In the main, the issues were not in themselves divisive – there were many good feminist demands to be made – but they did result in a dissipation of feminist energy across a wide field.[3]

WIL's purposes from the start had had a focus beyond the war, looking to the time of peace making and postwar international relations, so it should not be surprising that its founding leaders showed a high degree of loyalty to WIL, many remaining as officers or board members to carry it forward. Those remaining active included Swanwick, Marshall, Courtney, Royden, Emmeline Pethick Lawrence, Sheepshanks, and Ford, although not all were able to give WIL their full attention either because of ill health or the pull of other interests.

The second characteristic of democratic suffragism had been the developing vision that informed it. In that vision the campaign for the women's vote was not just about getting what women were entitled to, nor was it simply a means to the end of improving conditions for women. Rather women's suffrage was to form part of a broader concept of democracy which would give a voice to all people, which it was believed would in turn lead to a better world for all, not just for women; the best possible world for women could not exist in a vacuum, but must form part of a more just world for all. Democratic feminist ideals were seen as having an affinity to the socialist ideals of Labour, but only in so far as these pointed to equality and sharing of power and resources, not to class or gender warfare. When, in 1915, Marshall wrote passionately of the need to counter the spirit of domination and militarism wherever it might occur she was building on ideas which had been part of her thinking from before the war:

> Men have hitherto accepted the dominance of force as inevitable. ...
> The mark of your militarist is that he would rather get what he

wants by fighting than in any other way. He wants to force his enemy to yield, so that he may have him at his mercy and be able to impose what terms he choses. I have heard trade unionists talk like this of trade union rights. I have heard socialists, who were ardent pacifists on international questions, talk like this of class warfare. I have heard suffragists talk like this of the struggle for sex equality. *They were all talking pure militarism* – they were all moved by the desire to dominate rather than to co-operate, to vanquish and humiliate the enemy rather than to convert him into a friend.[4]

Speaking on a similar theme in 1917, Marshall elaborated on the role of women:

I am convinced that the great constructive task for us of the W.I.L. faith is not simply to oppose war in a negative way ... but to help to find an *alternative* to war that shall be as creative of free and fruitful life as war is destructive of them, that shall make as urgent a call on men's and women's courage and devotion and self sacrifice, and that shall abolish not only armaments, offensive and defensive, but the spirit of *domination* on the one hand and of *defensiveness* on the other. And to achieve this fruition of the pacifist faith we have got to have a 'revolution' of our whole social, industrial and political systems ... a revolution that will bring about ... change without resort to the methods or the spirit of war.
  Long before the war came upon us I had begun to feel that the great contribution which the women's movement could make to the world lay in this direction. It was with this idea in my mind that I was so keen about developing understanding and co-operation between the women's movement and organized Labour, and the same thing which made me so anxious to develop the Int[ernational] aspect of the women's movement.[5]

WILPF's leaders believed in equality, but not in sameness: this is an important concept. Women's influence would be felt in all spheres, balancing that of men and not limited to fields conventionally held to represent women's interests; both genders had a contribution to make across the board.
  It is beyond the scope of this work to follow the history of WIL within Britain, or indeed of WILPF in the international arena, but it is worth taking a look at the response to the making of the postwar set-

tlement since it provides both an illustration of the vision carried forward by WILPF into the international arena, and a striking clarification of the difference in scope of the WILPF perception from that of the conventional suffragist understanding that had won out in the NU at the time of the 1915 débacle.[6]

Already before the war was over, WIL had shown that its feminist concerns included an imperative to be heard on matters outside the range of narrowly defined women's issues; in sending envoys in 1915 to meet with heads of state and urge the opening of peace negotiations, they had claimed international relations, that most sacred of male preserves, as an area where women were entitled to respect for their opinions. Indeed, at the height of the 1915 divisions in the NU, it will be remembered, both sides had affirmed their interest in the international dimension of the women's movement, and the plan of the nascent WILPF to hold an international gathering whenever and wherever the statesmen came together to discuss peace terms had quickly been followed by a proposal from Fawcett to support a plan current in the IWSA for a postwar suffrage conference at that same time and place.

In the event, both plans bore some fruit, although both were modified. For those who had gathered at The Hague in 1915, the inclusion of women from both sides of the conflict was essential. Now that the statesmen's conference had become a meeting only of the victors, and now that travel to Paris – where the treaty would be hammered out at Versailles – was barred for women from the defeated nations, Paris was no longer an appropriate venue. Following a flurry of transatlantic cables, the founding conference of WILPF convened in Zurich in May 1919.

The IWSA, similarly hamstrung, found a different solution; working with the International Council of Women they called on those who could to go to Paris to lobby for women's interests. In response, an *ad hoc* organization calling itself the Inter-Allied Suffragists (IAS) was formed, whose membership encompassed only women from the victorious countries, providing women with at least a tenuous presence in Paris while the treaty was under discussion, and arriving there several months before the WILPF congress could convene in Zurich. From Britain Millicent Fawcett and Ray Strachey were among those who attended the first IAS gathering in Paris in early February, and Margery Corbett Ashby and Margery Fry remained there for some weeks.[7]

The British constitutional feminists who had been so seriously divided during the war were struggling to work together again. Far from rejecting the IAS initiative, leading members of WIL welcomed it with respect, and helped to clarify objectives to be sought by those who would lobby the statesmen in Paris. At the end of February 1919 WIL convened a conference in London to draw up a 'Minimum Feminist Programme'. This gathering, attended by some of the British representatives of the new IAS, became in effect a briefing session for the lobbyists in Paris, and passed resolutions embodying wide-ranging hopes for improvement in the political status and condition of women.[8]

In Paris, the experience of the IAS was frustrating. They first struggled to get representation for women in the peace-making process itself. The bulk of the work of the peace conference was done by commissions, meeting separately to make proposals on specific issues (such as minorities, mandates, reparations and borders), and the suffragists' hope was to see a special commission appointed, 'composed of women representing organized bodies of women in their respective countries, to whom questions bearing on the life and employment of women should be referred'[9] (WILPF would have preferred to have women represented on all commissions). Despite some initial encouragement from Woodrow Wilson – which proved to be verbal only – the women's effort to get any official forum was pushed aside or ignored. They achieved only two official hearings. One was before the Commission on International Labour Legislation, which was sympathetic and made a strong recommendation in favour of equal pay for work of equal value.[10] The other was before the commission on the League of Nations, and resulted in a major achievement. Rightly hailed as 'A Great Victory' by feminists, but passing almost unnoticed elsewhere, the draft Covenant was amended to include a clause declaring that 'All positions ... shall be open equally to men and women,' a demand also included in the minimum feminist programme. The concession was important even if – once more – its effect was to prove only a small step.[11]

Minimum feminism and beyond

Why had WIL labelled as 'minimum' the concerns taken to Paris by the Inter-Allied Suffragists? The minimum programme embodied hopes that the Congress of Powers would endorse equal suffrage, equal status in national and international bodies, equality of opportunity in training and employment, equal pay for equal work, woman's right to her own nationality independent of that of her husband, an equal share for both sexes in the rights and responsibilities of the guardianship of children, and the 'Endowment of Motherhood' (mothers' allowances).

Other resolutions addressed safeguards for consumers' rights, a minimum wage, the 'traffic in women', the 'abolition of State Regulation of Vice', international marriage laws, and the 'universal abandonment of conscription'.[12] Even now, this may sound like a remarkably comprehensive feminist catalogue.

Worthwhile as they were, however, almost all of these demands relate to traditional women's concerns. At no point did the IAS express a wish to be heard on questions of international power, whether military, economic, or political. They made no official comment on the draft Covenant of the League of Nations, published in British newspapers on 13 February 1919. Representation on all commissions was seen as less desirable than having a special women's commission; and their function in either case would be to look after women's interests (and who would have decided what would be referred to the women's commission?). Ironically, some of the most determined prewar anti-suffragists would have had no quarrel with the demands of the Inter-Allied Suffragists. Mrs Humphry Ward – the leading woman anti-suffragist in Britain, and herself active in social concerns – had readily conceded that, if it were practically possible, 'there would be a great deal to be said for a special franchise' which would limit women's votes to 'those matters where they were equally concerned with men', and keep them from those areas (such as foreign and imperial affairs) 'where [women's] ignorance is imposed by nature and irreparable.'[13]

Even so, the term 'minimum' used by WIL was not pejorative; WIL leaders supported the feminism of the IAS, but believed that, for themselves, feminism must go farther. When WILPF met in Zurich the causes addressed were not limited to obtaining rights and relief for women. Nor was WILPF prepared to wait until those in power recognized their claims to a voice before speaking out on international affairs – if they could not do it from inside the existing power structure, they would do it from outside. They did not wait for an invitation, nor pause to plead their worthiness, they simply went ahead with a critique of the peace terms emerging from Paris.

Here we can only draw attention to some of the points in the WILPF critique of the Covenant of the League of Nations and of the Peace Treaty that resonate with pre-war democratic suffragism. Perhaps the most significant overall feature is that no subject was accepted as outside the women's mandate. The best brains of WILPF – and notably Helena Swanwick – had devoted many hours of research to the forms of international organization that might follow the end of the war (a privilege not available to the statesmen meeting at Versailles, who had been busy conducting the war). As soon as the draft Covenant had been published in February 1919 it had been studied in WIL, and Swanwick's critique was available to the women gathered in Zurich; nevertheless debate was heated. The Congress resolution on the League of Nations forwarded to Paris welcomed the concept but was very critical of the form, urging that the League should become an instrument to 'represent the will of the people and promote international co-operation', open to all nations who would agree to the duties of membership, and with a constitution allowing for amendment.[14]

The resolution also included something of a 'wish list', outlining additional principles which the Congress held would greatly strengthen the League as an instrument of peace. Included are 'total disarmament … enforcement of the decisions of the League by other means than military pressure or food blockade … national ratification of treaties only by an elected legislative body … executive power of the League to be democratically elected … universal free trade', a plan of world economy to keep down the cost of necessities, guarantees for the civil and political rights of minorities, and the placing of colonized people under League guardianship with the mandatory powers to be required to take steps towards easing the way to self-government for their wards. They also urged that the League work towards 'complete freedom of communication and travel … abolition of child labour … abolition of government censorship in all League nations', and the 'establishment of full equal suffrage, and the full equality of women with men politically, socially and economically.'[15]

Since the draft Covenant of the League of Nations had been available for several months, the thorough review of its provisions conducted at Zurich, remarkable as it is, is no more so than the briefer commentary on the draft peace terms, which had only been released on the day before the Congress met. In fact, some of the most committed of the women at Zurich were surely among the first persons ever to read the document from beginning to end, not excepting the statesmen and officials gathered at Paris; it had been, 'in the end, thrown together in a tremendous flurry and … never properly co-ordinated. When it was rushed to the printers … nobody had read it in full and nobody was very sure of its contents.'[16] The resolution on the peace terms sent from Zurich to the statesmen at Paris is shorter than the one on the Covenant only because the women could find so little of good in the document on which to build positive suggestions. It condemns the overall departure from the Wilsonian principles on which the acceptance of the armistice had been based, and urges the Allied and Associated governments to accept amendments which will bring the peace into harmony with those principles. The women had a good grasp of the significant points of the document. By 'guaranteeing the fruits of the secret treaties to the conquerors,' the terms of the treaty are seen as sanctioning secret diplomacy, violating the principle of self-determination, 'recogniz[ing] the right of the victors to the spoils of war,' and creating 'discords and animosities, which can only lead to future wars.' The demand for disarmament of only the defeated countries is seen as denying justice and reinforcing the rule of force. And 'by the financial and economic proposals a hundred million people of this generation in the heart of Europe are condemned to poverty, disease, and despair, which must result in the spread of hatred and anarchy within each nation.'[17]

As the women at Zurich came from the defeated countries as well as from the victorious, there were those among them who bore first-hand evidence of the effects of the blockade in their own malnourished bodies, evidence driven home by the arrival in Switzerland of a train-load of starving children from Vienna. The WILPF response to the blockade went beyond the humanitarian: the resolution forwarded to the statesmen in Paris urged, in effect, that this opportunity be taken to help lay the foundation of peace, and to bring much needed political credit to the war-based organizations of the Allies by turning them to the purposes of relief, which in turn could 'bring about the permanent reconciliation and union of the people'.[18]

The feminism of the Inter-Allied Suffragists and of the WILPF both have validity. Neither had palpable success in 1919. In the following century, western political institutions have been more receptive to the objectives of the IAS than to the broader demands of the democratic suffragists, the feminist pacifists of WILPF. Yet, in the twenty-first century, it may be argued that the condition of women – and their brothers – is more rather than less uncertain than it was a century ago, faced as we are by nuclear weapons, an international climate of distrust, the consequences of global warming, gross poverty of more than half the human race, and continuing reliance on violence as the means of addressing international conflict. It may be legitimate to suggest that the approach to laying the foundations of a lasting peace advocated by WILPF's visionaries was a more realistic one than that which prevailed at Versailles. We may also wonder whether it is time for twenty-first century feminists concerned about women's well-being to move again beyond the minimum feminist programme.[19]

Notes

1 Introduction: The National Union of Women's Suffrage Societies before the First World War

1 The following account condenses much that can be found in more detail in Vellacott, *From Liberal to Labour with Women's Suffrage: The Story of Catherine Marshall*, 1993 (hereafter *Lib to Lab*), in which primary sources are fully referenced. Other relevant secondary sources on which I have drawn include Constance Rover, *Women's Suffrage and Party Politics in Britain: 1866–1914*; (1967); Jill Liddington and Jill Norris, *One Hand Tied Behind Us: The Rise of the Women's Suffrage Movement* (1978); Leslie Parker Hume, *The National Union of Women's Suffrage Societies, 1897–1914* (1982); Les Garner, *Stepping Stones to Women's Liberty: Feminist Ideas in the Women's Suffrage Movement, 1900–1918* (1984); Sandra Stanley Holton, *Feminism and Democracy: Women's Suffrage and Reform Politics in Britain, 1900–1918* (1986); David Rubinstein, *A Different World for Women: The Life of Millicent Garrett Fawcett* (1991); Harold L. Smith, *The British Women's Suffrage Campaign, 1866–1928*, (1998, new edition in preparation); Martin Pugh, *The March of the Women: a Revisionist Analysis of the Campaign for Women's Suffrage, 1866–1914* (2000).

2 The NU's move towards democratization took place at the same time as Emmeline and Christabel Pankhurst were rejecting attempts to introduce a more structured and democratic constitution in the militant Women's Social and Political Union. Jill Liddington's *Rebel Girls* sheds new light on the capricious nature of the support provided by the WSPU London office to suffragettes at the periphery.

3 Pugh, *March of the Women*, ch. 5, shows the growth of Conservative Unionist support for women's suffrage in the pre-war years, and shows also that this support was for a limited, class based suffrage; H. Smith, *British Women's Suffrage Campaign*, 18.

4 For more detail on the emergence of the revised constitution, see *Lib to Lab*, 65–6, 81–5.

5 NUWSS, *Annual Report*, 1910.

6 NU *Annual Report*, 1910 lists 15 federations already formed.

7 Caine, *From Bombay to Bloomsbury*, ch. 11, greatly enhanced my understanding of the nature of the suffrage contribution of Philippa and Ray Strachey, and will be explored below (ch. 3). Caine does not credit Oliver with as large a role as he played.

8 The following discussion draws closely on *Lib to Lab*, 312–15.

9 Lady Jane Strachey to James Strachey, cited by Caine *Bombay*, 182.

10 'Present Position of the London Society and its Branches', printed, with covering letter from Ray Strachey, n.d., marked by Marshall, CEMP.

11 A plea for understanding of the opposition to full federation came from Helen Ward, a member of the LSWS executive in a long private letter to Marshall. Ward vividly depicted the problems caused in London by the

multiplicity of different suffrage organizations, the constant presence of militancy, and the difficulty of obtaining any certainty of commitment to agreed policy where the climate within branches could be so variable. But although Ward made the Stracheys' case better than they did she came from a very different perspective; her concern lay with the political work especially among the working class and in the trade unions. [A. Helen Ward] to Marshall, 7 Dec. 1913. CEMP. The letter is damaged and the signature missing; Ward has been identified from the address. *Lib to Lab*, 311–15, 477–8, nn.10, 12.

12 *CC*, 19 Dec. 1913, 20 Feb. 1914.

13 Eleanor Rathbone led opposition within the NU executive and ultimately resigned over the EFF.

14 For the bumpy road to the agreement and a full account of the pre-war development of the EFF, see *Lib to Lab*, chs 8–15, passim; Holton, *Feminism and Democracy*, chs 4, 5.

15 Martin Pugh gives a useful assessment of the value of the EFF to the Labour Party, but is less reliable in his account of the actions and motives of the suffragists (see, e.g., his unreferenced statement on p. 292 about Marshall's view of the EFF in 1914), *The March of the Women*, 264–83.

16 Special EFF Committee, 19 July, 1915.

17 Rubinstein, *Different World*, 182–3; Harrison, *Prudent Revolutionaries*, 22.

18 Helena Auerbach, the treasurer, was as close a personal friend as Millicent Fawcett ever had; she was there for her when Fawcett needed a confidante, she did her job loyally and with integrity, but she seldom spoke out except on procedural questions.

19 I have found invaluable Elizabeth Crawford, *The Women's Suffrage Movement: A Reference Guide, 1866–1928* for some particulars of suffragists' lives. Alberti, *Beyond Suffrage*, ch. 2 contains insightful mini-biographies of most of our protagonists. See also Oldfield, *Doers of the World* (Oldfield has generously made available an affordable paperback edition of this useful collection). Rubinstein, *Different World*; Harrison, *Prudent Revolutionaries*; Swanwick, *I Have Been Young*; Hannam, *Isabella Ford*; Fletcher, *Maude Royden*. The last is also useful for the youth of Kathleen Courtney.

20 The same sense of responsibility shows in the life of Eleanor Rathbone, whose great wealth, however, made it difficult for her to attempt to walk in the shoes of the less fortunate; her contribution to the Victoria Settlement was as donor, educator, and policy maker. In the outcome, Rathbone was only able to identify with democratic suffragism to a limited extent. Pedersen: *Eleanor Rathbone and the Politics of Conscience*. For a description of the suffrage movement in Liverpool (Rathbone's home), see Cowman, 'Crossing the Great Divide'. Cowman indicates a sharp class and party political divide among Liverpool suffragists, with the Liverpool WSS (the NU affiliate), Liberal, constitutional and elite in constant rivalry with the Liverpool WSPU, Labour/socialist, militant and working class.

21 Fletcher, *Maude Royden*, 22–3.

22 Correspondence in WL.

23 Report of provincial council, 12 Nov. 1914, p. 14, CEMP. News also reached the Council that women's suffrage had been won in Montana and Nevada.

2 Response to War: August to October 1914

1 Cooper Willis, *England's Holy War*; Lindsay, 'The Failure of Liberal Opposition'; Hazlehurst, *Politicians at War*; Vellacott, *Bertrand Russell*, ch.2.
2 Auerbach to Marshall, 4 August 1914, CEMP.
3 S. Pankhurst, *Home Front*.
4 See, e.g. several newspaper clippings, ca. 14 August, mostly unidentified, CEMP; S. Pankhurst, *Home Front*, 23–9; Webb, *The War and the Workers*, 21.
5 The women's groups involved included the WCG, the WTUL, and the WLL, *Lib to Lab*, 360–1.
6 Playne, *Society at War*, 190.
7 'Schemes of Work Suggested by Societies and Individuals', August 1914, MPL/50/2/9/7.
8 NU executive, 6 Aug. 1914, CEMP; *CC*, 28 Aug. 1914. Angela K. Smith's work confirms the way in which suffrage continued latently or overtly to inform the thinking and action of most who had been committed to the cause in the pre-war years. Smith, *Suffrage Discourse*.
9 Kent, *Making Peace*, 15–16.
10 Edith Palliser at NU executive, 6 August 1914, CEMP.
11 Rejected by the British War Office, the Scottish Women's Hospitals offered to work under the French military authorities; Dr Elsie Inglis served with great distinction in Serbia, and died there in 1917. For an interesting discussion of the relation between this work and suffrage, see Smith, *Suffrage Discourse*, 81–2.
12 NU executive, 27 August 1914, CEMP; *CC*, 11 Sept. 1914.
13 NU executive, 6 Aug. 1914, CEMP.
14 NU executive, 27 Aug. 1914, CEMP.
15 E. Pankhurst to Nancy Astor, 3 May 1926, Nancy Astor MSS, quoted by Harrison, *Prudent Revolutionaries*, 35.
16 See, e.g., Hannam, 'I had not been to London'; Cowman, 'Crossing the Great Divide'; Cowman, 'Incipient Toryism?'; de Vries, 'Gendering Patriotism'; Purvis, *Emmeline Pankhurst*, ch.19; Rosen, *Rise Up Women!*, 246–54; Kent, *Making Peace*, 23–5; Smith, *Suffrage Discourse*, ch.2; *CC*, 28 Aug. 1914.
17 de Vries, 'Gendering Patriotism'.
18 Draft Syllabus: 'Women's Work in Time of War' [August 1914] MPL/M50/2/9/10; do. n.d., with a covering letter from Courtney to 'Members of the Education Sub-Committee', 18 Sept. 1914, CEMP; NU executive, 27 Aug. 1914. See also A.M. Williams, 'Workers', *CC*, 11 Sept. 1914.
19 An earlier draft, while reassuring to the men replaced (in a war still expected to be short), is far from feminist by our perceptions; for example, retired schoolmistresses who took over from departing schoolmasters might 'hand over all or part of the salary to the man's dependents'; other jobs were to be filled when possible by a relative of the soldier, keeping the position 'open for the man on his return from the war'. Although the (understandable) reassurance about keeping the position open was retained, the clause about the retired schoolteachers, which offended against the principle that the army should take care of its own as well as against the far-from-wealthy schoolmistresses themselves disappeared by the second draft, which presumably was closer to the one circulated.

20   Marshall to Miss Jebb, 18, 26 Aug. 1914; extensive material on the farming problem, CEMP.
21   'Women's Work in Time of War', MPL/M50/2, 9–10.
22   Material in CEMP and in NU executive minutes, WL; references in *CC*, *passim*.
23   Marshall to Miss A. Hobbs, 31 Aug. 1914, CEMP. Marshall describes her office as 'making special investigation with regard to unemployment and distress, particularly amongst women, to supplement the enquiries which are being conducted by the Government Intelligence Bureau, and the Labour Exchange Department of the BOARD of TRADE'.
24   The first few months of the war saw an intimidating outcrop of committees and sub-committees, central and local, government-sponsored, voluntary and hybrid, the names, acronyms, misnomers, and sometimes the functions of which changed with dizzying rapidity. Some of these bodies are usefully listed in Webb, *The War and the Workers*, 23. Official printed circulars (in CEMP), numbered W.E.R. 1, 2 and 3, defined the policies to be followed in the work for women.
25   Winter, *Socialism and the Challenge of War*, 184; Royden Harrison, 'The War Emergency Workers' National Committee,' 211.
26   The other women's groups listed were the Women's Trade Union League (WTUL), the Women's Labour League (WLL), and the Women's Cooperative Guild (WCG). By the time the WNC was formed, it was 'theoretically open to any organization affiliated or eligible to affiliate to the Labour party.' J.M. Winter, *Socialism and the Challenge of War*, 187, 223 n.4. The NU would have been ineligible from both this standpoint and that of its own constitution.
27   *Labour Year Book, 1916*, 37–9, 79–86.
28   Marshall to Caroline Marshall, 1 Sept. 1914, CEMP. Mary Macarthur came from a well-off Glasgow family, but embraced trade unionism while employed in her father's drapery business; she devoted the rest of her life to organizing women workers. She became joint secretary (with Margaret Llewelyn Davies of the Women's Cooperative Guild) to the People's Suffrage Federation (PSF), formed in 1909. She had served on the National Council of the ILP, and married W.C. Anderson, who was elected ILP MP for Sheffield in 1914. Lady Myddleton's name is not known to me. Lady Askwith was presumably the wife of Sir George Askwith, KC, noted for his skill in arbitration and conciliation. Susan Lawrence (1871–1947) was a Labour member of London County Council, a member of the external committee of the NU's EFF, and later a Labour member of parliament and chair of the Labour Party. Margaret Bondfield (1873–1953), a close friend of Mary Macarthur and Chair of the PSF, was also a trade union leader, active in the Women's Labour League, and a member of the executive both of the ILP and the WNC; she was well known to the NU, and had worked closely behind the scenes with the NU's principal organizer, Margaret Robertson (later Hills) to get a favourable suffrage vote at the Trades Union Congress of 1913; Bondfield too was later a Labour MP and was the first woman cabinet minister.
29   Marshall to Caroline Marshall, 1 Sept. 1914, CEMP.
30   Mimeo, CEMP.

31 For a table comparing the first government proposal, the proposed WNC scale and the final agreed scale, see Winter, *Socialism*, 226, n.53; NU executive minutes, 27 Aug. 1914, CEMP; for Sylvia Pankhurst's criticism of the rate of pay, see Smith, *Suffrage Discourse*, 40–1. The WNC even had to combat government attempts to 'raid' the Prince of Wales fund to provide allowances to soldiers' families, Winter, *Socialism*, 195. Kent sees what she interprets as the Women's Freedom League's willingness to provide relief to soldiers' families as more feminist than the work of the NU, which she stigmatizes as 'scurrying back to home and domesticity'. Kent, *Making Peace*, 21. The NU pressed the government to fulfil its responsibility towards the families, but directed its own efforts towards other victims of economic dislocation.

32 'The Queen's 'Work for Women' Fund: Work for Women in the Provinces', mimeo, n.d. Outside London, Lancashire was very hard hit; Charles Trevelyan reported that 'Half the factory chimneys are not smoking in the cotton towns', Trevelyan to E.D. Morel, 23 Sept. 1914, EDMI/BLPES; see also Frank Marshall (her father) to Marshall, 23 Sept. 1914, CEMP.

33 Correspondence between Marshall and the Agricultural Organisation Society, August to September, 1914; CCEW, 'W.E.R. 2: Memorandum on Schemes of Work for Women temporarily unemployed owing to the War'; 'W.E.R. 3: Memorandum on Training Schemes', October 1914, CEMP.

34 'Extension of Work for Women in the Civil Service', three drafts, revised by Marshall, n.d., CEMP. Before the war, the Post Office had opened up a number of jobs for women, but progress in other departments had been very slow.

35 Correspondence between Marshall and Helen Bardsley, Association of Midwives, 8 Sept. [*et alia*] 1914, and the Ninth Annual Report of the Association for Promoting the Training and Supply of Midwives, 1912, CEMP.

36 Webb, *The War and the Workers*, 2. Webb was a moving spirit in the work of the WNC. In some respects, Webb's tract reads curiously, emphasizing the need to maintain and create employment; Webb clearly did not anticipate that the war could create a shortage of labour. Despite his advocacy of women's representation, an unpleasant note of pitying contempt creeps in when he writes about what is to be done for women and girls thrown out of unskilled employment, *ibid.* 15.

37 Correspondence in CEMP refers. The relationship is complex between the dynamic, forceful Catherine Marshall (34 years old in 1914) and her parents, who shared her causes, supported her financially and emotionally, left her free in her day by day comings and goings, and yet controlled major areas of her life (with her apparent willing consent). It may have seemed less anomalous to contemporaries, see Smith, *Suffrage Discourse*, 80–1.

38 *CC*, 11 Sept. 1914; for the role of the SSFA, see Pedersen, 'Gender, Welfare and Citizenship'; Webb, *The War and the Workers*, 10; for rates paid to soldiers' families, Marwick, *Women at War*, 37.

39 'Rough copy', Marshall to *MG*, 15 December, CEMP. I have not found this letter in print.

40 Royden, 'Notes & News', *CC*, 13 Nov. 1914; NU exec. 4 Jan. 1915, MPL/M50/2/7/10.

41 NU, Weekly Notes, 28 Jan. 1915, WL; Women's Interests committee, MS Minute Book, 1 Jan. to 15 Apr. 1915, WL; Minutes of Professional Women's Patriotic Service Fund committee, WL; extensive material in CEMP including correspondence and notes for interviews with politicians and government officials. For a good summary and analysis of the civil rights issues, see Chrystal Macmillan to the *Nation*, 19 Dec. 1914.
42 See 'The Courage of Sanity', also leader on 'A Discredited System', and other items in *CC*, 16, 23 Oct. 1914; NU executive, 5 Nov. 1914 [incomplete, CEMP]; Smith, *Suffrage Discourse*, 41. Despite the abolition of the CDA in Britain, similar provisions had persisted where troops were stationed overseas, see Florence *et alia*, *Militarism versus Feminism*, 168, n.12.
43 Walshe to Marshall [Nov. 1914]; Sir Wilfrid Lawson to Marshall, 2 Dec. 1914, CEMP.
44 Material on Belgian refugees, CEMP.
45 WIC, minute book, WL; NU exec. 4 Jan. 1915. Members included Royden (chair), Marshall, Courtney, Fawcett, Rackham, Miss Clark, Chrystal Macmillan.
46 Kent, *Making Peace*, 17 and *passim*.
47 LSWS, *Annual Report*, 1914, WL.
48 Those who served on both executives included Lady Frances Balfour (President of the LSWS), Mrs Osler, Edith Palliser, Ray Strachey.
49 For Ray Strachey's earlier suffrage career, see *Lib to Lab*, 42–3, 55–6. For the feminism of the Strachey family, see Caine, *Bombay*, ch.11.
50 LSWS, *Annual Report*, 1914 (Dec. 1914), WL.
51 Holton, *Feminism and Democracy*, 132.; LSWS Minutes, 1914–15, WL.
52 Smith, *Suffrage Discourse*, 73. Although some women expected that training for skilled work might lead to permanent employment, Woollacott finds that government, trade unions and most employers set up training for women 'to do specific tasks for the duration', *On Her Their Lives Depend*, 93–4.
53 Quoted in B. Strachey, *Remarkable Relations*, 272.

3 Division Threatens

1 'Anglo-Indian' was used at that time to refer to those British families who served in India, rather than to those of mixed descent.
2 Rimmer: *Marshalls of Leeds, Flax Spinners*.
3 Crawford, *The Women's Suffrage Movement in Britain and Ireland*, 181, 25.
4 Margaret was relatively poorly educated and probably unbalanced, but her exposure to the contempt of the Stracheys can hardly have been helpful; what is known of her is filtered through their perceptions, with the exception of some correspondence. The letters quoted on the subject of her meetings with Bengali women show her to have had some insight. Later, as Margaret's mental health deteriorated, Pippa took charge of her children, her finances, and her household. Caine, *Bombay*, 39, 305–7, 217–18.
5 Caine, *Bombay*, 49; ch.1 *passim*.
6 Correspondence and other material in CEMP.
7 Marshall, 'The Labour and Woman Suffrage Entente', *Labour Leader*, 28 Aug. 1913; see also *Lib to Lab*, 293.

8 *Lib. to Lab,* 281; Beatrice ('Mrs Sidney') Webb, Introduction, *New Statesman,* 'Special Supplement on the Awakening of Women', 1 Nov. 1913.
9 See Smith, *Suffrage Discourse,* 51, citing *Jus Suffragii,* Sept. 1914.
10 Lord Robert Cecil to Mrs Fawcett, 5 Aug. 1914, WL; also in Smith, *British Women's Suffrage Campaign,* 87–8.
11 Marshall to Schwimmer, 22 Aug. [1914], NYPL/SLC, copy supplied by courtesy of Edith Wynner; Schwimmer to Marshall, 23 Aug. 1914; Marshall to Harper, copy, 31 Aug. 1914, CEMP.
12 Bessie Ford (one of Isabella's sisters) to Marshall, with copy of cable, 21 Sept. 1914, CEMP; Hannam, *Isabella Ford,* 164.
13 NU executive, 27 Aug. 1914, CEMP.
14 'Manifesto of the I.L.P.', 11 Aug. 1914, reprinted in Brockway, *Socialism for Pacifists,* 49–51.
15 For the role of the press at the beginning of the war, see Vellacott, *Bertrand Russell and the Pacifists,* 11, 12; Cooper Willis, *England's Holy War;* Koss, *Rise and Fall of the Political Press in Britain,* ch.7.
16 See Garner, *Stepping Stones,* 40–1.
17 Leading attenders at early planning meetings included some Liberal dissidents, ILP politicians, Quakers, journalists and political commentators, and intellectuals. Holton claims *(Feminism,* 136), that the UDC organizers saw the NU 'as a possible foundation on which to build up their own network of branches', but I have found no evidence of this, although the allegation was made by some opponents; and undoubtedly NU branches in some areas would have liked to affiliate to the UDC. Swanwick, although closely involved with the UDC, mistrusted its inclination to secrecy and its overcaution, and initially also E.D. Morel's attitude to women. For the UDC, see also Swartz, *The Union of Democratic Control;* Swanwick, *I Have Been Young,* 253–5; Hanak, 'The UDC during the First World War'; Vellacott, *Bertrand Russell,* ch.3.
18 E. Williams to Marshall, 6 Oct. 1914, CEMP. The same anxiety was being expressed in some other suffrage societies, esp. Manchester.
19 Harrison, *Prudent Revolutionaries,* 24; see also Rubinstein, *Different World,* ch.9; *Lib to Lab, passim.*
20 'Aunt Isabella' [I. Ford] to Marshall, 25 Oct. [1914], CEMP. Ford was not really an aunt of Marshall's, but the Fords and the Marshalls were longtime close friends. For Ford's reaction to the war, see also Hannam, *Isabella Ford,* ch.10. For Fawcett and the Boer War, see Rubinstein, *A Different World,* 120–8. For the public meeting of 22 Oct., see *CC,* 23 Oct. 1914.
21 *Lib to Lab,* 333–4.
22 Marshall, MS notes, marked 'Cambridge, Nov. 3: *Conclusion',* CEMP.
23 For a fuller development of my argument that resistance to war is a viable feminism, perhaps more so than seeking primarily to move into hitherto masculine roles, see 'A Place for Pacifism and Transnationalism in Feminist Theory'. For Ward's views, see Mary (Mrs Humphry) Ward, *England's Effort.*
24 Marshall, MS, 'Notes for Newcastle, Jan. 25 1915', CEMP.
25 See, e.g. 'Revised Edition of Miss Macmillan's resolution', nd; 'Proposed resolutions for agenda'; resolution submitted by Cambridge WSS, CEMP. Resolutions were received from the affiliate societies and from the executive itself, and were then sifted and sorted by the executive. Anne Wiltsher's

description of interaction among the members of the executive in executive meetings and at the Council is vivid and compelling; she recognizes Fawcett's internal struggle. Wiltsher, *Most Dangerous Women*, ch. 4.

26 Lady Frances Balfour (1858–1930), a long-time suffragist; for accounts of the life of this fascinating woman and her suffragist, political, and aristocratic connections, see Olive Banks, *Biographical Dictionary of British Feminists*, v. 1: 1800–1930; Crawford, *Women's Suffrage Movement*.

27 NU special executive, 4 Nov. 1914, CEMP. Minutes of executive meetings held between regular fortnightly meetings were headed 'Meeting of Special Executive'; there was no difference in those eligible to attend, and they would have been better titled 'Special Meeting of Executive'. Seventeen members were at the meeting of 4 Nov.

28 Swanwick's German descent was not made an issue within the NU; indeed, the NU went to her defence against such attacks from elsewhere. For press attacks on Swanwick's origins, in her capacity as a leading member of the UDC, see Swanwick, *Builders of Peace*, 90; for the general style of some attacks on peacemakers, *ibid.* 89–99; Swartz, *Union of Democratic Control*, ch.6.

29 Strachey, *Millicent Garrett Fawcett*, 282.

30 Report of Provincial Council at Wallasey, 12 Nov. 1914, MPL/M50/2/6/1; see also Wiltsher, *Most Dangerous Women*, 64–9. The short report does not say whether Courtney gave examples of previous campaigns, but she may well have referred to that of autumn 1913, when the NU undertook an extensive education campaign on the topic of 'The State and the Child', not to work for any specific legislation but to promote knowledge and discussion. Report of council at Exeter, 23 May, 1913, WL. See also A. Clark to Marshall, 15 Nov. 1914, CEMP; *Lib to Lab*, 294, 473 n80.

31 For example, Fawcett to Asquith, 13 Sept. 1913, 'formally, on behalf of this Society' urging appointment of women to the commission on venereal disease, CEMP; and see also her interest in the summer of 1914 in the 'Channing Arnold affair', involving the abuse of a young Malayan girl and the persecution of a journalist who had publicized the case, *Lib to Lab*, 336–40.

32 For example, in June 1912 the NU had held back from taking an official position on the government's treatment of suffragette prisoners.

33 A series on 'Problems of War and Peace' included articles by *inter alia* G. Lowes Dickinson, Aneurin Williams, Fenner Brockway and J.A. Hobson.

34 Auerbach to Fawcett, 9 Nov. 1914, WL; Fawcett to Auerbach, 16 Nov. 1914, IAV; Courtney to Marshall, 24 Nov. 1914, CEMP.

35 Auerbach to Fawcett, 9 Nov. 1914, WL.

36 A. Clark to Marshall, 15 Nov. 1914, CEMP.

37 Courtney to Marshall, 24 Nov. 1914, CEMP.

38 Holton, *Suffrage Days*, 213–5.

39 Courtney to Marshall, 13 October 1914, incomplete, CEMP. Courtney does not identify the gathering as a UDC organizational meeting but the names mentioned and the tone justify the assumption. Arnold Rowntree also favoured secrecy, Rowntree to Morel, 1 Oct. 1914, EDM/BLPES.

40 Rubinstein, *A Different World*, 217.

41 E. Rathbone to Marshall, 14 Nov. 1914, CEMP. Marshall had asked Rathbone if she would consider standing again for the executive, but

Rathbone replied that she was still too much hurt by the circumstances of her resignation in March 1914, which had left her feeling that she was not trusted. For Rathbone's resignation, see *Lib to Lab*, 325–8.

42 MS in Marshall's handwriting, CEMP. There is no proof that the letter was sent, but Marshall marked it 'From Letter to Mrs Fawcett, Nov. 28. 1914', which is a strong indication. No reply is known to me.

4 Crucial Forum: The National Council, February 1915

1 For Sheepshanks, see Oldfield, *Spinsters*.
2 For an interesting commentary on the unique nature of *Jus Suffragii*, see Smith, *Suffrage Discourse*, ch.4.
3 Fawcett, in *Jus Suffragii*, 1 Sept. 1914; Fawcett, letter to *CC*, 25 Sept. 1914; Fawcett, '1815 and 1915–16', *Nation*, 27 Feb. 1915.
4 E. Williams to Marshall, 31 Dec. 1914; Marshall to E. Williams, 11 Jan. 1915, CEMP; *CC*, 2 Oct. 1914.
5 Courtney to Marshall, 26 Nov. 1914, CEMP.
6 NU exec. 3 Dec. 1914, MPL/M50/2/7/9.
7 Fawcett to Catt, 15 Dec. 1914, WL, presumably a draft copy.
8 *CC*, 8 Jan. 1915.
9 Rubenstein, *A Different World*, esp. ch. 10; Fawcett, *Wanted, a Statesman*.
10 R. Strachey to Mary Berenson, 1, 5 February, 1915, BSH/WL.
11 'Questions to be addressed to candidates ...', with covering letter, R. Strachey to 'Madam', 31 December 1914, CEMP.
12 LSWS exec., 14, 21 Dec. 1914, WL. I have not found the O'Malley/Ward questions in LSWS records, but a set differing from Strachey's is in Marshall's papers (without attribution to LSWS or to any individual); it is much better worded and probably is the one referred to. 'Questions to candidates ... Annual Meeting, February 4th 1915', CEMP.
13 Marshall to R. Strachey, MS copy, faint carbon, 5 Jan. 1915, CEMP.
14 R. Strachey to Marshall, 9 Jan. 1915, CEMP.
15 Marshall to R. Strachey, 3 Feb. 1915, ts. copy, CEMP.
16 R. Strachey to M. Berenson, 5 Feb. 1915, BSH/WL.
17 The main documentation for my account of this Council is the printed 'Proceedings', MPL/M50/1/6/2, and Marshall's annotated copy of the agenda, CEMP. The former details motions in favour of 'the Previous Question' (i.e. to dismiss the resolution without any, or further, discussion), amendments, movers, seconders, speakers for and against, and whether carried or lost. Representatives voted by 'rising in their places'; the Chair declared the result; close votes might be challenged by the minority and a count taken, and only in this case was a numerical count recorded. The discussion was not minuted. Marshall's notes mostly include some assessment of the size of the majority, as 'large', 'considerable', 'huge', 'rather close'.
18 The added paragraph was not new, but was transferred from a separate resolution.
19 Marshall MS notes 'Re-remaining in N.U.', n.d., CEMP. See also Frank Marshall to Catherine Marshall, 5 Mar. 1915; Caroline Marshall to Catherine Marshall, n.d. [ca March 1915], incomplete, CEMP. Marshall's

proposed amendment, and her unsuccessful attempt to move it are noted in the margin of her agenda.

20 *Proceedings*, 4–6 Feb. 1915, MPL M50/1/6/2; '*Attitude of the N.U. to war*: interpretation of the decisions arrived at the Annual Council Meeting, February 1915', mimeo, MPL M50/2/9/38; NU exec. 18 Feb., 4 and 18 Mar., 1915.

21 Mimeo, dated January 22, 1915, CEM.

22 *MG*, 6 Feb. 1915; Rubinstein, *A Different World*, 219–20; Fawcett, notes on letter to Armstrong, 7 Feb. 1915.

23 Officers, 5:2 against; auxiliaries 6:4 against, but the Canadian section might support the conference if it were held in the USA. Hungary's favourable vote came 'through' Schwimmer. 'Letter from Mrs Chapman Catt', NU exec., 4 Mar. 1915, WL; Fawcett, 'The NUWSS and the Hague Congress', *Englishwoman*, June 1915, 197.

24 LSWS exec., 28 Jan.; 17 Feb. 1914, WL.

25 Mimeo of the addresses, CEMP.

26 Fry was an absolutist pacifist (until the rise of nazism), and a suffragist, but suffrage was never at the top of her priorities; she was working at this time for war victims, and later was active in prison reform. A friend of Rathbone, she may have felt that the NU was not the best place for the promotion of peace work, but she would surely not have stood in the way of any peace initiative. Her sister, Joan Mary Fry, served on the BCIWC. See Oldfield, *Doers of the Word*, pp. 83–6.

27 There are four losers whose views I do not know. No 'pacifists' have been conclusively identified among the unsuccessful candidates. Votes were allocated to constituent societies according to size of membership, but I am ignorant of some details as to how they might be distributed among candidates. *Proceedings*, 4–6 Feb. 1915, MPL M50/1/6/2; NU executive, 18 Feb. 1915, draft, WL. Marshall's (subjective) division into 'Obstructive' and 'Progressive, or at least not obstructive?' is in her notes for a later meeting, Marshall, MS, 9 May, 1915, CEMP.

28 George Armstrong of Manchester embarked on a highly critical correspondence with Fawcett, both in private and through the columns of the *Manchester Guardian*. Fawcett notes on letter to Armstrong, 7 Feb.; Fawcett, 13 Feb. 1915, copy, WL; Armstrong to Fawcett, 7 Feb., 12 Feb. 1915, WL; Fawcett to *MG*, 9 Feb. 1915.

29 'London Society Meeting: Mar. 2', Marshall, MS notes, CEMP.

30 Oliver Strachey also wrote an article for the *Englishwoman* in which he makes a great deal of use of a rather specious formal logic to prove that women's suffrage in no way implies pacifism, *Englishwoman*, No. 76, Apr. 1915.

31 Marshall to Stocks, 2 Feb. 1915, copy, CEMP.

32 Marshall, MS pencil notes, nd [Feb. 1915], CEMP.

33 'London Society Meeting: Mar. 2', Marshall MS notes, CEMP; Ida O'Malley, distressed at the thought of a quarrel with Marshall, wrote to try to make Oliver's speech more acceptable claiming that he had made it plain that he only used the offensive labels for convenience; but her personal affection for Marshall did not alter the fact that she was in agreement with his point of view in every respect. O'Malley to Marshall, 9 Mar. 1915, CEMP.

34 For the particular characteristics of the Liverpool Society, see Cowman 'Crossing the Great Divide'.

5 Disaffection and New Directions

1 Ingram, 'In Christ's Name – Peace!', 179–80.
2 Sheepshanks to Fawcett, 14 Apr. 1915, with note of reply in margin 'expressed my views about congress can do little good to peace and may do much harm to suffrage'. MPL/M/50/2/22/20.
3 *JS*, 1 Mar. 1915; *CC*, 5 Mar. 1915; M. Hills, 'Internationalism among Women', *LL*, 4 Mar. 1915; *WD*, 6 Mar. 1915; NUWSS, 'Weekly Notes', 3 Mar. 1915, WL; 'British Committee of the International Women's Congress', printed leaflet, n.d.
4 WLL, notice in *LL*, 25 Mar. 1915; the manifesto of the British Committee was published in the same issue. Oldfield, 'England's Cassandras'; Oldfield, *Doers of the Word*.
5 NU exec. 18 Feb. 1915, WL.
6 Caroline Marshall to Catherine Marshall, n.d. [ca. March 1915], incomplete; Frank Marshall to Catherine Marshall, 5 Mar. 1915; See also Armstrong to Catherine Marshall, 7 Feb., 17 Feb., 1915; Catherine Marshall to Armstrong, 9 Feb. (ts. copy), 19 Feb. (MS copy), 1915, CEMP.
7 NU exec. 4 Mar. 1915, WL; Marshall to Fawcett, marked 'copy not corrected', CEMP; MS amendment to minutes, NU exec. 4 Mar. 1915, WL.
8 Fawcett to Marshall, 6 Mar. 1915, typed document marked 'Private and Confidential: Correspondence between Mrs Fawcett and Miss Marshall. Circulated to Members of the Executive Committee', consisting of Marshall to Fawcett, 3 Mar. (her letter of resignation) and Fawcett to Marshall 6 Mar. 1915, CEMP.
9 NU exec. 18 Mar. 1915, WL. Marshall had meant there to be two copies of her resignation, one addressed to Fawcett, the other to Rackham (as indeed, Fawcett's letter of 6 Mar. shows to have been the case), but admitted that she had inexcusably failed to give clear instructions. Marshall's letter of 4 Mar. is not extant; the offensive expressions are known through having been quoted back to Marshall by Fawcett in her letter of 6 Mar. Whether the document was in fact circulated is uncertain; my guess is that it was not. See also Rubinstein, *Different World*, 220.
10 'Extract from the Minutes of March [18], 1915', 4 pp, printed, MPL/M50/2/7/14; NU executive, 18 Mar. 1915, WL. Fawcett to Catt, 21 July 1915, WL. See also 'Copy of a letter from Mrs Fawcett to a Secretary of a N.U.W.S.S. Society', 2 May 1915, mimeo, MPL/M50/2/9/46.
11 Swanwick to Marshall, 24 Mar. 1915, CEMP.
12 Crookenden to Hon. Secs. of federations and societies, 20 Mar. 1915, CEMP.
13 Courtney to Marshall, 6 Apr. 1915, CEMP.
14 Swanwick to Marshall, 22 Mar. 1915, CEMP.
15 Letters, between 11 Mar. and 26 Apr. 1915; NU exec. 18 Mar. 1915, CEMP.
16 NU exec. 15 Apr. 1915, WL.
17 NU exec. 18 Feb., 18 Mar., 1915, WL; copy in Fawcett's handwriting, marked 'Reproduction of letter from the Press Dept. which caused the misunderstanding', MPL/M50/2/9/47. See also Fawcett to Auerbach, 16 Mar. [1915], IAV.

18 Macmillan to Atkinson ('in train en route Stockholm to Petrograd'), 7 June 1915, MPL/M50/2/9/48, reprinted in *CC*, 25 June 1915.
19 Fawcett to Catt, 21 July 1915, MS (draft), WL.
20 R. Strachey to Mary Berenson, 21 Apr. 1915, BSH/WL; Oliver Strachey to Ray Strachey, 21 Apr. 1915, quoted by Susan Pedersen, *Eleanor Rathbone*, 146. There is an irony in Ray Strachey's unquestioned and apparently problem-free travel across the Channel to the Riviera: at about the same time the Englishwomen who wanted to go to the Hague conference found the North Sea closed to them.
21 R. Strachey to 'Aunty Loo' [Alys Russell], 5 Mar. [1915], BSH/WL.
22 On record are Mrs Fyffe, one of the two censured for not obeying executive instructions at the NU Feb. Council, who resigned from the executive, Mrs Spring Rice from executive and from the LSWS, Ethel Snowden from the LSWS. Kingston and Surbiton were the branches that withdrew. LSWS executive, 17 Feb. 1915, WL. Helen Ward resigned from the LSWS executive in April. LSWS executive, 15 May 1915, WL.
23 Accounts of participants include Addams, Balch and Hamilton, *Women at the Hague*; British Committee of Women for Permanent Peace, *Towards Permanent Peace*. See also Lela Costin, 'Feminism, Pacifism, Internationalism and the 1915 International Congress of Women'; Vellacott. 'Anti-War Suffragists'; Wiltsher, *Most Dangerous Women*.

6   No Way Back

1 Ashton to Marshall, 3, 5 May 1915, CEMP.
2 Schuster did not attend; she felt hopeless about the future of the NU, and had resigned as Chair of the Maidenhead WSS (a southern branch) when they passed a resolution of confidence in Fawcett. The only others missing were Kathleen Courtney and Katherine Harley (who wrote from her post with the Scottish Women's Hospitals in Troyes, France, close to the Front line, to express her support). Schuster to Marshall, 7 May 1915; Harley to Marshall, 10 May 1915, CEMP.
3 'Draft Resolution proposed by Miss Marshall as a basis for discussion'; Swanwick to Marshall, 5 Apr. 1915; MS in Frank Marshall's handwriting, nd; 'Suggested formation of Women's Independent Party', in Marshall's handwriting, nd, CEMP.
4 'Possibilities of a Special Council' in F. Marshall's handwriting, nd. CEMP.
5 'Informal Meeting of Ex-members of N.U. Executive and others', marked 'C.E.M.'s notes (by no means complete)' 9 May 1915, CEMP.
6 'Manchester Resn', draft brought by Ashton and Tomlinson 'as a basis for discussion', CEMP.
7 'Possibilities of a Special Council', nd, CEMP.
8 'Informal Meeting', 9 May 1915, CEMP.
9 Those listed as 'progressive' were Macmillan, V. Jones, Tuke, Fry, Osler and Rackham. The 'obstructive' members on the executive were O. Strachey, Uniacke, Palliser, Balfour; and among the officers, Fawcett, Auerbach, and Atkinson. R. Strachey had not yet been formally appointed.

10 E. Williams to Marshall, 7 May 1915; see also Frances Hardcastle, Secretary of the NE Federation to Marshall, 7 May 1915, CEMP.
11 R. Strachey to M. Berenson, 20 May 1915, BSH/WL.
12 Rackham to Fawcett, 19 Apr. 1915, WL; BLP/WIL/5/2; Swanwick, *Builders of Peace*, 56 n.1.
13 LSWS exec. minutes 14, 18, 28 May, 2, 11 June 1915, WL. I do not know exactly how votes were allocated between the societies, but it is safe to assume they were in proportion to the number of members.
14 Agenda; Proceedings, LSWS, 17 May 1915, May, WL.
15 Fawcett to Marshall, 11 May 1915; NU exec. 6, 20 May 1915, CEMP.
16 Ashton to Marshall, 2 June; Marshall to Ashton, 4 June [1915], draft, CEMP.
17 M. Conway to Katherine Harley and Ethel Williams, copy, [9 June 1915, misdated 9 May], notifying them that Manchester would now be unable to support their candidature. MPL/M50/1/2/90; Conway to Atkinson, [9 June 1915, misdated 9 May], MPL/M50/1/2/91; NU special exec. 14 June 1915, CEMP; *MG*, 9, 10 June 1915; Ashton to editor, *CC*, 18 June 1915; 'Position of Manchester Society', unsigned, *CC* 18 June 1915.
18 Fawcett to Conway, 9 June [1915], MPL/M50/1/2/92.; P. Strachey to Conway, 15 June 1915, MPL/M50/1/3/96. Ashton seems to have come from this defeat in a curious state of mind; within a day or two, she made a speech from an army recruiting platform, though she wrote to *CC* to explain that the report in *MG* was not wholly accurate (she had not said that the war was a necessary one), but it is nevertheless hard to read it as anything but a pro-war speech (Ashton to editor, *CC*, 25 June 1915; speech reported in *MG*, 11 June 1915, also reprinted *CC*, 25 June 1915), causing Fawcett understandably 'the greatest possible surprise ... with those views one wonders what all the trouble was about'. Fawcett to Conway, 12 June [1915], MPL/M50/1/2/93.
19 Marshall *et alia* to Rackham, 14 June 1915, CEMP.
20 'Final Agenda' and 'Proceedings' of the Special and Half-Yearly Council, 17–18 June 1915, MPL/M50/2/6/4, also WL; *JS*, 1 July 1915; *CC*, 25 June 1915; Marshall, MS 'from letter to Mrs Auerbach', 3 July 1915, CEMP. Rubinstein errs in saying that a vote of confidence in Fawcett was passed, *Different World*, 223.
21 P. Strachey to Roger Fry, 22 June 1915, WL, quoted by Caine, *Bombay*, 313–14. Caine is unaware that the occasion described was the Council.
22 Fawcett to Conway, 24 June 1915, MPL/M50/1/2/94; Fawcett to Atkinson, 19 Feb. 1916, WL.
23 I have not placed Margery Fry with north or south: she grew up in London but worked in Birmingham from 1904–14. I counted Leaf as a Londoner, because she was a long-time resident there, but much of her support came from northern suffrage societies. Assigning location is made more difficult by the fact that candidates (particularly the better known ones) often received nominations from many societies.
24 See note 13 above; NUWSS Nomination Paper, June 1915; NUWSS, Proceedings of the Special and Half-Yearly Council, June 17th and 18th, 1915, MPL/M50/2/6/4.
25 Strachey, *Cause*, 351.
26 Harrison, *Prudent Revolutionaries*, 103.

27 Pedersen, *Rathbone*, 145.
28 Rubinstein, *Different World*, 223.
29 Strachey, *Cause*, 351.
30 Marshall, 'Questions for Miss Addams', MS, marked [May 1915], but the content shows it to be actually June 1915, during Addams' second visit to Britain, SCPC/JA. The reference in the last sentence is to the story told in Genesis ch.27, but should surely have been to Jacob, not to Esau, since it was Jacob who deceived his father, Isaac, into giving him the blessing intended for and earned by his older brother Esau. Marshall's error may be seen as a poignant irony, illustrating how a righteous loser may disappear from history, or be misremembered as the offender.

7   Cutting Down the Election Fighting Fund

1 Holton, *Feminism and Democracy*, 101–2, 112–15; Fawcett, *The Women's Victory*, ch.3.
2 Marshall to Fawcett, 2 May 1915, rough MS draft, CEMP; NU, 'Weekly Notes', 28 Jan. 1915, WL; NU executive, 6 May 1915, CEMP.
3 R. Strachey to M. Berenson, 2, 7 Jun., BSH/WL; Marshall, notes of letter to R. Strachey, 20 Jun.; R. Strachey to Marshall, 24 Jun. 1915, CEMP; R. Strachey to M. Berenson, 26 Jun. 1915, BSH/WL.
4 NU executive, 1 Jul. 1915; Atkinson to Marshall, 2, 6 Jul. 1915; Marshall to Atkinson, 28 Jun., 3 Jul. 1915, copies; Marshall to Fawcett, 3 Jul., draft copy with many erasures; quotation is from Marshall to R. Strachey, copy, 4 Nov. 1915, CEMP.
5 EFF Agenda, 14 Jul. 1915, CEMP; Marshall to [Rackham], 14 Jul. 1915, MPL/M50/1/9/49; EFF minutes, 14 Jul. 1915, MPL/M/50/2/8/1.
6 The insistence of the Labour Party on avoiding the embarrassment of candidates' receiving direct funding from the EFF has probably contributed to the failure of mainstream political historians to notice the effective pre-war involvement of the EFF in by-elections.
7 'Report of interview with Mr John Hodge, M.P.', 3 Aug. 1915; 'Report of interview with Mr W.C. Anderson, M.P.', WL.
8 Only Marshall, Courtney, Atkinson, Coombe Tennant, and Ray Strachey seem to have been at the EFF meeting of 15 Sept. In the absence of minutes my account of what took place is based on comment in later documents. Courtney to Marshall 17 Oct. 1915, CEMP. Much of this history was revisited at an executive meeting part of which was joint with the EFF committee on 18 Nov. 1915, which was recorded almost verbatim (84 pages), Joint Meeting of Executive and EFF committees, 18 Nov. 1915, full report, in WL, and in CEMP (hereafter cited as JM, 18 Nov. 1915). There is also a 7 page mimeo 'Report of Statements made and Resolutions put to the Vote' at the Joint Meeting (hereafter cited as Report of Statements, 18 Nov. 1915).
9 JM, 18 Nov. 1915, 71, WL, CEMP; EFF, 5 Oct., agenda and minutes, CEMP.
10 Rough MS notes, nd [end of Nov. or early Dec. 1915: wrongly assigned in CEMP by the present writer, *mea culpa*, to Feb. 17–19, 1915], headed 'CEM's statement'; EFF minutes, 5 Oct. 1915; 'Report of the Position of the E.F.F. work of the National Union', 15 and (revised) 21 Oct. 1915, CEMP.

11 Ashton to Marshall, 19 Oct. 1915, CEMP.
12 JM, 18 Nov. 1915, 51, WL, CEMP; Report of NU interview with Jowett, 12 Oct. 1915, CEMP.
13 [Middleton] to Marshall, 14 Apr. 1915, carbon, LP/WOM/12/57.
14 NU executive, 1 Jul., 1915; letters from Tothill, secretary of East Bristol WSS, from Townley, and from Marshall, in minutes of NU exec., 1 Jul. 1915, CEMP. For Townley's pre-war EFF work see *Lib to Lab*, 300–01.
15 Holton says that it was Ayles's attitude to conscription that led to the controversy over East Bristol in October to November 1915 (Holton, *Feminism and Democracy*, 140–141). While his views became an added aggravation, the sequence of events (and the arguments) show that the focus on East Bristol came about because it was the one constituency where EFF work for a confirmed candidate was still steadily proceeding in mid-1915. Ayles was indeed a founding member of the No-Conscription Fellowship but the NCF's profile was low until near the end of 1915. Conscription came in early in 1916.
16 Marshall, notes headed 'Mrs Townley', 1 Oct. 1915; EFF minutes, 5 Oct. 1915, CEMP.
17 The old members of the EFF also thought that minutes sometimes omitted important points made by them, that Strachey's report to the branches was 'garbled', and that Strachey made herself hard to reach. Courtney to Marshall 17, 19 Oct.; Marshall to R. Strachey, 20 Oct.; Ashton to Marshall, 19 Oct. 1915, CEMP.
18 EFF committee, 20 Oct. 1915, agenda (annotated by Marshall) and minutes, much annotated, and second copy, amended, CEMP. Swanwick and Royden had resigned from the EFF in July 1915.
19 Townley to Marshall, 1 Nov. 1915; 'Interview with Representatives of E. Bristol on E.F.F. work', 25 Oct. 1915; EFF minutes, 5 Nov. 1915, CEMP.
20 Marshall to R. Strachey, 4 Nov. 1915, draft, CEMP.
21 'E.F.F. Report: Interview with representatives from East Bristol' nd, WL, CEMP. The subtitle is misleading; the text is a report of the discussion at the executive. Marshall's copy is annotated and marked 4 Nov. 1915; the interview was on 25 Oct. and is recorded separately, 'Interview with Representatives of E. Bristol on E.F.F. work', 25 Oct. 1915; EFF minutes 5 Nov. 1915, CEMP.
22 Marshall to Fawcett, 16 Nov. 1915, MS copy, CEMP; also included in minutes of NU special executive, 18 Nov. 1915, WL, CEMP; EFF minutes 5 Nov. 1915; see also Marshall to 'Ida' [O'Malley], 9, 11 Nov., [1915]; O'Malley to Marshall, 10, 17 Nov. 1915, CEMP.
23 JM, 18 Nov.; Marshall to Shaw, 11 Nov.; Shaw to Marshall, 11 Nov.; A. Clark to Shaw, 14 Nov.; Ashton to Shaw, 14 Nov.; Ford to Shaw, 14 Nov.; Courtney to Shaw, 15 Nov. 1915, CEMP. Mr Shaw was a Labour member of the EFF committee, on whom I have little further information.
24 'Resolution', 2 Dec. 1915, enclosed with Atkinson to Marshall, 2 Dec. 1915; EFF report at NU executive, 16 Dec. 1915, CEMP.
25 JM, 18 Nov. 1915, 4, WL, CEMP.
26 'Report of Special Executive Committee Meeting', 18 Nov. 1915, WL.
27 EFF minutes, 19 Jan. 1917; Ayles to Fawcett, 25 Feb. 1917, WL.
28 Atkinson to Marshall, 2 Dec. 1915, CEMP.

29 Quoted, n.d., in Berenson, biography, BSH/WL.
30 Marshall to R. Strachey, 4 Nov. 1915, draft, CEMP.
31 Williams to R. Strachey, 10 Nov. 1915, WL. For more on Marshall's view, see Marshall to Fawcett, 16 Nov. 1915, CEMP, also reproduced in NU executive, 18 Nov. 1915.

8   Relations with Labour: Women's War Work

1 Woollacott, *'On Her Their Lives Depend'*, ch.7 and *passim*.
2 R. Strachey to M. Berenson, 15 Oct. 1915, BSH/WL. 'Educated' was short-hand for middle or upper class, someone presumed to be educated beyond the primary level of free public education at that time.
3 Smith, *Suffrage Discourse*, 72–6 and ch.5 *passim*.
4 Caine, *Bombay*, 314.
5 R. Strachey to Marshall, 26 Jul. 1915, with marginal comment by Marshall, CEMP.
6 'Report of interview with Mr W.C. Anderson, M.P.', WL.
7 See, e.g. *Lib to Lab*, 299–302.
8 Special EFF, 3 Aug. 1915, 5.30 pm, MPL/M/50/2/8/2; see also Liddington, *Rebel Girls*, 113–14.
9 NU executive, 5 Aug. 1915, MPL/M50/2/17/19; R. Strachey to Marshall, 6 Aug. 1915; NU executive, 7 Oct. 1915; EFF 5 Nov. 1915, CEMP.
10 NU executive 5 Aug. 1915; 'Private Notes re-employment of Women on Munition Work', typed by Lloyd George's secretary (Frances Stevenson) from rough notes left by Marshall after a meeting with Lloyd George [ca 22 July 1915], amended and returned by Marshall. Lloyd George papers.
11 NU executive, 16 Sept. 1915, annotated by Marshall; Marshall to R. Strachey, 9 Oct. 1915, CEMP.
12 Harrison, *Prudent Revolutionaries*, 165.
13 E. and C. Pankhurst acted in this, as ever, without consulting with their organization. Purvis, *Emmeline Pankhurst*, 276–9; Rosen, *Rise Up*, 252–3.
14 See, e.g., Mrs Humphry Ward, *England's Effort*.
15 MS notes and correspondence with E. Pethick-Lawrence, June–July 1915, CEMP.
16 Winslow, *Sylvia Pankhurst*, ch.4.
17 NU Women's Interests committee, 5 Mar. 1915, WL.
18 NU WIC, reports from several areas, 26 Aug. 1915, CEMP.
19 Presumably one of the local joint committees of trade unionists and factory owners set up in the treasury agreement, supposedly to give unions a share in the direction of industry, but in fact, as A.J.P. Taylor says, 'used only to organize dilutions'. Taylor, *English History*, 29.
20 Tomlinson to Marshall, 11 Aug. 1915, CEMP.
21 Tomlinson to Marshall, 13 Aug. 1915, CEMP.
22 Tomlinson to Marshall, 20 Oct. 1915, CEMP. Current increased research into regional suffragist activities may shed more light on the followup to the June Council.
23 Harris (Home Office) to Marshall, 23 Sept.; Marshall to Harris, 24 Sep. 1915, CEMP.

24 Rathbone to Marshall, nd [ca Sep. 1915]; 4 Sep. 1915, CEMP.
25 Crookenden to Marshall, 11 Oct. 1915, CEMP.
26 Crookenden to Marshall, 11, 21 Oct.; WIC, 12 Oct.; Marshall to Lloyd George, draft, 14 Oct.; Marshall to Ll. George, copy (more civil than the draft) 18 Oct.; Marshall to 'Dear Crookie' 19 Oct. 1915. Crookenden was right in seeing this as 'something of a triumph' for Marshall, but she made comparisons between the running of the Ministry of Munitions and the old NU office, to the serious disparagement of the former. After a while the 'mess and muddle' became more than she could stomach and in early 1916 she resigned, Crookenden to Marshall, 1 Jan. 1916, CEMP.

9 Separate Ways

1 Vellacott, *Bertrand Russell*, chs 3, 4.
2 Addams, Balch and Hamilton, *Women at the Hague*, 110; Addams, *Peace and Bread*, 15–20; Randall, *Improper Bostonian*, 166–212; Marshall, 'The Women Envoys' in *Towards Permanent Peace*; Wiltsher, *Most Dangerous Women* ch.6.
3 Marshall to Addams, 21 Jun. [1915], JA/SCPC. A list dated 'June 26?' supplied by Edith Wynner, and based on her research in the Schwimmer/Lloyd papers, NYPL, includes 48 individual names of people seen by Addams during the past week, not including '180 members of English Committee, Settlement people etc.'.
4 Material in CEMP and JA/SCPC refers.
5 L. Bennett to Marshall, 19 Oct., 1915, CEMP. A year later the Irish women were able to establish their own branch and direct representation to the ICWPP.
6 'Women's International League. Objects', ICWPP *News-sheet VI*. WILPF/Col.
7 Marshall, 'Questions for Miss Addams' [June 1915], misdated [May 1915], SCPC/JA.
8 Fletcher, *Maude Royden*, chs 6, 7.
9 Courtney to Macmillan, 15 Jun. 1915, incomplete, CEMP.
10 WIL report for Jan. 1916, in *International*, March/April 1916, WILPF/Col.
11 Swanwick to Marshall, 28 Mar., to Caroline Marshall, 29 Mar. 1916, FMP. For more on Marshall's work for the NCF, see Vellacott, *Bertrand Russell*.
12 Rathbone to Marshall, 4 Sept., 14 Oct. 1915, CEMP.
13 Rathbone to Marshall, nd [Sep. 1915], CEMP.
14 Rathbone to Marshall, 4 Sep. 1915; NU exec. 16 Sept. 1915; Marshall, notes for speech at Liverpool, 3 Sep. 1915, CEMP.
15 Fawcett to Addams, 11 May 1915, JA/SCPC.
16 Fawcett to Miss Conway, 24 Jun. 1915, MPL/M50/1/2/94.
17 Marshall, 'Questions for Miss Addams' [June 1915], SCPC/JA.
18 Fawcett to Catt, 21 Jul. 1915, MS [probably a draft for typing], WL.
19 Oldfield, *Spinsters*, 187
20 Leaf to Courtney 8 Jun. [1915]; similar in Leaf to Marshall [ca 10 Jun., 1915], CEMP.
21 Sheepshanks 'Woman Suffrage and Pacifism', extract from unpublished autobiography, seen by courtesy of Sybil Oldfield; Frank Marshall to Catherine Marshall, nd; Hawse End Guest Book, which shows Sheepshanks

visiting 24–28 May 1915. Graham Wallas, J.A. Hobson, G.B. Shaw, and Sydney and Beatrice Webb were also at the Fabian conference.
22 Leaf to Courtney, 8 Jun.; to Marshall [ca 10 Jun.], CEMP
23 Coit to Fawcett, 5 Sep. 1915, MPL/M50/2/22/45.
24 Oldfield, *Spinsters*, 186.
25 NU exec., 21 Oct. 1915, CEMP; NU exec. 18 Nov. 1915, WL. Osler did not attempt to overturn the executive decision, but introduced a resolution that important resolutions should not be brought forward without notice (as the condemnation had been) at the end of long meetings when many had already left. Extensive correspondence in MPL relates to Sheepshanks, Fawcett, and *Jus Suffragii*, MPL/M50/2/22.

10 Back to the Franchise

1 The United Suffragists and the WFL had not paid even lip service to suspending the campaign and had continued to urge the passage of a bill without waiting for the end of the war.
2 Marshall to J.S. Middleton, 29 May 1916; to Asquith, 24 May, copy enclosed with above. LP/WNC/29/5.
3 See Morgan, *Suffragists and Liberals*, ch 10, for a lucid account of the cabinet's difficulties and their final resolution, 1915–1917. Lord Curzon (1859–1925) had played a leading role in the National League for Opposing Women's Suffrage. Harrison, *Separate Spheres*, passim.
4 WIL *AR*, BLP/WIL/2/1; Alberti, *Beyond Suffrage*, 62, citing NU exec. 3 Dec. 1915, 3 Feb. 1916.
5 Holton, *Women's Suffrage*, 143–4.
6 Caroline Marshall to Marshall, [June 1916], CEMP.
7 Pedersen, *Rathbone*, 146–7; Holton, *Women's Suffrage*, 184 n.44.
8 WIL *AR*, BLP/WIL/2/1.
9 The Military Service Act made provision for conscientious objection but left the decision as to whether a man's objection was genuine to tribunals of variable competence, and in particular provided inadequately for those who could not accept non-combatant military service. Vellacott, *Bertrand Russell and the Pacifists*; Kennedy, *Hound of Conscience*; Rae, *Conscience and Politics*.
10 Marshall to Middleton, 29 May, 6, 14 June 1916, LP/WNC 29/5.
11 Holton, *Women's Suffrage*, 184 n.55.
12 Fawcett to Asquith, 4 May 1916, copy, WL, also in *CC*, 19 May 1916; *Times*, 16 May 1916.
13 Marshall to Asquith, 24 May, copy, LP/WNC/29/5/6.
14 Swanwick to 'Dear Sir' [Henderson?], 1 June 1916, LP/WNC/29/5/8; Marshall to Middleton, 6, 14 June 1916, LP/WNC/29/5/15, 16.
15 'Resolutions passed at preliminary suffrage conference', and 'Committee pro tem' (with signatures) on WIL letterhead, 16 June 1916, LP/WNC 29/5/18, 19, 20; *Times*, 31 May 1916.
16 For details on the political manoeuvering see Morgan, *Suffragists and Liberals*, 137–43; David Rolf, 'Origins of Mr Speaker's Conference during the First World War'; Pugh, *Electoral Reform in War and Peace*, chs 5–9; for a

short overview of the renewed suffrage issue see Marwick, *The Deluge*, 100–12.
17 Swanwick in WIL Monthly News Sheet, Sept. 1916.
18 Pugh, *Electoral Reform*, 71.
19 Close, 'The Collapse of Resistance to Democracy'; Holton, *Feminism and Democracy*, 185, n.58.
20 Swanwick to Asquith, nd [27 July 1916]; 'The Claim for Adult Suffrage' [9 Sept, 1916]; Swanwick letter 'Votes for all', 9 Sept.; Swanwick to Middleton, 11 Sept, 1916; all in LP/WNC/29/5; NCAS 'Report of First Year's Activities', Dec. 1917, CEMP. The WNC section of the Labour Party archives is my main source for information about the NCAS.
21 Among many others who signed 'The Claim for Adult Suffrage' were Margaret Ashton, the Countess of Carlisle, the Reverend John Clifford, Isabella Ford, Margaret Macmillan, H.W. Massingham, Sylvia Pankhurst, Ethel Snowden, Beatrice and Sydney Webb, Dr Ethel Williams, and Leonard Woolf. 'The Claim for Adult Suffrage', nd [ca. Aug. 1916], LP/WNC/29/5/27.
22 Swanwick to Middleton, 11 Sept. 1916, LP/WNC29/5/39.
23 Leaf to Fawcett, 2 Nov. 1916, WL.
24 Fawcett to Leaf, copy, 3 Nov. 1916; Auerbach to Fawcett, 11 Nov. 1916. WL. Writing to Auerbach, Fawcett names 'the other two' as 'Miss Ashton and Mrs Schuster', adding 'but Mrs S. did not address me with personal insult – she only compared me with Bethman Hollweg! which was rather comic. Anyway I did not care anything for her. But the other two I had looked upon as friends and Miss Courtney as a close and intimate friend.' Fawcett to Auerbach, 4 Nov. 1916, IAV. Cary Schuster had been a member of the NU executive before the debacle of April 1915. Had I not come on this letter, I would have assumed that the other unforgiven member was Marshall.
25 Courtney to Fawcett, 26 Nov. 1916; rough copy or draft of letter from Fawcett to Courtney, nd [ca. 27 Nov. 1916] incomplete, WL.
26 For a list of the founding organizations of the CCCWSS, see Holton *Feminism and Democracy*, 184 n.44. Holton has a good account of the re-emerging suffrage action but does not comment on the significance of the NCAS or its genesis in WIL, via VFA.

11   The Vote at Last

1 For details of the party affiliations and special interests of those appointed to the Speaker's Conference, see Pugh, *Electoral Reform*, 72–5. For the Speaker's Conference and the parliamentary aspects of the campaign see also Morgan, *Suffragists and Liberals*; Rolf, 'Origins of Mr Speaker's Conference'; Close, 'The Collapse of Resistance.'
2 Rolf, 'Origins', 43.
3 Caroline Marshall to Marshall, nd [ca Sept. 1916], CEMP; WFL view quoted in Pugh, *Electoral Reform*, 73. For the Speaker's role in 1913, see *Lib to Lab*, 203–6.
4 See Pugh, *Electoral Reform*, ch. 6 for a good account of its deliberations as far as they are known.

5   Rolf, 'Origins', 44
6   Close, 'Collapse', 900; Pugh, 'Politicians and the Women's Vote', 362; Morgan, *Suffragists and Liberals*, 144–5.
7   Purvis, *Emmeline Pankhurst*, 286–7.
8   Mimeo, marked 'Confidential', 15 Dec. 1915, WL, quoted by Holton, *Feminism and Democracy*, 147.
9   'Proposals of the Speaker's Conference, 1917', in Pugh, *Electoral Reform*, Appendix 7.
10 'Attitude of other organisations,' 5 Feb, 1917, CEMP.
11 *Ibid.*
12 'N.C.A.S.: Notes for Executive Committee Meeting, Feby. 5th', CEMP.
13 Strachey to Dickinson, 6 Feb. 1917, Dickinson Papers, cited by Pedersen, *Eleanor Rathbone*, 147.
14 Marshall to Lloyd George, 6 Feb. 1917, copy, CEMP.
15 Marshall, note to Russell [ca 1 Apr. 1917] referring to a telegram from Simon inviting her to dinner 'to talk suffrage', BRA; not quite sharing Swanwick's anathema towards Lloyd George she also breakfasted with him, Marshall, notes for breakfast with Lloyd George, 17 Feb. 1917, CEMP.
16 'N.C.A.S.: Notes for Executive Committee Meeting, Feby. 5th', CEMP.
17 Marshall, rough notes on interview with Dickinson, 13 Feb. [1917], CEMP. Swanwick also met with many politicians but Marshall left more of a paper trail.
18 Marshall, rough notes of NCAS Kingsway Hall meeting, 10 Feb. 1917; and of another meeting with Simon and Dickinson, [17? Feb, 1917], CEMP.
19 Marshall to Swanwick, cc Courtney, 11 Feb. 1917, CEMP.
20 R. Strachey, report, NU exec. 29 Mar. 1917, CEMP.
21 NU exec. 29 Mar. 1917, CEMP; Holton, *Feminism and Democracy*, 149; Rendel, 'Contribution of the Women's Labour League', 77 and *passim*.
22 Caroline Marshall, MS notes on meetings of the KWSA and the NWF [May, June 1916], CEMP; *Lib to Lab*, 292 and *passim*.
23 Letter to Secretaries of NU Societies and Federations, 15 February, 1917, MPL/M50/2/9/52.
24 See chapter 2 above. This was not the first time that the 'as is or may be' policy had been set aside, but previously only after discussion.
25 Letter to Secretaries, 15 February, 1917, MPL/M50/2/9/52.
26 H. Smith, *British Women's Suffrage Campaign*, 64.
27 Thoday to Caroline Marshall, 14 Feb, 1917, CEMP. Thoday says that this resolution was passed by the executive on 3 Feb.
28 Marshall had drafted an impassioned plea to promote an age clause, if there must be one, which would give the vote to young women and withdraw it from the older women, but the Council Proceedings do not show her as speaking; a second part to the urgency resolution committing the NU for working for 25 as the specified age was withdrawn. Proceedings of Annual Council, 21–23 Feb 1917; Marshall, MS notes on 'K.D.C.'s Urgency Resn', [21–3 Feb. 1917], CEMP. I appreciate Margaret Kamester's help in transcribing these and many others of Marshall's all but illegible MS notes.
29 Fawcett 'The Special Council on Electoral Reform', *Contemporary Review*, March 1917.
30 H. Smith, *British Women's Suffrage Campaign*, 65–6.

31 Marshall, part of a letter, addressee unknown, nd, CEMP, incorrectly dated there (by the present writer) as [19 Feb. 1917], now dated by external and internal evidence as ca 19 March 1917.

32 Marshall to Swanwick, 29 Mar. 1917, CEMP.

33 Marshall to Asquith, 28 Mar. 1917, copy, CEMP. Marshall, apparently quite seriously, suggested that the estimated number of women voters might legitimately be reduced by the number of women who would be incapacitated (for three weeks) by child birth at any one time.

34 H. Smith, *British Women's Suffrage Campaign*, 65–6; Pugh, *Electoral Reform*, 96. Proportional Representation was also left without Government protection, although it had been unanimously approved by the Speaker's Conference; this potentially history-changing reform was narrowly defeated (150:143) by a Unionist amendment, *ibid.* 109.

35 See Vellacott, *Bertrand Russell*, ch. 11, for the response to the Russian Revolution; extensive material in CEMP refers.

36 NU exec. 29 Mar, 1917.

37 Marshall to B. Russell, 1 Apr. 1917, BRA.

38 In August 1917, when Russian delegates were received in Britain, a delegation of women, including leading figures from WIL and the WFL, met with them. Swanwick to Marshall, 26 Aug., 1917, CEMP.

39 P. Strachey to R. Strachey, nd, BSH/WL.

40 NU exec. 29 Mar. 1917; flyer 'England Can Do Better', CEMP.

41 NU exec., 29 Mar. 1917, CEMP.

42 NU exec. 29 Mar. 1917, WL; Swanwick to Marshall, 28 Mar. 1917; Marshall to Swanwick, 29 Mar. 1917, CEMP. Marshall's name appears in the report among the more than 80 women listed as present, but it is clear from correspondence with Swanwick that she was not there. Pankhurst used the occasion to emphasize her absolute cooperation with whatever measure the government might put forward. Purvis, *Emmeline Pankhurst*, 288–91.

43 NU exec. 29 Mar., 19 Apr., 24 May 1917; Ayrton Gould to Marshall, 25 May; NCAS *AR*, 1917. I do not have much information about the work of this Joint Committee. Marshall, who was named to it, may have been prevented by pressure of work and illness from taking part, but Courtney, Sharp, and Macarthur were also appointed from the NCAS.

44 NU exec. Feb., Mar., especially 29 March 1917, WL; Mary Berenson: Biography of Ray Strachey, BSH/WL.

45 Mary Berenson: Biography of Ray Strachey, BSH/WL.

46 Rathbone, reporting at NU exec. 19 Apr. 1917; Purvis, *Emmeline Pankhurst*, 289–90.

47 NU exec. 19 Apr. 1917, CEMP.

48 *Ibid.*

49 *Ibid.*

50 Pugh and Close have both analysed the divisions in detail, coming to different conclusions about the number of conservative antis converted. Pugh, *Electoral Reform*, 148–9; Close, 'Collapse', 904–5.

51 Pugh, *Electoral Reform*, 146.

52 Pedersen uses fresh research to show Rathbone's role, *Rathbone* 148–50; Pugh, *Electoral Reform*, 150–1; H. Smith, *British Women's Suffrage*, 68; in *The Cause*, 362–3, Strachey avers that the change to the local franchise seemed

to the NU 'to be a perfectly reasonable demand' and claims much credit for the NU for the success; she does not mention either the NU's initial foot-dragging nor Rathbone's instrumentality in turning things around.

53 Close, 'Collapse of resistance', 905–6.

54 Gullace, *Blood of Our Sons*.

55 Conservative Unionist MPs numbered many more serving officers among them throughout the war than did the other parties.

56 Those who believed conscription was a panacea for social unrest must have known something of the casualty rate at the Front, but did not, of course, know how many of the young men experiencing the futility of war in the trenches would not fall into line, but would be disillusioned, would desert, would suffer irreparable mental or physical harm, would commit suicide or be shot for cowardice, or were, even as the House debated the Bill, among the 10,000 troops mutinying that summer at Etaples. The mutiny was kept from the public, as was (possibly in part for more humane reasons) the nature of the deaths of those shot for desertion or cowardice. See Pugh, *The Making of Modern British Politics*, 191–4, where he also discusses the political implications of the radicalization of some British troops. For pre-war arguments in favour of conscription (euphemistically named 'National Service') see Hayes, *Conscription Conflict*. An interesting research project, not as far as I know yet attempted, would be to assess the overlap in membership and concepts between the National Service League and the National League for Opposing Women's Suffrage.

12   Conclusions

1 During the war women won the vote in several other western nations; few countries bothered to hedge the franchise around with unequal limitations. Canada was an exception, granting the first instalment of the women's federal vote strictly for reasons of political advantage. Prime Minister Robert Borden, wanting support for the introduction of conscription, put through a bill in 1917 enfranchising only women who had a close relative serving in the armed forces. Adult suffrage followed in 1918.

2 Until I re-examined the evidence I shared the general view that the suffragists had made a wise and inevitable decision in accepting the narrow measure offered.

3 Unmarried women had a sharp need for the vote: all teachers and civil servants were unmarried; and the deaths of so many men in war had increased the imbalance between the sexes.

4 H. Smith, *British Women's Suffrage Campaign*, 69.

5 H. Smith, 'Sex versus Class'; P. Graves, 'An Experiment'.

6 Relevant Labour documents are reprinted in Kellogg and Gleason, *British Labor*.

7 Adelman, *Growth*, 48–51.

8 Vellacott, 'Feminism as if All People Mattered'.

9 In her lectures on 'Technology and Pacifism' (given in the Russell Peace Lectures series at McMaster University in February 1995, unpublished)

Ursula Franklin further developed the idea that people claiming to be politically practical are responsible for the trouble that the world is in and
that the people who are concerned about ecology, social justice, and peace
advocate the only truly realistic route to survival.

10 In the same passage Fawcett credited Ray Strachey as honorary parliamentary secretary as 'the best occupant of that difficult and exacting post that
we have ever had'. Fawcett, 'What I Remember', XLVI, in *Women's Leader*,
28 July 1924.

11 Rubinstein, *A Different World,,* 252–3; *ibid.* chs 18–20 is the best source for
Fawcett's later life.

12 Pedersen, *Eleanor Rathbone*.

13 Caine, *Bombay*, 315.

13   Epilogue

1 Alberti, *Beyond Suffrage*, 92. Note the difference between the relationship of
the NU to the IWSA and the relationship of WIL to WILPF. The NU was a
national body affiliated to an international organization which had come
into existence later than itself for mutual support and to facilitate the objective of its members – the gaining of the vote, an objective which was by its
nature national; the WIL was an integral founding member or section of a
body formed to serve an international purpose – that of giving a common
transnational voice to women.

2 P. Graves, 'An Experiment'; H. Smith, 'Sex vs. Class'.

3 See Alberti, *Beyond Suffrage*, ch. 4, for a good picture of the many demands
and options faced by suffragists in the immediate post-war years.

4 Marshall, 'The Future of Women in Politics', *Labour Year Book*, 1916;
reprinted in Florence *et alia*, *Militarism versus Feminism*, 45–52; MS (1915) in
CEMP.

5 Marshall, 'The Pacifist contribution to Revolution', MS notes for speech to
Cambridge W.I.L., 1 Nov. 1917, CEMP.

6 The following discussion draws on some of my previous articles; more
detail can be found in 'Feminism as if All People Mattered' and 'A Place for
Pacifism'.

7 Alberti, *Beyond Suffrage*, 88–9; Fawcett, *What I Remember*, 253–6; Margery
Corbett Ashby, preface to D.M. Northcroft's *Women at Work in the League of
Nations*.

8 'Conference to draw up a Minimum Feminist Programme'; *Proceedings*;
material in Col/WILPF.

9 *Proceedings*, Col/WILPF; report by Ray Strachey, *CC*, 21 February 1919.

10 *CC*, 4 April 1919. The phrasing of the recommendation goes beyond what
had been claimed in the 'Minimum Feminist Programme' where the resolution had asked only 'that women should receive the same pay as the men
for the same job'.

11 *CC*, 4 April 1919; Czernin, *Versailles 1919* contains a useful chart placing three successive versions of the Covenant side by side [140–163,
unpaginated].

12 *Proceedings* of Minimum Feminist conference, Col/WILPF

13 Mary Ward, *Speech by Mrs Humphry Ward* (London: Women's National Anti-Suffrage League, 1908).

14 WIL, *Towards Peace and Freedom*, 7

15 *Ibid.* 18–19. The League of Nations envisaged by WILPF has a good deal in common with the much later – and geographically more circumscribed – European Union, where membership is contingent on acceptance of certain standards regarding political and civil rights, economic conduct and international relationships, and where the union parliament is democratically elected by the people.

16 Sally Marks, *The Illusion of Peace*, 10–11; for more on the problems facing the statesmen at Versailles, see Margaret Macmillan, *Paris 1919*.

17 For the text of the resolution on the peace terms, see *Towards Peace and Freedom*, 18–19.

18 *Ibid.*

19 In her new anthology, *The Ursula Franklin Reader: Pacifism as a Map*, Professor Franklin powerfully develops the concepts both of the inseparability of pacifism from feminism, and of the essential practicality of the pacifist approach.

Select Bibliography

Archival materials

Collections

Barbara Strachey Halpern Papers, now in WL. (BSH/WL)
Bertrand Russell Archives. McMaster University, Hamilton, Ontario. (BRA)
British Library of Political and Economic Science. (BLPES)
Catherine E. Marshall Papers. Cumbria Record Office, Carlisle, England. (CEMP)
Clifford Allen papers. University of South Carolina, Columbia, S. Carolina. (CAP)
David Lloyd George Papers. House of Lords. (Ll G)
E.D. Morel papers at BLPES. (EDM/BLPES)
Fonds Duchêne, Bibliothèque de documentation internationale contemporaine (Nanterre). (BDIC)
Frank Marshall Papers. Seen by courtesy of Frank Marshall. (FMP)
International Archive for the Women's Movement. Amsterdam. (IAV)
Jane Addams papers, SCPC. (SCPC/JA)
Labour Party Archives. (LP)
Manchester Public Library: Suffrage papers. (MPL)
Schwimmer-Lloyd Collection. New York Public Library. (SL/NYPL)
Swarthmore College Peace Collection. (SCPC)
Women's International League papers, at BLPES. (WIL/BLPES)
Women's International League for Peace and Freedom papers, at the University of Colorado. (WILPF/Col.)
Women's International League for Peace and Freedom (USA) at SCPC. (WILPF/SCPC).
The Women's Library, London. (WL)

Newspapers and periodicals

Common Cause
Daily Express
Englishwoman
The Friend [Britain]
Herald
Jus Suffragii
Labour Leader
Manchester Guardian
Nation
New Statesman
Britannia (formerly *Suffragette*)
The Times
Tribunal (New York: Kraus Reprint, 1970)
Votes for Women
Women's Dreadnought

Unpublished material

Berenson, Mary. 'Biography of Ray Strachey' (unpublished, incomplete), BHP. Seen by courtesy of Barbara Strachey Halpern.

Hawse End Guest Book, seen by courtesy of Frank Marshall.

James E. Lindsay. 'The Failure of Liberal Opposition to British Entry into World War I'. PhD dissertation, Columbia University, New York, 1969.

Sheepshanks, Mary. 'Woman Suffrage and Pacifism'. Extract from unpublished autobiography, seen by courtesy of Sybil Oldfield.

Published sources

Addams, Jane. *Peace and Bread in Time of War* (New York: King's Crown Press, 1945).

Addams, Jane. Emily Balch and Alice Hamilton. *Women at The Hague: the International Congress of Women and Its Results* (New York and London: Garland reprint, with new introduction by Mercedes Randall, 1972; original, New York: Macmillan, 1915).

Adelman, Paul. *The Rise of the Labour Party: 1880–1945*. 3rd ed. (London and New York: Longman, 1996).

Alberti, Johanna. *Beyond Suffrage: Feminists in War and Peace, 1914–1928* (London: Macmillan, 1989).

Banks, Olive. *Biographical Dictionary of British Feminists*, vol. 1: 1800–1930 (New York: New York University Press, 1985).

Bentley, Michael and John Stevenson (eds) *High and Low Politics in Modern Britain: Ten Studies* (Oxford: Clarendon Press, 1983).

Black, Naomi. *Social Feminism* (Ithaca and London: Cornell University Press, 1989).

Briggs, Asa, and John Saville. *Essays in Labour History, 1886–1926* (London: Macmillan, 1971).

British Committee of Women for Permanent Peace. *Towards Permanent Peace* (London, June 1915).

Brockway, A.F. *Socialism for Pacifists* (Manchester: National Labour Press, 1916).

Brunt, Rosalind, and Caroline Rowan (eds) *Feminism, Culture and Politics* (London: Lawrence and Wishart, 1982).

Bussey, Gertrude, and Margaret Tims. *Women's International League for Peace and Freedom* (London: Allen and Unwin, 1965).

Chatfield, Charles, and Peter van den Dungen (eds) *Peace Movements and Political Cultures* (Knoxville, Ten.: University of Tennessee Press, 1988).

Caine, Barbara. *Bombay to Bloomsbury: A Biography of the Strachey Family* (Oxford: Oxford University Press, 2005).

Close, David. 'The Collapse of Resistance to Democracy: Conservatives, Adult Suffrage, and Second Chamber Reform, 1911–1928'. *Historical Journal* 20 (1977): 893–918.

Cook, Blanche Wiesen (ed.) *Crystal Eastman on Women and Revolution* (Oxford: Oxford University Press, 1978).

Costin, Lela B. 'Feminism, Pacifism, Internationalism and the 1915 International Congress of Women', *Women's Studies International Forum*, vol. 5, no. 3/4 (1982): 301–15.

Cowman, Krista. '"Giving Them Something to Do": How the Early ILP Appealed to Women'. In M. Walsh (ed.) *Working Out Gender: Perspectives from Labour History* (Aldershot: Ashgate, 1999), pp. 119–34.
—— '"Incipient Toryism"? The Women's Social and Political Union and the Independent Labour Party, 1903–1914'. *History Workshop Journal* 53 (2002): 129–48.
—— '"Crossing the Great Divide": Inter-organizational Suffrage Relationships on Merseyside, 1895–1914'. In Eustance, Ryan and Ugolini, *A Suffrage Reader* (London and New York: Leicester University Press, 2000), pp. 37–52.
—— '"A Party Between Revolution and Peaceful Persuasion": A Fresh Look at the United Suffragists'. In Joannou and Purvis, *The Women's Suffrage Movement: New Feminist Perspectives* (Manchester: Manchester University Press; New York: St Martin's, 1998), pp. 77–88.
Crawford, Elizabeth. *The Women's Suffrage Movement: A Reference Guide, 1866–1928* (London and New York: Routledge, 1999).
—— *The Women's Suffrage Movement in Britain and Ireland: A Regional Survey* (London and New York: Routledge, 2006).
Culleton, Claire A. *Working Class Culture, Women, and Britain, 1914–1921* (New York: St Martin's, 2000).
Czernin, Ferdinand. *Versailles 1919* (New York: Capricorn Books, 1964).
de Vries, Jacqueline. 'Gendering Patriotism: Emmeline and Christabel Pankhurst and World War One'. In Oldfield (ed.) *This Working-Day World*, pp. 75–88.
Eustance, Claire, J. Ryan and L. Ugolini. *A Suffrage Reader* (London and New York: Leicester University Press, 2000).
Fair, John D. 'The Political Aspects of Women's Suffrage during the First World War.' *Albion* 8, no. 3 (Fall 1976), 274–93.
Fawcett, Millicent Garrett. *What I Remember* (London: T. Fisher Unwin, 1921; reprint. Westport, Conn.: Hyperion, 1976).
—— *Women's Suffrage: A Short History of a Great Movement* (London: T.C. and E.C. Jack, 1911).
—— *The Women's Victory – and After: Personal Reminiscences, 1911–1918* (London: Sidgwick and Jackson 1920).
—— 'Wanted: A Statesman', pamphlet (London, 1901).
—— 'The NUWSS and the Hague Congress'. *Englishwoman*, June 1915, 197.
—— 'The Special Council on Electoral Reform'. *Contemporary Review*, March 1917.
—— 'What I Remember' XLVI. In *Women's Leader*, 28 July, 1924.
Fletcher, Sheila. *Maude Royden* (Oxford: Blackwell, 1989).
Florence, Mary Sargant, Catherine Marshall, and C.K. Ogden. *Militarism versus Feminism* ed., Margaret Kamester and Jo Vellacott (London: Virago, 1987).
Franklin, Ursula. *The Ursula Franklin Reader: Pacifism as a Map* (Toronto: Between the Lines, 2006).
Garner, Les. *Stepping Stones to Women's Liberty: Feminist Ideas in the Women's Suffrage Movement, 1900–1918* (Rutherford, N.J.: Fairleigh Dickinson University Press, 1984).
Graves, Pamela. 'An Experiment in Women-Centered Socialism; Labour Women in Britain'. In H. Gruber and P. Graves (eds) *Women and Socialism – Socialism*

and Women: Europe between the Two World Wars (Oxford: Berghahn, 1998), pp. 180–214.

Gullace, Nicoletta. *'The Blood of Our Sons': Men, Women, and the Renegotiation of British Citizenship during the Great War* (New York and Basingstoke: Macmillan, 2002).

Hanak, H. 'The UDC during the First World War'. *Bulletin of the Institute of Historical Research*, 36 (Nov. 1963): 168–80.

Hannam, June. '"I had not been to London": Women's Suffrage – A View from the Regions'. In Purvis and Holton (eds) *Votes for Women*, pp. 226–45.

—— *Isabella Ford* (Oxford: Blackwell, 1989).

Hannam, June, and Karen Hunt. *Socialist Women: Britain, 1880s to 1920s* (London and New York: Routledge, 2002).

Harrison, Brian. *Prudent Revolutionaries: Portraits of British Feminists between the Wars* (Oxford: Clarendon Press 1987).

—— *Separate Spheres* (London: Croom Helm, 1978).

—— 'Women's Suffrage at Westminster 1866–1928'. In Michael Bentley and John Stevenson (eds), *High and Low Politics in Modern Britain: Ten Studies* (Oxford: Clarendon Press 1983), pp. 80–122.

Harrison, Royden. 'The War Emergency Workers' National Committee, 1914–1920'. In Asa Briggs and John Saville (eds) *Essays in Labour History, 1886–1926* (London: Macmillan, 1971), pp. 211–59.

Hayes, Denis. *Conscription Conflict* (London: Sheppard Pres, 1949; reprint, New York: Garland, 1973).

Hazlehurst, Cameron. *Politicians at War, July 1914 to May 1915: A Prologue to the Triumphs of Lloyd George* (London: Jonathan Cape, 1971).

Holton, Sandra Stanley. *Feminism and Democracy: Women's Suffrage and Reform Politics in Britain, 1900–1918* (Cambridge: Cambridge University Press, 1986).

—— *Suffrage Days: Stories from the Women's Suffrage Movement* (London and New York: Routledge, 1996).

House of Commons Debates (Hansard), fifth series, 1914–17.

Hume, Leslie Parker. *The National Union of Women's Suffrage Societies, 1897–1914* (New York: Garland, 1982).

Ingram, Angela. '"In Christ's Name – Peace!" Theodora Wilson Wilson and Radical Pacifism'. In Ingram and Patai (eds) *Rediscovering Forgotten Radicals*, pp. 175–204.

Ingram, Angela and Daphne Patai (eds) *Rediscovering Forgotten Radicals: British Women Writers, 1889–1939* (Chapel Hill: University of North Carolina Press, 1993).

Jalland, Pat. *Women, Marriage and Politics: 1860–1914* (Oxford: Clarendon Press, 1986).

Joannou, Maroula and June Purvis: *The Women's Suffrage Movement: New Feminist Perspectives* (Manchester: Manchester University Press; New York: St Martin's, 1998).

Kellogg, Paul U. and Arthur Gleason. *British Labor and the War; Reconstructors for a New World* (New York: Boni and Liveright, 1919; reprint, New York and London: Garland, 1972).

Kennedy, Thomas C. *The Hound of Conscience: A History of the No-Conscription Fellowship* (Fayetteville: University of Arkansas Press, 1981).

Kent, Susan Kingsley. *Making Peace: The Reconstruction of Gender in Interwar Britain* (Princeton: Princeton University Press, 1993).

—— *Sex and Suffrage in Britain 1860–1914* (Princeton: Princeton University Press, 1987).

Koss, Stephen. *The Rise and Fall of the Political Press in Britain*, vol. 2: *The Twentieth Century* (Chapel Hill and London: University of North Carolina Press, 1984).

Labour Year Book, 1916 (London, 1916).

Leventhal, F.M. *Arthur Henderson* (Manchester: Manchester University Press, 1989).

Liddington, Jill. *The Long Road to Greenham* (London: Virago, 1989).

—— *The Life and Times of a Respectable Rebel: Selina Cooper, 1864–1946* (London: Virago, 1984).

—— *Rebel Girls: Their Fight for the Vote* (London: Virago, 2006).

Liddington, Jill, and Jill Norris. *One Hand Tied Behind Us* (London: Virago, 1978).

MacMillan, Margaret. *Paris, 1919* (New York: Random House, 2001).

Marks, Sally. *The Illusion of Peace: International Relations in Europe, 1918–1933* (London: Macmillan, 1976).

Marshall, Catherine E. 'The Future of Women in Politics'. In *Labour Year Book, 1916*.

—— 'The Women Envoys to the Governments of Europe and the United States'. In WIL, *Towards Permanent Peace*, 2nd ed. September 1915.

—— 'The Labour and Woman Suffrage Entente'. *Labour Leader*, 28 Aug. 1913.

Marwick, Arthur. *The Deluge: British Society and the First World War* (Harmondsworth: Penguin, 1965).

—— *Women at War, 1914–1918* (London: Fontana, 1977).

Middleton, Lucy (ed.) *Women in the Labour Movement* (London: Croom Helm, 1977).

Morgan, David. *Suffragists and Liberals: The Politics of Woman Suffrage in England* (Oxford: Blackwell, 1975).

Northcroft. D.M. *Women at Work in the League of Nations* (Keighley: Rydal, 1927).

Oldfield, Sybil. *Doers of the Word: British Women Humanitarians 1900–1950* (London: Continuum, 2001).

Oldfield, Sybil. *Spinsters of this Parish: The Life and Times of F.M. Mayor and Mary Sheepshanks* (London: Virago, 1984).

—— 'England's Cassandras in World War One'. In Oldfield (ed.) *This Working-Day World*, pp. 89–100.

—— *Women Against the Iron Fist* (Oxford: Blackwell, 1989).

Oldfield, Sybil (ed.) *This Working-Day World: Women's Lives and Culture(s) in Britain 1914–1945* (London: Taylor and Francis, 1994).

Pankhurst, E. Sylvia. *The Home Front* (London: Century Hutchinson, 1987, first published 1932).

Pedersen, Susan. 'Gender, Welfare, and Citizenship in Britain during the Great War'. In *American Historical Review* 95, no. 4 (Oct. 1990) pp. 983–1006.

—— *Eleanor Rathbone and the Politics of Conscience* (Cambridge: Cambridge University Press, 2004).

Playne, Caroline. *Society at War, 1914–1916* (London: Allen and Unwin, 1931).

Pugh, Martin. *Electoral Reform in War and Peace, 1906–18* (London: Routledge and Kegan Paul, 1978).

—— *The Making of Modern British Politics, 1867–1939* (Oxford: Blackwell, 1982).

214 *Select Bibliography*

—— *The March of the Women: A Revisionist Analysis of the Campaign for Women's Suffrage, 1866–1914* (Oxford: Oxford University Press, 2000).
—— 'Politicians and the Women's Vote 1914–1918'. *History* 59 (1974): 358–74.
—— *Women's Suffrage in Britain, 1867–1928* (London: Historical Association pamphlet, 1980).
—— *Women and the Women's Movement in Britain: 1914–1959* (London: Macmillan, 1992).
Purvis, June. *Emmeline Pankhurst: A Biography* (London and New York: Routledge, 2002).
Purvis, June, and Sandra Stanley Holton (eds) *Votes for Women* (London and New York: Routledge, 2000).
Rae, John. *Conscience and Politics: the British Government and the Conscientious Objector to Military Service, 1916–1919* (London: Oxford University Press, 1970).
Randall, Mercedes. *Improper Bostonian: Emily Greene Balch* (New York: Twayne, 1964).
Rendel, Margherita. 'The Contribution of the Women's Labour League to the Winning of the Franchise', in Lucy Middleton (ed.) *Women in the Labour Movement* (London: Croom Helm, 1977) pp. 57–83.
Rimmer, W.C. *Marshalls of Leeds: Flax Spinners* (Cambridge: Cambridge University Press, 1960).
Rolf, David. 'Origins of Mr Speaker's Conference during the First World War', *History* 36 (1979): 36–46.
Rosen, Andrew. *Rise Up, Women!: The Militant Campaign of the Women's Social and Political Union, 1903–1914* (London: Routledge and Kegan Paul, 1974).
Rover, Constance. *Women's Suffrage and Party Politics in Britain: 1866–1914* (London: Routledge and Kegan Paul, 1967).
Rowan, Caroline. '"Mothers, Vote Labour!" The State, the Labour Movement and Working-Class Mothers, 1900–1918'. In Brunt and Rowan (eds) *Feminism, Culture and Politics*, pp. 59–83.
Rubinstein, David. *A Different World for Women: The Life of Millicent Garrett Fawcett* (New York and London: Harvester Wheatsheaf, 1991).
Rupp, Leila J. 'Constructing Internationalism: The Case of Transnational Women's Organizations, 1888–1945'. *American Historical Review* 99, no. 5 (Dec. 1994): 1571–600.
—— *Worlds of Women: The Making of an International Women's Movement* (Princeton: Princeton University Press, 1997).
Schott, Linda. '"Middle-of-the-Road" Activists: Carrie Chapman Catt and the National Committee on the Cause and Cure of War'. *Peace and Change* 21, no. 1 (Jan. 1996).
Smith, Angela K. *Suffrage Discourse in Britain during the First World War* (Aldershot: Ashgate, 2005).
Smith, Harold L. *The British Women's Suffrage Campaign 1866–1928* (London and New York: Longman; 2nd edition, forthcoming 2007).
—— 'Sex vs. Class: British Feminists and the Labour Movement, 1919–1929'. *The Historian* [US] 47 (Nov. 1984): 19–37.
Stocks, Mary D. *Eleanor T. Rathbone: A Biography* (London: Gollancz, 1949).
Strachey, Barbara. *Remarkable Relations: The Story of the Pearsall Smith Family* (London: Gollancz, 1980).

Strachey, Rachel. *The Cause: A Short History of the Women's Movement in Great Britain* (London: Virago, 1978; first published 1928).
—— *Millicent Garrett Fawcett* (London: John Murray, 1931).
—— *Women's Suffrage and Women's Service: The History of the London and National Society for Women's Service* (London: The Society, 1927).
The Suffrage Annual and Women's Who's Who 1913 (ed.) A.J.R. (London: Stanley Paul, 1913).
Swanwick, Helena M. *I Have Been Young* (London: Gollancz, 1935).
—— *Builders of Peace: Being Ten Years' History of the Union of Democratic Control* (London: Swarthmore Press, 1924; New York and London: Garland, 1973).
Swartz, Marvin. *The Union of Democratic Control* (London: Oxford University Press, 1971).
Tanner, Duncan. *Political Change and the Labour Party, 1900–1918* (Cambridge: Cambridge University Press, 1990).
Taylor, A.J.P. *English History, 1914–1945* (Oxford: Oxford University Press, 1965).
van Wingerden, Sophia A. *The Women's Suffrage Movement in Britain, 1866–1928* (Basingstoke: Macmillan, 1999; New York: St Martin's Press, 1999).
Vellacott, Jo. *Bertrand Russell and the Pacifists in the First World War* (Brighton: Harvester; New York: St Martin's, 1980).
—— *From Liberal to Labour with Women's Suffrage: The Story of Catherine Marshall* (Montreal: McGill-Queen's University Press, 1993).
—— 'Anti-War Suffragists.' *History* 62, no. 206 (Oct. 1977): 411–25.
—— 'A Place for Pacifism and Transnationalism in Feminist Theory: The Early Work of the Women's International League for Peace and Freedom', *Women's History Review* 2, no. 1 (1993): 23–56.
—— 'Feminism As If All People Mattered: Working to Remove the Causes of War, 1919–1929', *Contemporary European History,* 10, pt. 3 (Nov. 2001): 375–94.
—— 'Feminist Consciousness and the First World War.' *History Workshop Journal* 23 (Spring 1987): 81–101.
—— 'Historical Reflections on Votes, Brooms and Guns: Admission to Political Structures – On Whose Terms?' *Atlantis* 12, no. 2 (Spring 1987): 36–9.
—— 'Women, Peace, and Internationalism, 1914–1920: "Finding New Words and Creating New Methods"'. In Charles Chatfield and Peter van den Dungen (eds), *Peace Movements and Political Cultures* (Knoxville: University of Tennessee Press, 1988), pp. 106–24.
Ward, Mary (Mrs Humphry Ward). *England's Effort: Letters to an American Friend.,* 2nd ed. (New York: Scribner, 1916).
—— *Speech by Mrs Humphry Ward* (London: Women's National Anti-Suffrage League, 1908).
Webb, Beatrice. Introduction, *New Statesman,* 'Special Supplement on the Awakening of Women', 1 Nov. 1913.
Webb, Sidney. *The War and the Workers.* London: Fabian Tract no. 176, 1 September 1914.
Willis, Irene Cooper. *England's Holy War: A Study of English Liberal Idealism during the Great War* (New York: Knopf 1928; Garland reprint, 1972).

Wiltsher, Anne. *Most Dangerous Women: Feminist Peace Campaigners of the Great War* (London: Pandora, 1985).

Winslow, Barbara. *Sylvia Pankhurst: Sexual Politics and Political Activism* (New York: St Martin's, 1996).

Winter, J.M. *Socialism and the Challenge of War, Ideas and Politics in Britain, 1912–1918* (London and Boston: Routledge and Kegan Paul, 1974).

Women's International League. *Towards Permanent Peace: A Record of the Women's International Congress held at the Hague, April 28th–May 1st, 1915* (London: WIL, June 1915; 2nd ed. Sep. 1915).

Women's Who's Who. See *The Suffrage Annual.*

Woollacott, Angela. *On Her Their Lives Depend: Munitions Workers in the Great War* (Berkeley: University of California Press, 1994).

Index

House of Commons: conference on
suffrage, 138; debate on franchise
bill, 154–5, 157–8, 161–3
House of Lords, 159, 163
Hudson, J.A., 156
Hunt, Karen, 170

Independent Labour Party (ILP), 13,
39, 99; anti-war policy, 42, 99,
172; EFF support for candidates
of, 9, 98–9, 101–3, 105–7; suffrage
policy, 98–9, 161, 170. *See also*
Labour Party
Inglis, Dr Elsie, 187n11
Inter-Allied Suffragists (IAS), 174,
180–2, 184; Paris conference
(1919), 179–80
International Conference of Women
for Permanent Peace (ICWPP), 82,
123, 124, 125, 128, 131, 177. *See
also* British Committee of the
International Women's Congress;
Women's International League
for Peace and Freedom (WILPF)
International Council of Women, 180
International Manifesto of Women,
40–1
International Women's Relief
Committee (IWRC), 30–1
International Women's Suffrage
Alliance (IWSA): and BCIWC, 91,
128; board visit to London
(1914), 14; decision on 1915
(Hague) conference, 59–62, 68;
Fawcett's role in, 59–62, 68, 74,
77, 91, 127–30, 180; and ICWPP,
128; International Manifesto of
Women, 40–1; relationship to
NU, 41, 61–2, 207n1; women's
anti-war meeting (Aug. 1914), 17,
40. *See also* Hague conference
Ireland, 123; Irish Nationalist Party,
148, 161

Jacobs, Aletta, 61, 123
Jowett, Frederick W., 104–5
Jus Suffragii, 47, 59–60, 61, 74, 129–30

Kent, Susan Kingsley, 18, 31, 189n31

Keswick (Cumberland): Fabian
conference in, 129; Women's
Suffrage Association, 3–4, 6, 38,
134
Labour Leader (LL), 15, 42, 74, 122,
170
Labour Party: in coalition
government, 99, 135, 172;
Committee on Electoral Reform,
135; EFF support for candidates,
9–10, 12, 64, 98–100, 198n6;
National Executive Committee,
24; NU pre-war relationship with,
8–9, 13, 28, 94–5, 98–9, 168–9;
Parliamentary Labour Party (PLP),
10, 102, 149, 150, 171; policy on
franchise bill, 149–50, 157–9,
161, 169–71; policy on suffrage,
9, 102, 135–6, 143; policy on
war issues, 42, 172–3; postwar
development, 171–3; Speaker's
Conference representatives, 143;
suffrage conference (Mar. 1917),
149; and WIL, 135–6. *See also*
Independent Labour Party
Lansbury, George, 140, 156
Law, Hugh, 148
Lawrence, Susan, 13, 25, 28, 188n28
Leaf, Emily, 91, 141, 142, 197n23;
and Hague conference, 73, 122–3;
and Mary Sheepshanks, 129–30;
in NU 'pacifist' faction, 79, 91,
141–2; as NU press secretary, 11,
79
League of Nations, 172, 173, 175–6,
208n15; Covenant, 176, 181,
182–3
Liberal Party: in coalition
government, 88, 99, 135, 172;
and EFF, 8–9, 101; Marshall
family's work in, 3–4, 39, 126;
members in NU, 3, 9, 94, 95, 126;
policy on suffrage, 2–4, 8, 10,
136, 161, 164; policy on war
issues, 15, 42, 99, 136; in
Speaker's Conference, 143;
wartime disillusionment with, 39,
42, 74, 94, 172; Women's Liberal
Association, 3, 4

(Special), 83–97, 100; Nov. 1914 (Provincial), 47, 49–54, 56–7; Nov. 1914 (proposed), 44–6
executive committee: election at Feb. 1915 Council, 62–3, 68–70, 92–3, 95; election at June 1915 Council, 87–9, 92–4; London members of, 2, 5, 81, 86–9, 90, 92–3, 95–6, 111–13, 120; pre-war members of, 11–12, 94–5; relationship to constituency, 96–7, 152, 153; rump members (Feb. to June 1915), 83, 86–9; views expressed as individuals, 46–7
National Union of Women Workers, 127
Nevinson, Henry, 140, 145, 156
Newcastle, 44, 72, 87
New Zealand, 14, 167
No-Conscription Fellowship (NCF), 125–6, 147–8, 156, 199n15
North-Eastern Federation, 84, 85, 110
North of England Society for Women's Suffrage, 11
North of England Suffrage Society, 93
Northwest Federation (NWF), 134, 151

Oldfield, Sybil, 74–5
O'Malley, Ida, 11–12, 63, 72, 194n33
Osler, Mrs, 88, 93, 130, 131, 202n25

pacifism and pacifists: feminist perspective of, 179; link with suffrage, 124, 194n30; role during franchise bill debate, 147. *See also* peace issues and peace education
'pacifist or 'peace' faction (of NU): differing views among, 56; membership support for, 95–6; at NU Council Feb. 1915, 65–8, 69–72; and NU Council June 1915, 84–6, 87, 88
Paget, Violet, 74
Palliser, Edith, 11, 61, 72, 196n212

Pankhurst, Christabel, 20–1, 42, 48, 115, 145, 185n2
Pankhurst, Emmeline, 145, 159, 185n2; support of war effort, 20–1, 42, 48, 115
Pankhurst, Sylvia: anti-war views, 20, 43, 116; and BCIWC, 74, 82; break with Emmeline and Christabel Pankhurst, 20; and Lloyd George, 158; and NCAS, 140–1; relief work in London's East End, 16, 31; wartime suffrage work, 133, 140–1, 145, 157, 158, 159
Parmoor, Lord, 156
patriotism: link with worker's rights, 115–16; Marshall's views on, 52, 53
'patriot' or 'pro-war' faction (of NU), 46–7, 80; membership support for, 95–6; at NU Council Feb. 1915, 69–72. *See also* Strachey, Oliver; Strachey, Philippa (Pippa); Strachey, Ray
peace issues and peace education, 49–50; growing interest in, 121–2; as integral with suffrage, 47–9; link with international suffrage movement, 41, 60–2; resolutions at NU Council Feb. 1915, 65–8; split in NU as lost opportunity for, 79–80; as unpatriotic or treasonous, 51–2, 67, 76. *See also* pacifism and pacifists
Pedersen, Susan, 174
People's Suffrage Federation (PSF), 3, 188n28
Pethick-Lawrence, Emmeline, 133; in BCIWC and WIL, 82, 115–16, 123, 125, 178; in NCAS, 140; in WFL, 43
Pethick-Lawrence, Frederick, 43
physical force argument, 47, 50, 65, 85
Playne, Caroline, 74
Ponsonby, Mrs Arthur, 74
Prince of Wales' Fund, 17, 19, 25, 189n31

Printed in the United States
131475LV00001B/147/P

9 780230 013353